Dictionary of the Occult

The Wordsworth Dictionary of the Occult

—

André Nataf

Wordsworth Reference

This edition published 1994 by Wordsworth Editions Ltd,
Cumberland House, Crib Street, Ware, Hertfordshire SG12 9ET.
First published in France as *Les maîtres de l'occultisme*, 1988.

ISBN 1-85326-333-8

Printed and bound in Denmark by Nørhaven.

The paper in this book is produced from pure wood pulp, without the use of chlorine or any other substance harmful to the environment. The energy used in its production consists almost entirely of hydroelectricity and heat generated from waste materials, thereby conserving fossil fuels and contributing little to the greenhouse effect.

Acknowledgements

Translated from the French by John Davidson

Adapted for the English edition by Katharine Boyd
Roger Smith
Paul Wright

New entry on Dennis Wheatley written by Roger Smith

Chambers Compact Reference Series Editor Min Lee

Illustration credits

Page	
7	© Roger Viollet – Archives Photeb
9	© Bibliothèque nationale, Paris – Photeb
22	© Bibliothèque nationale, Paris – Archives Photeb
26	© Bibliothèque nationale, Paris – Photeb
32	© Bibliothèque nationale, Paris – Photeb
36	© Collection Viollet – Archives Photeb
39	Rocco Pedicini © Archives Photeb
42	© Bibliothèque nationale, Paris – Photeb
53	Jeanbor © Photeb
75	© Archives Photeb
79	© Roger Viollet – Archives Photeb
87	© Collection Viollet – Archives Photeb
97	© Bibliothèque nationale, Paris – Archives Photeb
108	© Bibliothèque nationale, Paris – Photeb
113	© Bibliothèque nationale, Paris – Photeb
119	Jeanbor © Photeb
123	© Bibliothèque nationale, Paris – Photeb
127	© Bibliothèque nationale, Paris – Photeb
133	Jeanbor © Photeb
135	© Bibliothèque nationale, Paris – Archives Photeb
142	© Collection Viollet – Archives Photeb
157	© Bibliothèque nationale, Paris – Archives Photeb
178	Jeanbor © Photeb
187	© Bibliothèque nationale, Paris – Photeb
193	© Bibliothèque nationale, Paris – Photeb
195	© Bibliothèque nationale, Paris – Photeb
206	Jeanbor © Archives Photeb
209	© Bibliothèque nationale, Paris – Archives Photeb
213	© Bibliothèque nationale, Paris – Archives Photeb © by SPADOM, 1989
223	© Bibliothèque nationale, Paris – Archives Photeb © by SPADEM, 1989
225	© Collection Viollet – Archives Photeb

Contents

Examples of Occult Thought in Literature

Introduction

According to the Oxford English Dictionary, the term 'occult' in the sense of 'not understood or able to be understood by the mind, beyond the range of ordinary knowledge', dates from 1545. By 1653, the accepted meaning of the word had extended to cover those would-be sciences of the ancient and medieval worlds, such as magic, alchemy, astrology and theosophy, which were supposed to contain some knowledge of, or to have power to activate, the secret and mysterious forces of nature. However, it took the work of Eliphas Lévi in 19th century Europe to develop occultism into a way of looking at the world, with its own rites. In fact, the beliefs, theories and techniques embraced by the terms 'occultism' or 'esoterism' were already widely known in later antiquity and some of them, such as magic, astrology, theurgy and necromancy, had been invented and systematized some 2000 years earlier in Egypt and Mesopotamia. Occult practices were also known in Asia and India, as witnessed by the divinatory methods of the Chinese *I Ching* and the alchemy of Tantric yoga.

The historical field of occultism might remain very imprecise but for one point which happens to circumscribe it: the written history of occult philosophy does not start until more or less the dawn of Christianity. Following in the wake of Judaism, Christianity separated religion from magic which had, up until then, gone together hand in hand. Measures were taken against the occult, in an attempt to root out these persistent old beliefs and practices. The result was that they became esoteric (hidden); Jung tells us that they took refuge in the collective unconscious.

Occult philosophy was created, as Lévy-Bruhl points out so clearly, by purging magical thinking of its aberrations and lack of realism; however, quite unlike strictly rational thought, it retained what the French poet André Breton calls the 'unshatterable kernel of darkness'. This philosophy, like poetry, is based on the belief that the world of dreams possesses a reality which does not contradict science, but simply follows a different course. This explains the fascination exercised on writers and artists by occultism. We have mentioned Breton; we might add Nerval, Baudelaire, Hieronymus Bosch, Mozart, Balzac and many more, whose names will crop up as we discuss one or other of the masters.

Occultism is based on two types of reasoning, indispensable to spiritual life, but for which science, based as it is on logic, has no use: these are intuitive knowledge and reasoning by analogy. Although the two worlds (the magical and the rational) are independent, there are nonetheless bridges between them which allow us to move from one to the other and which, further, prevent us from rejecting occultism absolutely. Marcelin Berthelot views alchemy as an 'experimental dimension which made continuous progress throughout the Middle Ages until modern, practical chemistry arose from it'. After all, were they not adepts who discovered artificial gems, phosphorus, the techniques of industrial dyeing, etc.? Even Isaac Newton spent more time at his alchemist's furnace than working on his theory of universal gravitation. The eminent astronomers Tycho Brahe and Kepler were, at the same time, convinced astrologers. As for medical history, it cannot be understood without taking into account the contributions of the school which stood out against official (dogmatic) medicine. This tendency often rested on an esoteric form of Christianity, the Cabala or alchemy.

As early as the first century AD, Gnosticism, the heart of hermetic philosophy, sought to uphold a cultural legacy rejected by the Church as pagan or heretical. The Gnostics evoked a tradition that the initiated, who possessed hidden — even secret — knowledge, passed this down from age to age. This tradition, they claim, is found in all the ancient religions (Egyptian, Persian and Indian among others) even in an esoteric form of Christianity. This was the sacred tradition St Paul entrusted to Timothy, and among its most faithful supporters were: Dionysius the Areopagite, initiated into the mysteries of Isis before he became Bishop of Athens; Julian the Apostate, the Christian emperor who wanted to restore the cult of Cybele; and Synesius, Bishop of Ptolemais, who knew the philosophers of Alexandria. Some eternal philosophy was, therefore, absolutely essential, so that thinkers could identify a common spirit in the various cults they defended. They were encouraged in this by the example of Jewish mystical thought which, under the name of Cabala, based itself on traditions predating Moses.

The body of occult knowledge was nurtured and diffused in curious ways, often by groups gathering round a master and sometimes in spite of persecution. We must not forget that the history of occult philosophy is quite distinct from that of the secret societies like the Catharian Church, the Rosicrucians or freemasonry. The rise of these movements can be put down to motives ostensibly of a sociological nature, although this has not stopped masons using occultism as an elitist ideology.

The Nature of Occultism

Agartha

At the centre of the Earth

The notion of the centre of the world is to be found in Greek and Hebrew cultures. It also exists in occultism.

The Tibetan word 'Agartha' means 'the underground kingdom placed at the centre of the Earth, where the king of the world reigns'. This place is evidently symbolic. (The Greeks sometimes used the word *omphalos* to mean Delphi as the centre of the earth; it literally means the navel.) All the great city states attached sacred legends to the area surrounding them and, as their very construction possessed a religious significance, they were said to be the 'centre' of the world. The coexistence of several such centres caused a problem which had to be solved by political means.

The notion of a centre is interesting, for it brings us back to the coincidence of microcosm and macrocosm, or to the philosophical coincidence of universal singularity. It alludes to a myth which Jules Verne was able to exploit in his *Journey to the Centre of the Earth* and about which many other authors have fantasized. This myth also recalls the claim of the explorer F. Ossendowski that, in 1922 in Mongolia, he had met emissaries from the 'king of the world', who hides in Agartha.

The Ages of the Earth

The occult view of history

Occultism's view of history is bound up with mythology.

According to the traditions, the age of gold came first. The age of gold (or Great Age) was of indeterminate length, because it was outside time. There was, furthermore, no division between heaven and earth. This is the myth of the earthly paradise. Hesiod tells us in his poems that 'The first race of mortal men created by the immortals were the men of gold. They lived like gods, their hearts carefree and untroubled; old age did not weigh upon them.'

There followed in succession the age of silver, the age of bronze, the age of the heroes and the age of iron (in which we live today). Each of these ages marks a progressive reduction in the human state but, according to the myth of eternal renewal, it is all part of a cycle which repeats itself indefinitely.

> **Myth and Marxism**
> 'Marxism has resurrected the primitive myth of the age of gold, but has placed it exclusively at the end of the historical process instead of placing it also at the beginning.' M. Eliade, *Mythe de l'éternel retour* (The Myth of Eternal Renewal)

Alchemy

The makers of gold have something to teach us

We all think we know what alchemy is. In fact, many people do not realize that it is a spiritual way of life.

The origins of alchemy are lost in the mists of time. Were the first alchemists smiths or perfumers? Is alchemy the forerunner of modern chemistry? Traces of it can certainly be found in all civilizations, and the enigma of its origins is a long way from being solved because alchemy, like speech, is perhaps as old as the human race. Alchemy is, in effect, a metaphor for the human state.

Alchemy is not chemistry for the layman

'Vulgar chemistry is the art of destroying compounds which nature has formed, while the chemistry of the hermetists is the art of working with nature to perfect them', says Dom Pernety (in *Greek and Egyptian Fables Revealed*, 1786). The alchemist indeed perfects nature. In his eyes — in simple terms — metals such as copper and lead are diseased (or leprous) gold. His work is to restore them to their original state prior to the Fall. Why does he go to so much trouble? What is he seeking when he tries to turn lead into gold? It is impossible to reach any kind of understanding without appreciating that the best of the alchemists were not striving after 'vulgar gold'. The philosopher's stone was, in fact, the symbol of a state of inner freedom.

From Savoret
'The physical philosopher's stone and the mystical philosopher's stone are similar but not identical. To achieve the second, is to be able to achieve the first supremely; having achieved the first, one knows which way may lead to the achievement of the second but it does not necessarily mean that the journey has been made. The distinction is essential.' *Qu'est-ce que l'alchimie?* (What is Alchemy?)

But what was the nature of this state? Some writers, notably Jung, have tried to stress its religious side. However, Nicolas Flamel himself shows in his *Book of Hieroglyphic Figures* that, if religious feeling — to speak in psychic terms — constitutes the 'raw material' of the work, then alchemy by its spiritual nature transcends religion and morality. The alchemist exposes his own solitude, plunges himself into the universe and then invents his own morality (he becomes 'the child of his works').

Alchemy and eroticism

Another thesis, developed by the author of this article, can be summed up as follows:

> Passing from primitive craftmanship and magic to spirituality and nuclear chemistry, from the beginnings to Hiroshima . . . , the secret most alchemists pursued was an erotic one. How could physical love be used to create a work of art? The process known as 'distillation' symbolizes that which we call (incorrectly) mastery of the sex drive and working in the black conjures up ideas of entering the unconscious . . . The fire burning in the alchemist's furnace represents passion which has become a creative force . . . By devoting himself to alchemy, the alchemist is able to 'work' on his emotions, forebodings and even instincts, just as a painter works with shape and colour.

If eroticism was holy to the alchemists, what exactly is eroticism? And how is true eroticism the sign of creative freedom? How is it identified with spirituality? Or rather, how 'does the alchemist complete nature'? (Also, how does he convert the religious into art?) According to the sexual mythology of alchemy, the metals (which, in mythology, are gods) sleep together, torture one another, marry and give one another pleasure. We must examine these obscure, but illuminating and intriguing texts, which will prompt us to ask ourselves numerous questions. Alchemy is neither a list of recipes, nor a dogma, nor yet an ideology. It is existential poetry. It is spiritual knowledge, refined to the point where it can penetrate the dark corners where our strongest and most urgent desires lurk.

In producing the black colour, the alchemist, the adept or the artist reaches the 'centre of the earth' where metals 'sleep'. He enters the unconscious which he is going to 'burn' with his passion ... He is going to discover his bisexuality, which is symbolized by the hermaphrodite, will pass through the stages of exaltation (represented by the colour white) and finally arrive at the colour red. But the alchemistic operation, being a work of love, is a task for two. In producing the red colour, a kind of orgasmic circuit is set up; the current passes through the lovers as they embrace and helps them to discover the universe. The crowned hermaphrodite symbolizes the orgasm, just as the royal child symbolizes childhood finally rediscovered i.e. the gift of poetry. Seen in this way, alchemy is simply the conquest of love, an 'alloy' of the erotic and the spiritual. But is this conquest so simple? Is it not also an initiation, or a way of contacting the universe?

AZOTH,
OV LE MOYEN DE FAIRE
l'Or caché des Philosophes.
De Frere Basile Valentin.
Reueu, corrigé & augmenté par Mr. L'agneau Medecin.

A PARIS.
Chez PIERRE MOET, Libraire Iuré, proche le Pont S. Michel à l'Image S. Alexis.

M. DC. LIX.

Title-Page *The two triangles show the analogy between what is above and what is below, and the alchemist's tree has the seven planets as its fruit. (Wood-engraving)*

The philosopher's gold

'Thus the philosopher's gold, full of impurities, surrounded by thick darkness, covered in sadness and mourning, must nevertheless be considered the true and unique raw material of the Work, even as its own true and unique raw material is mercury, from which this gold, invisible, miserable and unnoticed, sprang.' Fulcanelli, *Les Demeures* (The Houses of Philosophy)

From Le Trévisan

'To have an understanding of this subject, one must first know that in the beginning God made matter confused and without any order, and He willed that it was full of diverse matters.' *Le Livre de la philosophie naturelle des métaux* (Book of the Natural Philosophy of Metals)

A Text on Alchemy

The following extract from Flamel's *Le Livre des figures hiéroglyphiques* gives an excellent introduction to alchemy. It refers to figures the alchemist had painted in the Cemetery of the Innocents in Paris, which can be interpreted, without any contradiction, either theologically or alchemistically.

The theological interpretation

On the other side, on the left hand, is St Peter with his key, dressed in orange-red, holding the hand of a kneeling woman. This woman, also dressed in orange, is a drawing of Perrenelle from the life, with her hands clasped and holding a scroll bearing the words *Christe precor esto pius* ('Christ, I pray, be merciful'). Behind her is an angel, kneeling, with a scroll which says *Salve Domine angelorum* ('Hail the Lord of the angels'). There is also another angel kneeling behind the drawing of me beside St Paul, also holding a scroll saying *O Rex sempiterne* ('O eternal King'). All of this can, quite obviously, be interpreted in terms of the Resurrection and the Last Judgment. Furthermore, it seems that this arch has been painted only for this reason, and that is why there is little point in dwelling on it, since people of lesser importance and the ignorant will surely give it that interpretation.

After the three people who have risen, there are two angels, also in orange and on a blue background, on whose scroll is written *Surgite mortui, venite ad Iudicium Domini mei* ('Arise, ye dead, come to the Judgment of my Lord'). This again helps the interpretation of the Resurrection, as do the last figures which follow. On a purple background, there is a man in vermilion, holding the foot of a lion, also painted vermilion, which has wings and is opening its mouth as if to devour him. It can be said that the man represents the unhappy sinner who, sleeping slothfully in the corruption of vice, dies without repenting or confessing. On this terrible day he will certainly be given to the Devil, here painted in the shape of a roaring red lion, who will swallow him and bear him away.

The alchemistic interpretation

I wish with all my heart that he who seeks this secret of the wise men, having considered in his mind these ideas of the life and resurrection to come, should draw profit from them; secondly, that he should be wiser than before, that he should carefully analyse my figures, colours and scrolls — especially my scrolls, for in this art one does not speak in vulgar fashion. [He should do all this] so that he asks himself later, why the figure of St Paul is on the right, where St Peter is usually painted, and why that of St Peter is in St Paul's place. Also, why the figure of St Paul is dressed in an orangey white colour and that of St Peter in orangey red. And, again, why the man and woman at the feet of the saints, praying to God as they would on the Day of Judgment, are dressed in various colours and are not depicted as bare bones, as if they had just risen. Why, on this Day of Judgment, this man and woman are painted at the feet of saints, when they ought to be lower down on Earth and not in Heaven. Why also the two angels in orange, bearing the scroll with the inscription *Surgite mortui, venite ad Iudicium Domini mei* ('Arise, ye dead, come to the Judgment of my Lord') are dressed in this colour and are not in their proper place, which ought to be up in Heaven with the two others playing their instruments. Why they are on a purple and blue background; but especially, why their scroll, which speaks to the dead, ends in the open mouth of the winged red lion. So I would like him, after considering these questions and others one might ask, to open the eyes of his spirit completely and to reach the conclusion that this has not been done without a reason; that is to say, that these forms have been used to represent some great secrets which he must pray to God to reveal to him.

Having thus advanced his belief by degrees, I wish further that he should understand that these figures and explanations are not meant for those who have not seen the Books of the Philosophers; such people, ignorant of the Metallic Principles, cannot be called Children of Science. For, if they wish to understand these figures, yet ignore the first agent, they will doubtless make mistakes and never understand anything. Therefore let no one blame me, if he does not understand me easily; for he will be more deserving of blame than me, especially since, without initiation into these sacred and secret interpretations of the first agent (which is the key to the doors of all the sciences), he nevertheless wishes to understand the most subtle concepts of the philosophers. The philosophers are very jealous and have written them only for those who know these Principles, which are never written in any book, because they leave them to God, who reveals them to whom He pleases, or else causes them to be taught *viva voce* by a master in the Cabalistic tradition, which does not happen often. Now, my son (I can call you this, for I am advanced in years and, besides, perhaps you are a Child of Science), God lets you learn and then work to His glory, therefore listen attentively to me. But go no further if you are ignorant of the principles of which I have just spoken.

Nicolas Flamel and Perrenelle his wife *'Trois traictez de la philosophie naturelle'* Le Livre des figures hiéroglyphiques, *trans. P. Arnauld, Paris, 1612. (Wood-engraving, National Library, Paris)*

Analogy

Analogy is occultism in action

Occultism lies on the fringes of poetry and religion. Reasoning by analogy is its royal road.

Rationalist causality associates two events in a cause and effect relationship; for example, I push this glass and it falls. Analogy, on the other hand, brings these elements together, to accentuate a feature which these two events or objects or beings share in common. The important thing about analogy is the emphasis on the features shared by the two objects under consideration. This is found throughout esoterism, where notions of sympathy, exorcism and love are essential. According to Péladan, analogy allows us to pass from the known to the unknown, from the phenomenon to the noumenon and from the visible to the invisible.

Asceticism

Let us make no mistake: hermetic asceticism is no less valid than scientific asceticism. The delirium of analogy, revealed most frequently through superstition, is due to the hold over a thinker of his own lack of understanding. In fact, the reality revealed by analogy, and highlighted through its association of ideas, is always an invisible one; it can only be perceived by someone who has been prepared (or initiated). Analogy involves the participation of the analyst as part of the process.

In hermetic thought, the method of analogy begins simply by bringing two ideas together; it ends with an intuitive grasp of the relationship between the ultimate realities of knowledge (the analogy between the microcosm and the macrocosm). The criterion of truth remains 'a clear and distinct concept', but here it becomes more of an existential illumination. On the other hand, analogy does not provide us with definitive proof, for the truth revealed is symbolic; it can, and must, be enriched over and over again. Truth in hermetism is sometimes represented by an asymptote, a line that continually approaches a curve without ever actually reaching it.

Let us take the example of Zeus and Jehovah, the unifying principles of the two philosophies to which they refer. Paradoxically, the method of analogy begins with a rather confused identification between the two figures, and finishes with contrasting details. The aim of analogy is not to get bogged down in some comparison, which might after all become quite banal, but to reach an intuitive grasp of the similarities between Zeus and Jehovah. In artistic terms, the process of displaying both figures against a uniform background serves to reveal the specific colours of each. So, in conclusion, scientific causality proceeds by means of the dogmatic division of the world, whereas analogy takes each fragment of the real world and fits it into the whole of which it is part. The two procedures are complementary and it is a great pity to neglect either one of them.

A dynamic process

'Complete identification by analogy is never achieved; by definition, the analogy can never be complete. So, analogy remains open to the interplay of consequences and changing relationships brought about by the introduction of additional experimental or conceptual information into the concrete whole. The dynamic process of analogy therefore has a legitimate place within any dialectic process.' R. Alleau, *La Science des symboles* (The Science of Symbols), Ch. IV, *La logique de l'analogie* (The Logic of Analogy)

Androgyny

At the heart of hermetism lies androgyny

Androgyny or hermaphroditism is an awareness of one's bisexuality and is the ultimate goal of the alchemist's search.

All the disciplines grouped under the general heading of hermetism or occultism — magic, alchemy, initiation, etc — suppose that the human being, once he is rid of his innermost darkness and lack of understanding, realizes that he is bisexual. This bisexuality is what enables him to relate to other people and the universe. From this point of view, the hermaphrodite symbolizes bisexuality controlled, refined and harmoniously integrated.

Active and passive

'Thus the two lights of divine being have this particular feature: that one, the active light, is male and the other, the passive light, is female.'
Zohar

In sexual magic, or in alchemy, the hermaphrodite represents the orgasm which, in turn, represents the universe, created by and in the act of love. In magic, the hermaphrodite, freed from customary human sexual polarity, represents that state of purity in which occult work may take place. It should be noted that black magic, with its techniques of alienation, aims to obscure the (potential) state of hermaphroditism.

The myth of hermaphroditism is very ancient and perhaps this is what Greek philosophy meant by 'self' and 'other'. Whatever its origin, it highlights many paradoxes which have long perplexed man: How can I remain myself? How can I grow while 'becoming' the being whom I love? How, quite simply, can I enter into relationships with the world while still preserving my own integrity?

Arithmancy

When numbers take on a new meaning

The search for the secrets of history through arithmancy has nothing to do with arithmetic.

The attribution of a special significance to numbers has given rise to a a great deal of speculation. Taking this line of thought to its limit, the use of magic numbers claims to be the science of the rhythms of man and the universe.

Human rhythms

In *De Crisibus* (1593), André de Laurens explains, for example, that every illness reaches its crisis on the seventh day and comes to an end on the 21st day. Roch le Baillif describes the 'seven year cycle of man from the womb'. He thinks that the cycles of human life can be measured in multiples of seven years: 'At four times seven, a man stands four square. At five times seven, he is at the peak of his strength. At six times seven, he keeps his strength and hair grows in his ears. And at seven times seven, he is at the peak of his wisdom.' Malfatti goes further: 'The four ages of man develop in a cycle of three times seven: twenty-one — youth; forty-two — manhood; sixty-three — old age; eighty-four — decay.'

The calculation of cosmic cycles turns out to be more complicated. From Judeo-Christianity, the end of the world was calculated at 6000 years from its creation, since the world was created in six days and each day of God is equivalent to 1000 years. But in the 19th century, the calculation became divorced from its Judeo-Christian references. In 1852 Mouësan de La Villirouet established seven laws. His first law states: 'There exists a constant correlation between the effective number of heads of any state, or of the princes of a dynasty, and the sum of the numerals of the first or the last date, or of these two dates combined.' Another law is based on the principle or reversing dates: 'Inversion of the numerals of a given date quite regularly gives either the exact duration of a given empire or dynasty, or the precise date of its fall, or a great political change, or some other event of the first order.' For example, the first year of the Capetian monarchy in France was 987 and its fall occurred in (1) 789, the numerical reversal of the first date.

The magnetism of the Earth

Captain Rémi Bruck invented a formula for calculating historical rhythms, based on the magnetism of the Earth (see 'Electricity or the Magnetism of the Earth', Brussels, 1851). He wrote: 'No one will seriously claim that the magnetic current found in every part of the Earth is there simply to direct a magnetic needle ... The magnetic system of the Earth has far more important functions to fulfil.' After a series of complicated calculations, he concluded that the birth of Christianity could not take place until 2041.

Astrology

Just what is astrology?

There is a lot of fantasy in astrological practice, but there is also an enigmatic truth.

Could an embryonic form of astrology have existed in pre-history? Whatever the case may be, the Venus of Luassel is holding a lunar crescent and it is 25 000 years old. It is known that astrology had great importance in Sumeria where it was used to reveal the portents on which the king based his actions. The ancient Egyptians used astrology in the same way, as well as the Greeks (especially Ptolemy in the third century BC) and the Arabs. Modern astrology dates from Morin de Villefranche, the author of *Astrologica gallica* (1661).

A network of correspondences

The astrologer believes in links between the stars and human beings. From these links, he deduces significant tendencies which help him to make predictions. The basic axiom of astrology is that everything living is under the influence of the stars. Proof is drawn from the influence of the moon on the tides, on women in childbirth, etc. In this way, a cause and effect relationship was proved between a person's 'map of the heavens' and his constitution — even his path through life. This is known as 'casting a horoscope'.

This way of working, though, is quite foreign to normal procedure in the occult sciences. Indeed, astrology is a cosmology. The belief is in the unity of the universe, held together by a network of correspondences and analogies: the microcosm (man) echoes the macrocosm (the universe). However, the relationship is not shown in terms of some mechanical causality — as in the profane sciences — but by analogy. Astrology, therefore, differs greatly from its popular perception. Could it even be an exact science?

Symphonic harmony

'The order of the astrological cosmos is not the order of the scientific world. The elements of the astrological cosmos do not act upon one another whereas, in the eyes of science, they exert an influence upon one another. For, the astrological cosmos is a harmonious world ... A symphonic harmony or agreement binds beings and things in a different way from that in which they influence one another. Each being and each thing has its own sign ... Nothing can escape this principle of universal symbolism ... However, here, correspondence is taken to mean anology, and not causality, agreement, and not influence.' R. Amadou, *La Tour Saint-Jacques* (The Tower of St James) No. 1, May–June 1956

A base and a support

Like the tarot, astrological practice brings together chance and meaning (see 'The Tarot'). For a creative imagination, the 'map of the heavens' is an extremely stimulating support for divination. The astrologer can lay open the subconscious of the person who is consulting him and reveal, albeit clumsily, his secret desires. He is rather in the position of Pythia, the priestess of Apollo, and obliged to stammer. Like the tarot, astrology appears to be able to make astonishingly accurate predictions; analogy reveals concrete reality by chance. This means that astrology succeeds by chance. This is not to condemn astrology absolutely, for, without art, this chance connection would not have been noticed. Could there, though, be some way of achieving correct predictions without believing in the other aspects of astrology? The question remains to tantalize us, even if — for the time being — the answer is in the negative.

'The Astrologers'

This extract from Marcus Manilius, a Latin poet of the first century, takes us to the very heart of the concepts of astrology.

'Summing up the long centuries in their vast arrangements, the astrologers allocated to each moment the event which appeared appropriate; they noted the day on which each man had been born, the vicissitudes of his life, the connection between each incident and the time at which it had taken place and the surprising differences that a moment more or less might have produced in human destiny. Then, when they had worked out the place in the heavens where each star was to be observed, and the nature of the power which every star exercised over the course of our life, they established rules based on long experience: observation of the past showed the way for the future. After much thought, they realized that the stars had an influence over man and that this influence obeyed hidden laws. They recognized, further, that the movements of the universe were governed by periodic causes, and that the vicissitudes of life were the result of different celestial conjunctions.

'Indeed, before these wise observations were made, men, with neither discernment nor guiding principles, and with nothing to go on but the evidence of their senses, were ignorant of the causes of all they saw around them. The rising of the sun seemed to them an amazing phenomenon; the setting of the stars was for them a grave loss, and their reappearance, a reason for joy. They had no idea what caused the days and nights to be of unequal length; they had not even any idea why the length of shadows varied, according to whether the sun was nearer the earth or further away. The wisdom of the human spirit had yet to give birth to the arts: the earth yielded nothing for the needs of inhabitants who did not cultivate it; gold was buried in the depths of remote mountains; and new worlds were separated from us by an ocean on which no one sailed. No one risked his life on the sea, or gave voice to his hopes: they thought it was enough for a man to know himself. But, after long centuries had trained the spirit of mankind, when hardship had given rise to thought, and the fickle hand of luck, without thwarting the desires of man, had convinced him of the necessity of looking out for himself, his mind turned to the way in which he could apply his knowledge. Every experience he rationalized then became a source of public usefulness; furthermore, each derived pleasure from communicating the results of his research to his neighbour. Thus, the language of the Barbarian peoples became polished and obeyed laws; the earth was cultivated and produced all sorts of bounty; the restless sailor braved the unknown seas and made possible trade between nations which did not know one another.'

Atlantis

A fabulous continent

It is through fictions like this that thought progresses. These fictions are transmitted by occultism.

A fabulous continent, an earthly paradise, the home of all knowledge and all civilization, Atlantis is of interest nowadays only to a few visionaries. The question seems to have been settled for all time: Plato, one of its 'inventors', was lying, or at best merely spinning a tale, when he wrote, 'In this island, which is bigger than Libya and Asia together, kings formed a great and admirable power which extended its domination ... from Libya as far as Egypt and from Europe as far as Tyrrhenia. It was an immense power whose armies marched insolently against all Europe and Asia, coming from another world situated in the Atlantic Ocean. ... But there were terrible earthquakes and floods and, in the space of one dreadful day and night, Atlantis sank into the sea and disappeared.' *Timaeus*

Myth and prejudice

'The myth of Atlantis has caused so much ink to flow (on freaks and fantasies, if not worse) that every rational person setting out to speak of Atlantis must first of all remind the reader that it is a myth and obeys the logic of myth, and not in any way the legendary echo of a historic fact; secondly that it is a platonic myth, and not some popular legend that Plato simply took up for his own purposes. This is even more tiresome, because it has been done so many times, apparently in vain, for prejudices about myths in general and this one in particular are more tenacious than historic proof; however strongly it is stated that all mythology is popular, the dream-like strength of this particular myth poses as an allegation of truth.' Sir Francis Bacon, *The New Atlantis*

The myth of the origins

Plato's 'story' may well contain traces of ancient legends, and in turn have fostered a myth about the beginnings of the world, taken up again in the 19th century by Fabre d'Olivet, who writes:

> 'Since it is proved that the Atlanteans had accepted a dogma of only one principle, which was in complete harmony with their circumstances, the obvious conclusion is that they had reached the highest degree of civilization. Their empire had set the earth alight. But after they had flourished, when the brilliance of their civilization was becoming dim, the Celts conquered them ... Egypt was the last country remaining under the domination of the Atlanteans. Therefore, in Egypt, the memory of this people was kept alive; and even after Egypt came under the domination of Phoenician shepherds, it retained the knowledge of two important traditions ... The first tradition enabled it to preserve the memory of an earlier world, together with some ideas about the southern race ... This earlier race, to which perhaps the original name of Atlantis belonged, had perished completely in the midst of a terrible flood which covered the earth and ravaged it from pole to pole ... These traditions, which the Egyptian priesthood alone possessed, justifiably gave it superiority over all others.' *Histoire philosophique du genre humain* (The Philosophical History of the Human Race).

We may be sure that Fabre d'Olivet was not Plato's only successor in this domain. The reference to Atlantis, that legendary land possessing the true knowledge of man's beginnings, occupies an important place in collective beliefs, some with frankly reactionary interpretations. However, *The New Atlantis*, by Sir Francis Bacon (1561–1626) gives surprising new life to the question: not because it throws any new light on the presumed existence of the island, but because it invites us to rethink the question entirely.

A modern myth

What does *The New Atlantis* tell us? A ship arrives at an island forgotten by the rest of the world, and the subject of the book is the description of this fabulous country and its inhabitants. This type of tale was particularly popular during the Renaissance. Bacon was neither an explorer nor a public entertainer, which prompts us to ask ourselves whether he was trying to pass on some sort of message through fiction, as was the current fashion. Many commentators have argued that Bacon simply exploited this medium in order to convey his main theme, the creation of a community of scholars. The central pages of *The New Atlantis*, describing the house of Solomon, do indeed show us how a multidisciplinary laboratory might work — something which was obviously completely unknown at that time.

Further proof that this is the way in which the book should be interpreted comes from Diderot and Kant, who greatly admired it, and took up the theme themselves (the first dedicated his *Encyclopédie* to Bacon, the second his 'Critique of Pure Reason'). Moreover, Bacon only bears a remote resemblance to Agrippa von Nettesheim, another researcher of his own period. The main resemblance between the two men comes from their encyclopedic knowledge. However, Agrippa is firmly on the side of magic, whereas Bacon seems to foresee the development of modern science.

But, however interesting this explanation may be, it is not entirely convincing. One question remains. Why did Bacon not simply say what he meant? Why did he have to dress it up as fiction? Perhaps the reason is so simple that no one thought of it. *The New Atlantis* is much more than mere allegory. Bacon makes no bones about wanting to reach the source of scientific endeavour. For him, this source can be summed up in one word: dialogue. By this he means not only the dialogue among the scholars themselves, but also the dialogue with nature. But what does it mean, to hold a dialogue with nature? How does this differ from Descartes' 'mastery and possession of nature', on which Western civilization is founded? Does this difference have any bearing on scientific processes, or affect our interpretation of them? This is not the place to go into these questions, but it should be noted in passing that Bacon is here describing a utopia which underlies many secret societies, including modern freemasonry. Indeed, the aim of all initiation ceremonies is to put the mystic once again in contact with a 'lost speech', from which the world is now cut off.

The Beyond

The initiatory mystery

By 'the beyond', does occultism mean life after death? Or is it simply a symbol? Opinions are divided.

Mircea Eliade writes that:

> Initiatory death is necessary for the beginning of spiritual life; it lays the foundation for rebirth to a higher level of 'being'. It is symbolized by darkness, by cosmic night, by the earthly womb, by the dark cell, by the belly of the monster. All these images are based on the return to an earlier state, rather than total annihilation ... The images and symbols of ritual death come from germination and embryology; they indicate that a new form of life is being prepared
> *Mystic Rebirth*

Death to the world sets up an analogy with the vital process. It initiates a rebirth, or rather the desire for rebirth because placed, as it is, symbolically at the heart of death it is placed equally at the very point where death is supposed to topple over into its antithesis. The fundamental belief is that there exists a source, or a being, above and beyond life and death. Journeys into the beyond are journeys towards that source, and are a conquest of immortality.

A subtle body

Does the beyond exist? Hermetism has no answer, for this problem does not concern it directly. However, this has not stopped writers from stating that initiation is the substitute for immortality which some of us can attain (initiation, that is to say immortality, symbolizes a real state, even if we usually cannot attain it). Can those who believe in the existence of the beyond provide any proof? With some justification, they often reply that the existential is something which is not proved, but is experienced. When asked how it is to be experienced, they reply that hermetism makes one sensitive to the beyond, for the question to which hermetism gives no answer, its founding myth, is the belief in immortality. To be more precise, the most important thing is not whether or not one believes in the beyond, but is to divest oneself of one's dark misunderstanding in order to acquire 'a subtle body': that is to say, to enter the invisible before the end of this life.

Spiritualism (see **Spiritualism**) and other ways of calling up the dead have only a very remote link with hermetism. Similarly, the theory of reincarnation is quite foreign to it. So, the *Bardo Thödol* — like the Egyptian 'Book of the Dead' — speaks of earlier life or after-life only in symbolic terms. So what does come after death? Once again, hermetism provides no answer. Entry into the invisible, the philosopher's stone and initiation are all concerned only with deliverance from the sicknesses of death, that is to say from the fantasies which are attached to it. It is these fantasies or fears which hinder us as much from living as from accepting our true death. The initiate echoes Rilke, who spoke of wishing to 'mature his own death'.

Man as a spirit

'All these creative equivalences, symbols and metaphors, consequences of the raising of death to an exemplary model for all important transitions, underline the spiritual function of death, because death transforms man into a spirit — whether soul, or breath of life, or an ethereal body or some other similar thing.'
Mircea Eliade, *Occultisme, sorcellerie et modes culturelles* (Occultism, Sorcery and Culture)

Black Magic

Conjuring up devils

Sometimes called 'goety', from the Greek goes, *'wailer', because of the shrieking of incantations which was supposed to bring the spirits out of their lair.*

Throughout history, it is only second-rate magicians who have practised black magic. However, in the Middle Ages, everybody, witches and the Church alike, believed in the possibility of calling forth spirits. It was, according to Alexandrian, in his *Histoire de la philosophie occulte*, a 'general belief backed by the law.'

A sinister ceremony

The ceremony takes place at night in a cemetery or amongst ruins or, better still, in a place where a crime has been committed. The officiant wears a black cloak and a lead skull-cap and he holds a hazel wand on which are engraved the letters of the sacred tetragram (God's name in Hebrew). On the ground he draws a protective magic circle which he must on no account leave. The 'signatures' of the demons who are to be invoked (represented by letters and geometric figures) have already been drawn outside the circle. A dreadful smell, 'the sooty stink of Saturn', hangs in the air. An animal — dog, cat or cock — is sacrificed and its blood, held in a copper vessel, attracts the demons. The officiant has rubbed his body with a magic ointment and he now reads aloud the incantation from a book of spells. The demons are now supposed to appear; the magician has only to touch them with his wand to force them to come into the circle and obey him.

A former companion of Joan of Arc, the notorious Gilles de Rais, devoted himself to black magic from 1426 to 1440, assisted by a priest, Eustache Blanchet and an alchemist, Prelati. Children were sacrificed at these rituals, and Gilles de Rais would go into the magic circle trembling in every limb. One day his cousin, Gilles de Silé, assisting on this occasion, leapt from the window when he thought he saw the devil in person. Black magic became a fairly common practice with certain feudal overlords; Henry III, for example, was reputed to have a demon called Terragon in his personal service.

The invocation

'I, (say your name), summon you, the spirit (say the name of the spirit), in the name of the great and living God, to appear to me in the shape of (say what shape the spirit is to take); if not, St Michael the archangel, invisible, will strike you down into the depths of hell. Come therefore, (say the name of the spirit), come, come, come, to do my will.' Collin de Plancy, *Dictionnaire des sciences occultes* (Dictionary of Occult Sciences)

Fanciful books of spells

The oldest known such book is the famous 'Key of Solomon'; it was compiled in Byzantium and Latin copies were in circulation as early as the 12th century. In it, King Solomon tells his son, Roboam, the methods revealed to him by 'a light in the shape of a burning star' to secure 'enjoyment of all earthly treasures and all natural things'. Solomon 'discovered the secret of how to shut a million satanic spirits in a bottle of black glass, together with seventy-two of their kings, among whom the first was Bileth, the second Belial and Asmodeus the third'.

The Black Mass

Spirituality in reverse

The black mass has nothing to do with occultism, but it is an old custom to link them.

Originally, the black mass was a particular part of the ceremony of the sabbath, when witches were seen riding on their broomsticks and copulating with Satan in person. It is a real act, made its own by the aristocracy, whereas for the people the sabbath remains in the realm of fantasy. In simple terms, the black mass is a revolt against religion, not by breaking rules or abandoning religion, but by inverting its meaning, so that God is no longer venerated, and the Devil is worshipped in His place.

A satanic ritual

Gilles de Rais, marshal of France, condemned to death in 1440, used to hold wild black masses before any ritual had become established. As Satan refused to appear, he tried to entice him by offering, wrapped in white linen, the hands, hearts, eyes and blood of children he had killed after abusing them in sadistic orgies. However, if the historians are to be believed, the ritual of the black mass was invented in the time of Louis XIV by Catherine Monvoisin, known as la Voisin, who was an abortionist, astrologer and reputed magician. Part of her clientele was made up of ladies from the court, and the Duchess of Bouillon, who wanted to kill her husband in order to marry the Duke of Vendôme, consulted her. La Voisin procured the fat of hanged men from the public hangman in Paris. Among her specialities, she included that of 'burning the faggot': a mixture of incense and alum was put on a faggot which was then set alight and, when it was burning fiercely, was sprinkled with wine and salt. In this way, it was believed, all wishes could be granted. La Voisin also dabbled in sexual black magic, abortions and poisoning. The most interesting point is that she had priests amongst her disciples, for sacrilege committed by a priest was considered necessary to make the spell work.

Abbé Guibourg, main acolyte and lover of la Voisin, used to celebrate black mass over a naked woman. Assisted by another naked woman, between two consecrations he would say conjurations to Asmodeus and Ashtaroth, two propitious demons. Abbé Gilles, who took his place sometimes, did not always resist temptation: 'While saying mass, he kissed her shameful parts, and he was not alone in doing such things, for Gérard, the priest of St-Sauveur, also said mass over the belly of a shopkeeper's daughter from the rue St Denis whom he had debauched.' Abbé Guibourg sometimes killed children. The Duchess of Vivonne, who wanted to see the statesman Colbert die, had an abortion and offered the foetus to the Devil, in the belief that this would bring about the fulfilment of her wishes; whether or not this caused Colbert's death shortly thereafter must, however, remain mere speculation.

Far removed from occultism

The practices of the black mass or sabbath have no connection with occultism, even if it is true that la Voisin and her accomplices knew the works of Agrippa very well. However, it would be disgraceful to link Agrippa's philosophy with such practices. This has been attempted, by people whose only excuse can be the most rigid dogma.

The Cabala

The mysterious Cabala is a form of Gnosticism

The secret of the Cabala is that of Gnosticism.

The Cabala, essentially of Jewish origin but sometimes assimilated into Christianity, is first and foremost a 'quest for the secrets of the faith', according to the *Zohar*, its most famous book. It relates to every domain of creation: from the secrets of the faith to the secret of the universe, from the knowledge of God to knowledge of man. The Cabala is based on a commentary on sacred texts and the *Torah*, and on the 'marrow extracted from them'. The *Zohar* says that 'ignorant people consider only the clothes that are the story; they see nothing more than that and do not realize what the clothes conceal. Those who know a little better, see not only the clothes, but the body beneath them. The wise — the servants of the supreme king and the same people who were present in Sinai — consider only the soul, which is the essence of the real *Torah*.' So there is a hidden meaning in the sacred texts, and we must discover it in order to approach the mysteries of the Creation.

The ten *sefirot*

The novelty of the Cabala lies in the 'secrets of divine truth'. The divinity described by Cabalists, though, is quite different from the other forms found in Judaism. The Cabala is a heresy at the heart of Judaism, as Catharism was for Christianity. Isaiah Tishby writes, 'Instead of the severe law-giver and guide, the forgiving father, the King raised up for the initiates of the chariot (in Ezekiel's vision), the necessary Being and the mysterious Motor . . . , instead of all these, the Cabala presents a many-faceted and complex face of God, at first view quite foreign to the genius of Israel'. In the beginning, according to the Cabala, 'God wished to see God'. By a free act of creation, he drew back the absolute All (*Ain Sof*) and contracted it to allow a hole to appear in it where the mirror of existence was to emerge. This act is called *Zimzum* ('contraction'). A rabbinic saying holds that 'the place of God is the world, but the world is not the place of God'. From the *Ain Sof Or* (the light without end surrounding the void), a ray of light *Kav* shone out at ten different levels, known as the *sefirot*. The root of the Hebrew word *sefira*, singular of sefirot, is similar to that of 'cipher' and 'sphere'. The sefirot have been presented as the receptacles, or the tools, of God; or as his ten faces or hands, or his clothes. All agree, however, that they represent overlapping divine attributes.

The practical Cabala

'M. Scholem does not agree that the influence of the practical Cabala should be underestimated although it lies in the domain of mythology, alchemy and magic. It is as valuable as the speculative Cabala, or at least, in his eyes, the two branches make up one and the same doctrine. It therefore serves no purpose to dissociate them. Whether the practical Cabala corresponds to the truth or not is of little importance; it rests on historical fact.' H. Serouya, *La Kabbale*

According to the Cabala, the **dibbuk** is a spirit which takes possession of a living person. A famous legend tells how a young Cabalist was in love with a certain girl. He died and subsequently took possession of her body. This legend appears in a fine play, *The Dibbuk*, by Charles Anski.

Relations between the sefirot are governed by three principles, the hidden Splendours (*Zazahot*). These are: Will, which keeps balance; Mercy, which spreads the flux of the emanation; and Severity, which contains it. In this way, the Splendours organize the sefirot, according to a model known as the Tree of Life or Cabalistic tree: this is the archetype by which Creation is ordered. The sefirot are God's attributes, but they can also be understood in terms of human experience; they are the common measure between the Creator and his creation. The Cabala is a type of Gnosticism, as man seeks to find divinity within himself. First of all, he discovers nothingness, symbol of the nearness of God; this is when the mystic empties himself to become a receptacle for transcendence.

The first sefira is called *Keter Elyon*, the crown. As the point of the original emanation and final reabsorption — for in the end the world will return to its non-manifest state — it is expressed as 'I am, I was, I shall be', i.e. the name of Jehovah (often translated as 'I am who I am'). Under the influence of the Splendours, the shining light spreads to create the second sefira, *Hokhma*, or Wisdom which is also called 'Veiled Thought' and is the thought of God. It contains the general plan of the construction of the world, which is manifested concretely in the third sefira, *Bina* or Intelligence. Thereafter come *Hesed*, or Grace; *Gevura*, or Power; *Tiferet*, or Beauty; *Nezah* or Permanence; *Hod*, or Reverberation; and *Yesod*, or Foundation. The last one is *Malkhut*, or Royalty and receives the outpouring of the last three. The theoretical problem of the Cabala is how to preserve the unity of the Creator, while taking account of the Splendours of his epiphany: the emanation might after all seem to fragment the divine Being. The *Zohar* refutes this by stating that 'in creating this world below, the world above lost nothing. It is the same for each sefira: if one is illuminated, the next loses none of its brilliance.'

Letters and numbers
'Nobody should be surprised', writes Agrippa von Nettesheim, 'that things can be divined by the numerical value of letters. According to the Pythagoreans and the Hebrew Cabalists, in numbers there are hidden mysteries which few understand. The Most High created all things by number, dimension and weight; by these numbers it is possible to work out the essence of letters and names.' *La Magie céleste* (Celestial Magic).

A world of symbols

The sefirot have often been likened to symbols — they look like 'a priori categories' (in Kant's sense) of mystical experience. The Cabalists pursue their quest for symbols by deciphering the *Torah*, in which the divine light is clothed in consonants and words. There is a way of reading the Bible, according to Tishby, which 'reveals a fabric of sacred names which shine through countless combinations'. This has given rise to some quite extraordinary speculation: a meld of the most uninhibited surrealism and the purest poetry. However, the superstitious numerology of the Cabala is not limited to the *Torah*, for the earth and its inhabitants are ordered according to a divine archetype.

In the *Zohar*, we read that 'the human dimension contains all things, and all that exists in accordance with that . . . Man contains all that is in heaven above and on earth below, both heavenly and earthly creatures.' This is not mere anthropomorphism. The Cabala reminds us, beautifully and despairingly, that man remains the measure of everything. Every experience of the 'other' — and God is the absolute 'other' — is but an experience of the same, that of the being of the experimenter. This holds true unless the experimenter discovers the nothingness which invests him and he then places himself simultaneously at the very tip of his own being. Truth is what roots a man to the earth and, at the same time, enables him to transcend it.

Doctrinal sources

'Cabala' means tradition or reception. In mythology, it begins with the oral tradition given to Moses in Sinai. Some writers go even further back, and place the beginning

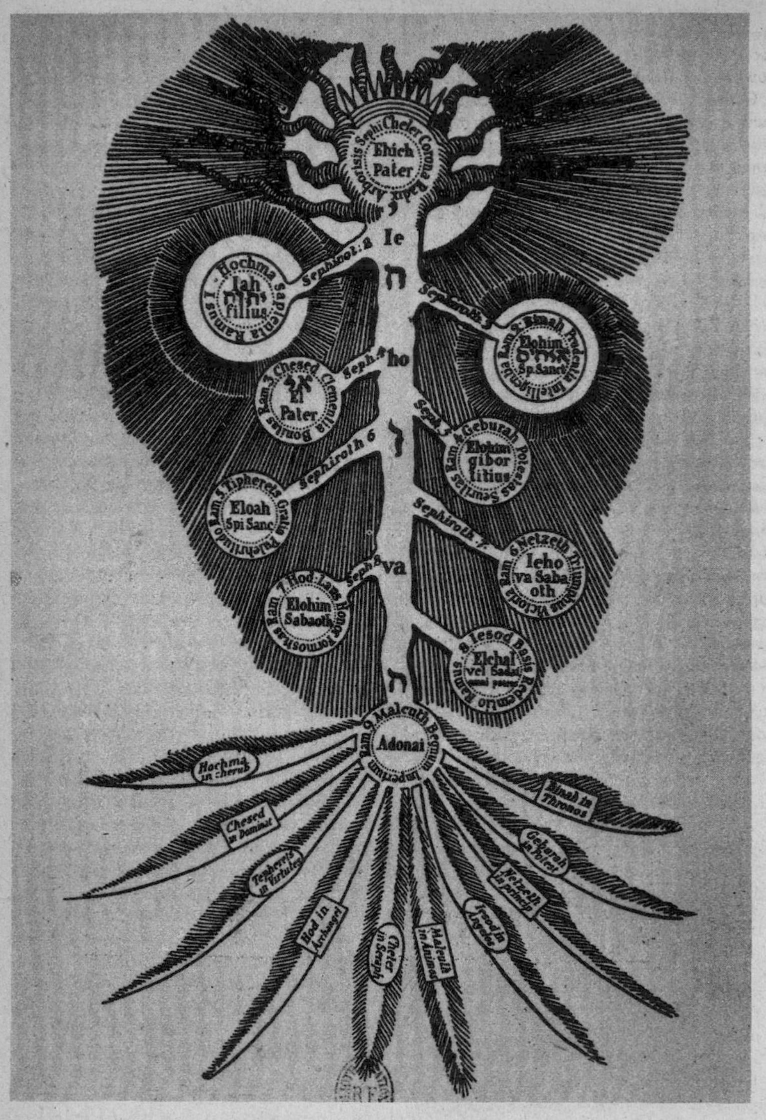

The Cabalistic tree and the sefirot
represent the scheme of creation in Jewish esoterism. (National Library, Paris)

of the quest of the Cabala with Abraham or even the Assyrians, and perhaps its roots are in prehistory. Historical criticism, however, relies on texts. There is certainly a Gnostic approach in the *Merkaba*, the meditation on Ezekiel's vision; but it was only in the 12th century that Abraham ben Huya wrote down the doctrine in the *Sefer Bahir*, by drawing together earlier materials. The *Sefer Bahir* even contains a fragment of the *Sefer Yetsira*, which was not published until 1562, although it dates back to between the second and the fifth centuries.

The *Zohar* appeared in the 13th century, the period when the Cabala flourished, and is probably the work of Moses of León. It is placed under the (symbolic) authority of Rabbi Simeon bar Yokhai, who codified the second century BC Cabala with the help of visions transmitted by the prophet Elijah, who is supposed to have left the after-life to help him. In the time of the Cathars, doctrinal renewal came from Provençal writers such as Abraham ben Isaac, Abraham ben David and his son, Isaac the Blind, who helped to explain the relationship between God and his manifestation; from Italian writers, including Juda Ben Yagar, Ezra ben Solomon, and the brothers Isaac, who defined the nature of intermundane space (that is the dwelling-place of mythical and demoniacal creatures); and finally from German writers, in particular Abraham Abulafia, who added a technique of spiritual experience to the doctrine.

In the Christian world, notably at the time of the Renaissance, many people began to take an interest in the Cabala, including Pico della Mirandola (1463–94), Reuchlin (1455–1522), Guillaume Postel (1510–81), Paracelsus (1493–1541), Robert Fludd (1574–1637), Jakob Böhme (1575–1624) and Kircher (1601–80). 'The Cabala, whether accepted or rejected, is as important a discovery as the New World', as P. Secret put it in *Le Soleil chez les Kabbalistes Chrétiens* (The Sun and the Christian Cabalists).

In the Cabala, the **Golem** is an automaton, or rather a 'clay being', to which a rabbi gave life by slipping a piece of paper between its lips with the name of God written on it. This legend was particularly current in the Prague ghetto in the Middle Ages, and has given rise to numerous novels and films.

There is also a **dream of Golem** in medieval Christian literature, with a 'homunculus' or little man, to which a magician — often St Albert the Great — had managed to give life. The Golem helped to protect persecuted Jews, while the homunculus took care of the domestic tasks of the magician. (See Gustav Meyrink, *Le Golem*.)

A primordial speech?

The Cabala is, by nature, Gnostic, a search for the secret of Creation. Like all Gnosticism, it proposes a cosmogony in which man is an actor with a major role to play, even that of a collaborator with God. In this way, the Cabala attempts to answer the problem of evil. The creation of the world does indeed cause a break in divinity (and the symbol of the shattering of vases occurs here). But whereas the Gnosticism of Alexandria, for example, is manifested in a profusion of images, the Cabala adopts a nonfigurative form. Cabalistic speculation sets out to be rigorous, combinative and mathematical. Under the jumble of obscurities and poetic flights of fancy, it may even contain the (unconscious) elementary structures of scientific thought. It could even be, for our civilization, the source, albeit at times confused, of a primordial speech.

It is hardly surprising that Cabalistic writings — and they are legion, even if the best known examples date only from 12th and 13th century Provence and Spain — embrace all spheres of knowledge, containing reflections on astrology (viewed with little favour), alongside those on the government of the world, the metaphysics of numbers, geological phenomena and life after death. We should, at this point, note two theories which have attracted a lot of comment: according to one, God based the creation of the world on the letters of the Hebrew alphabet; and according to the other, a numerical value was assigned to each Hebrew letter so that words with the same 'value' were equivalents.

The division of the soul

One theory dominates the *Zohar* — that of the division of the soul into three parts: *nefech*, the organic breath; *rouah*, the spirit; and *nechama*, the power of man. The soul which comes down to animate a body refuses to leave its original place, but in the end it must always obey God's will. It must win its complement of perfection from the material world and, at the same time, it is charged with the task of impregnating matter with a share of spirituality in order to purify it and draw it upwards. Thus, the body is a combination of saintliness and stain; it is a mediator of cosmic forces.

> Rabbi Eleazar asked Rabbi Simeon, 'Knowing that men must die, why does God send their souls down here?' The answer given is: firstly, so that they may know His glory (by studying the *Torah*); and secondly, in order to fulfil the text, 'Drink waters out of thine own cistern and running waters out of thine own well' (Proverbs 5:15). The cistern is a dry place; water only appears in it when the soul is perfected. Thus, the soul rejoins its source; all is perfect above and below and the ascension of the soul is accomplished by the wakening of the passion of the feminine for the masculine. The waters well up from below and the cistern is transformed into a source of living water. The identification of passion and desire is accomplished. The soul of the just man transforms the dry place; love and passion are awakened above, and all is Unity. *Zohar*

The cosmic drama always tells a story of love. All the texts and all the evidence point in this direction. The Cabalist has to fight against the darkness of the world and his quest is to try to illuminate it. The intense passion which guides him shows that love and knowledge are often synonyms. The dryness of the heart is the enemy, the face of that evil which the initiate must root out from within himself. The secret, in the end, lies beyond morality: it is the secret of the source the *Zohar* describes, and which the Cabala calls upon us to rediscover.

Gematria

Along with the notarikon, gematria is a process of Cabalistic magic. The object is to bring together words with the same numerical value. Each letter of the Hebrew alphabet has a corresponding numerical value, so that the value of each word is the sum of the value of its letters. Words with the same value can be brought together in order to reveal their hidden meaning. Thus, in Hebrew, where 'one' is *ehad* and 'love' is *ahaba*, the two words refer to the same transcendental reality because they have the same value (in one case $1 + 8 + 4 = 13$ and in the other $1 + 5 + 2 + 5 = 13$).

The **notarikon** is a method using the first, middle or last letters of a word to form another. **Temura** combines both gematria and notarikon.

Divination

From coffee grounds and tea-leaves to tarot cards

The methods of fortune-telling are numerous; only the support varies.

Eliphas Lévi writes that 'divination, in its widest sense, as well as its literal meaning, is the exercise of divine power and realization of divine science. It is the priesthood of the magi. This implies the need for religious feeling, turned to different ends from those of conventional religion. The devote worshipper serves a divine force; the magus uses it.

The term 'divination' denotes all types of knowledge, paranormal and esoteric: knowledge of the future, of the past, of things far away, of things hidden from normal sight and of the occult. Divination can proceed either through a medium or directly: a medium may use astrology, read the entrails of a sacrificed animal (haruspicy), use cards or any other support; direct knowledge of the future may be gained by intuition, vision, or the second sight. Cicero writes in *De Divinatione* 'There are two types of divination: one comes from art, and the other from nature.'

The art of divination

Apart from astrology, the arts of divination include several specialities, some of which are listed below.

Geomancy is the art of telling the future through observations of land forms or of the patterns made by dust thrown at random on to a flat surface. **Physiognomy** is reading a person's character according to the shape of his features. **Chiromancy** is the knowledge of the character or destiny of a person gained by reading the lines on his hand. **Metascopy** is fortune-telling using the lines on the forehead. The future can also be told by interpreting dreams (**oneiromancy**), by using mirrors (**catoptromancy**), and by using playing cards (**cartomancy**). **Rhabdomancy**, or dowsing, is the art of finding springs, hidden treasure or mines, using a rod which twitches at the moment of the discovery, or a pendulum which swings over the object sought. **Necromancy** claims to call forth the dead to obtain from them revelations about the future.

We should note in passing that oneiromancy (the interpretation of dreams) finds its scientific expression in Freudian psychoanalysis. There were, however, many precursors, the most remarkable of whom was perhaps Synesius, a Greek born at Cyrene about 370, who was a pupil of the female philosopher Hypatia, who taught at Alexandria. In his treatise *Concerning Dreams*, Synesius writes, 'Sleep is offered to all; it is an oracle, which is always there and ready, an infallible and silent counsellor. In the mysteries of sleep everyone is, at one and the same time, his own priest and initiate.' Another remarkable work is *Le Palais du sommeil*, written by Célestin de Mirbel, a magistrate under Louis XIV. This work is less rational than Synesius', and more interested in telling the future from dreams.

From Paracelsus

'There are many ways of fortune-telling, other than palmistry, which enable a man's inclinations and destiny to be discovered, or the good and the bad which will befall him to be foretold ... Other means include using herbs, leaves, wood, stones and spirits, or even divination by landscapes, roads and rivers.'

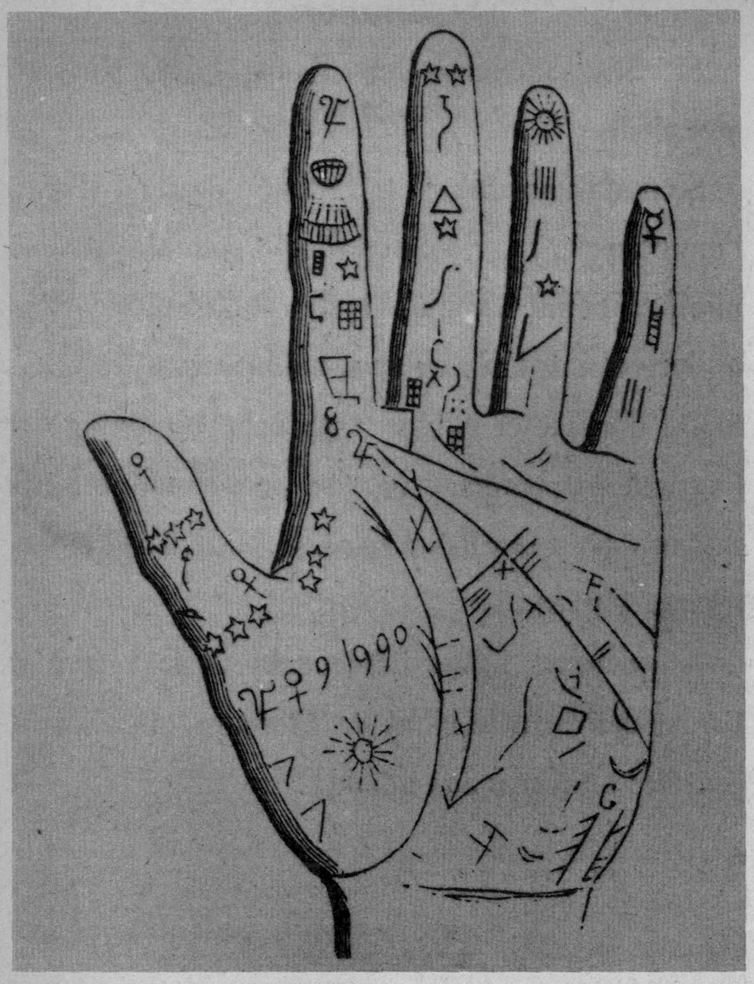

Study of the left hand of Napoleon I *in 'The Complete Handbook of Chiromancy', attributed to Marie-Anne Lenormand, Volume II (Paris, 1845): 'Here is the complete explanation in its minutest detail. I examine this hand with great curiosity. It might have rested with pride on the most glorious period of his reign.' (National Library, Paris)*

The Elements

The building-bricks of the universe

The four elements of ancient philosophy are neither matter nor principle, but both at the same time.

In traditional alchemy, as in Aristotle's physics, the universe is made up of four elements — fire, water, air and earth. It is of more than passing interest that the number four symbolizes firmness or stability (see **Numbers and Symbolism**). We have the four points of the compass, by which we define our place in the world, four seasons, four gospels, etc. Therefore, according to the lights of the ancient world, there could only be four constituent elements for the universe. However, according to Heidegger, who takes as his basis pre-Socratic thought, these four constituents are only modes or aspects of a single form of matter, which he calls 'being'.

Squaring the circle

In hermetism, the four elements are types of operation (see **Initiation**). They are not to be identified in terms of their earthly forms; in alchemy, fire does not mean fire, but symbolizes passion (human as well as divine, at the joining of which the fire blazes). So the four elements are simultaneously qualities of the physical world and psychological projections. It seems that they might symbolize the four typical modes of existential penetration: the alchemists sought only to restore to the elements their purity in chemical, not moral, terms.

The alchemists speak sometimes of the squaring of the circle, an important symbol in alchemy. They do, however, find it difficult to talk in such terms. This is not surprising, for every operation in alchemy is first and foremost an existential operation. But is the existential really indescribable? Does it not fall within the domain of a special, esoteric, form of mathematics? Perhaps the answer can be found in t'ai chi where, by alternation, the square (the earth) and the circular (heaven) are made to produce one another.

T'ai chi

According to Taoism, the world is governed by a cosmic energy made up of two opposite forces: yin (feminine and negative) and yang (masculine and positive). Marcel Granet explains the famous diagram of t'ai chi in this way: 'The double (yin) and the indivisible (yang), the square (symmetrical) and the round (centred) produce one another, or rather alternate in rhythmic fashion. The geometric ideal is an assimilation (succeeding an opposition) of the straight line and the curve, of the diameter and the semi-circle, of two and of three; that is to say a complete refusal to give a value to one.'

Esoterism

Questions of vocabulary

Keep the dictionary handy!

'Esoteric' was the adjective applied in ancient Greece to teaching in certain schools, and used also of any particularly well-qualified pupils; the esoteric completed and deepened the doctrine. It could be applied to any doctrine or body of knowledge which was transmitted by oral tradition to qualified adepts.

In university philosophy, the esoteric is first and foremost the initiated disciple of Pythagoras. According to Iamblichus in his *Life of Pythagoras*, if the disciples had been judged worthy by their way of life and their civility, after a silence of five years, they became known as esoterics and were entitled to hear Pythagoras, wearing a linen garment and with the advantage of seeing him.

The esoteric is also the occult sense of a work of art. According to the Shi'ite 'Hadith of the Sixth Imam', 'Our cause is the truth of truth. It is the exoteric, the esoteric of the exoteric and the esoteric of the esoteric. It is the secret of the secret; it is the secret of that which remains veiled, a secret which remains wrapped in secret.' In short, the esoteric is the hidden content of a doctrine, teaching, or any given thing.

Esoterism

Esoterism may be defined as a 'doctrine, according to which knowledge cannot or must not be vulgarized, but only communicated to a few disciples.'

The central hypothesis of most occultists is that esoterism constitutes a whole body of knowledge. 'Traditional esoterism is at one and the same time doctrine and practice. It implies for the whole of the being, body, soul and spirit, a fundamentally different way of existence.' R. Abellio, *La Fin de l'ésotérisme* (The End of Esoterism).

Pseudo-esoterism is a parody, even trickery. According to René Guénon, 'This pseudo-esoterism, of which we have perhaps a few examples in the fancies and diversions we have been talking about (occultism, theosophy etc), is probably still quite some way from the mark.' His follower, Schuon, for his part, gave a definition of 'pre-esoterism':

'The distinction must be made between esoterism proper and what we might call 'pre-esoterism': the latter is no more than exoterism, ascetic, strict, subtle, internalized and excessively refined; whereas the former is built on higher concepts which therefore prevent moral and social extravagance.' *Philosophic Review* No. 1032, 1974

So, is there any objective criterion which would enable us to distinguish between esoterism and its counterfeits? There is, unfortunately, no absolute answer, as esoterism is more of an art than a science.

Closed language

'In traditional African societies, this philosophy is presented in two quite separate forms: knowledge which is expressed but remains esoteric, and underlying themes which are implied. The most perfect example of the first type is the cosmology of the Dogon, which was revealed to Marcel Griaule by an old initiate (see *Dieu d'eau. Entretiens avec Ogotemmeli* The God of Water. Conversations with Ogotemmeli, 1948). These esoteric traditions are expressed, as are all sacred texts, in a language which is rich in images and closed to the non-initiate and which thus needs detailed exegesis.' J. Maquet, *Dictionnaire des civilisations Africaines* (Dictionary of African Civilization)

Freemasonry

Its historic role

There are three aspects to freemasonry — the initiatory, the historical and the psychosociological.

Although an impressive number of books have been devoted to it — at least 60 000 to date — freemasonry remains largely misunderstood, especially in Latin countries. Modern freemasonry (we have no knowledge of earlier forms) came into being on 24 June 1717, the Feast of St John, when the Grand Lodge of London was created. Having united four lodges of operative masons, the Grand Lodge codified four ancient charters and produced the texts known as *The Anderson Constitutions*, which remain to this day the central tenets of freemasonry.

The centre of union

One of the founding texts of modern freemasonry, *The Anderson Constitutions*, published in 1723, says:

A *mason* is obliged, by his Tenure, to obey the moral Law; and if he rightly understands the Art, he will never be a stupid Atheist, nor an irreligious Libertine. But though in ancient Times Masons where charged in every Country to be of the religion of that Country or Nation, whatever it was, yet 'tis now thought more expedient only to oblige them to that Religion in which all men agree, leaving their particular Opinions to themselves; that is to be good Men and True, or Men of Honour and Honesty, by whatever Denominations or Persuasions they may be distinguished, whereby Masonry becomes the centre of union, and the means of conciliating true Friendship among persons that must have remained at a perpetual Distance.

A history shrouded in mystery

How far do we have to go back to find the real origins of freemasonry? Anderson, the editor of the *Constitutions*, tells us in both symbolic and historical terms. He tells us that the institution goes right back to Adam and at the same time he tells us that the first charters were granted to masons by the Anglo-Saxon king, Athelstan (895–940). In this way he alludes to a historical chronology, which we can see for ourselves, and also to an extra-historical chronology (in which Adam symbolizes the mists of time). We shall see that this double reference constitutes the essential originality of the masonic movement. Freemasonry develops in an ambivalent manner; more precisely, there is a continual coming and going between visible, or concrete, reality and invisible, or mythological, reality.

Practically everyone agrees that modern *speculative* freemasonry derives directly from historical *operative* freemasonry. But when we try to discover the origins of the latter, we are faced with legends, that is to say a strange, sometimes crazy, symbolism, mixed up with historical memories. Moreau wrote in 1837 that God was the first freemason, and that the society of freemasons existed before the creation of the earth. However, the main story is that of Hiram, the architect whom King Solomon brought from Tyre to build the Temple of Jerusalem and of whom we read in the Old Testament, in the first book of Kings and in Chronicles. This story — or myth — is so important that modern freemasonry has seized upon it as its central mystery, and the ceremony to confer the degree of master is a re-enactment of it. Hiram, to whom Solomon had entrusted the supervision of the work on this temple, according to the biblical legend, had under his command such a great number of workmen that he could not recognize them all. To distinguish between them, a system of different *words, signs* and *touches* was devised. Modern masonry still embodies a hierarchy along these lines, each degree having its own signs. The legend goes on to tell how three journeymen all wanted to be put in command. When Hiram refused, they killed him. In the ceremony of *elevation*, the man who is being made into a master mason identifies himself in succession with the three journeymen who symbolize his inner darkness and with Hiram who is his light. He dies to the world, killed by his alienation, in order to be reborn in freedom.

The choice of a symbol is never arbitrary. Why did the freemasons choose the legend of Hiram instead of, say, the legend of Osiris? René Guénon responds by pointing out that Hiram is a builder and that the temple in Jerusalem symbolizes the will of the Jewish people to take up residence there. This is clearly a builder's initiation. The journeymen referred to it in a concrete, or operative, manner and the freemasons in an intellectual, or speculative, manner. A curious detail is that the transformation from operative to speculative freemasonry corresponds to the period of the centralization of the initiating lodges. The Grand Lodge of London united a number of scattered lodges which had up until then been self-governing, thus enabling the initiating phenomenon to be adapted to the modern age.

The early history of freemasonry is difficult to separate from the history of the trade groups, Roman collegia, brotherhoods and corporations. It was in the 13th century that the trades began to organize themselves, and the earliest texts which mention freemasons are from England. There is one mention of freemasons in 1376, and in 1396 the Archbishop of Canterbury made a distinction between freemasons and vassal-masons. We should remember that in the Middle Ages, the word 'free' could be applied to any person who was not bound to a feudal overlord.

Freemasonry was, however, never exclusively operative. Religious and initiatory preoccupations were always side by side with the concrete, professional preoccupations — the transmission of technical skill and defence of members' interests, as in modern trade unionism. To these, we could add helping members in distress, charity and the duty of looking after the good behaviour of initiates. The dual nature of the movement became accentuated by the admission of 'accepted' members, that is to say those who did not belong to the trade, and lodges sometimes became a meeting ground for tradespeople and men of culture. Two things — the disappearance of the work sites where the great cathedrals were built, and the Renaissance — were to bring about the decline of the brotherhoods, thereby leaving vacant a structure, of which people of a more speculative turn of mind could take advantage.

Britain, France and Europe

As soon as modern freemasonry was created, it found itself torn between various tendencies, which gave rise to schisms, reunifications and conflicts. The first quarrel between the ancients and the moderns arose in 1753. The ancients recalled the guiding principle 'of the free mason in the free lodge', which seemed to be running counter to the current trend of centralization, but principally they accused the moderns of secularizing the ritual. This is a quarrel which persists to this day, in another form, between various rites, within rites and sometimes even within lodges, but which will not be pursued in detail here. To complete the early part of the history of freemasonry, it is sufficient to note that the quarrel between the ancients and moderns, at least in England, was settled by the fusion of the two groups under the name of the United Grand Lodge of the Ancient Freemasons of England. However, the Grand Lodge of England, with members of the Royal Family among its dignitaries, claims even today to be the only one to hold 'masonic regularity' and to have the right to attribute 'patents' to different lodges in various parts of the world.

Modern masonry was introduced to France, from Scotland, in 1649, in an earlier form than that which resulted from the fusion under the Grand Lodge of London. This freemasonry crossed the Channel when Henrietta Maria, widow of Charles I, took refuge in the Palace of Saint-Germain. In 1721, a specifically English form of freemasonry entered France and the first lodge appears to have been set up in Dunkirk. We can be certain that various lodges were set up in 1729, among them 'St Thomas with the Silver Louis', which used to meet in the house of the famous Parisian caterer, Landelle, in the rue de Buci; it received its patent from London or perhaps from the *Parfaite Union* ('Perfect Union') of Valenciennes. By 1753, there were 200 lodges in France, of which 22 were in Paris.

In 1735, the 'English' lodges wanted to remain under the control of London, while organizing themselves into a group within France. London refused, principally because they were on good terms with the Scottish lodges. Faced with this refusal, French freemasonry took the bull by the horns and set up a specifically French rite, the provincial Grand Lodge, with the Duke of Antin as its Grand Master. In 1772 a certain number of the brothers, a minority, grouped themselves into a rival organization, the Grande Loge de France.

The rapid development of freemasonry could not help but draw attention to itself: secret societies always have a bad reputation, especially if they have connections with foreign countries. However, at long last, the masonic movement became accepted. At the time immediately prior to the Revolution, freemasonry occupied a very prominent position in France, with its membership numbering such important people as La Fayette, Brissot, Condorcet, Talleyrand and Voltaire. The same was true in America, where Washington, Franklin and all the 'Fathers of Independence' were members, and later, in Europe, where Mozart, Goethe, Lessing and Nerval were all masons.

The masonic system

'Various degrees of freemasonry can be distinguished:
Blue (the first three degrees:
Apprentice, Journeyman and Master);
Red and Black (degrees 19 to 30, according to the Accepted and Ancient Scottish Rite);
White (grades 31, 32 and 33);
Masonry of the Templars, of the Rosicrucians, Hermetic Masonry and Egyptian Masonry.' P. Riffard, *Dictionnaire de l'ésotérisme* (Dictionary of Esoterism), 1983

Freemasonry and revolution

A number of writers, including the notorious Abbé Barruel (see his *Memoirs to Help in Understanding the History of Jacobinism*, London 1797), believe that the movement of freemasonry actually started the French Revolution. This theory was especially popular with the enemies of the Republic, who never understood that the French Revolution, far from being the result of a plot, was really a groundswell of public opinion. On the other hand, there is no doubt that freemasonry, along with the *Encyclopédistes*, paved the way for the event by creating 'clubs' whose very existence ran counter to the customs of the Ancien Régime. Certainly, the activities of the lodges foreshadowed the spirit of democracy. In the closing days of the Ancien Régime, freemasonry was one of the few spheres where free speech was enjoyed and shared by all, irrespective of rank. It is not for nothing that the motto of the 1848 Republic — *Liberté, Égalité, Fraternité* — is still the cry of most of the brothers at the end of their meetings. Joseph de Maistre wrote that 'freemasonry, in the several centuries of its existence, certainly had nothing in common with the Terror, but its general aim coincided with the principle of democracy!' This is particularly evident in a country like France where, as Karl Marx noted, political struggles are seen in their purest, clearest form.

Freemasonry cannot, however, be wholly reduced to political terms, for it never loses its concern for an invisible, mythological reality. The initiation ceremony of the freemasons seeks to bring together the feelings of freedom and spirituality in postulants. Is this utopianism? Is the 'lost speech' sought by the masons, the wording that will open the hidden door of the temple, a figment of poetic imagination? It is difficult to get to

Symbolic representation of the thirty-three degrees of freemasonry, as in the Scottish Rite (National Library, Paris)

the heart of this question to discover the initiating, psychological and social secret, but we can at least show how the different rites define themselves with reference to it.

Let us turn once again to history. As soon as the Terror in France was over, some brothers attempted to revive freemasonry. On 22 June 1799, at the end of lengthy discussions, the order was reconstituted 'one and indivisible' with the title of 'Grand Orient and Grand Lodge', so the new lodges were a fusion of the old Grand Orient and Grand Lodge. Meanwhile, 'Scottish' lodges were setting up the 'Scottish General Grand Lodge of the Accepted and Ancient Rite'. In 1806 Cambacérès, arch-chancellor of the Empire, was Grand Master of the Grand Lodge and deputy Grand Master of the Grand Orient at the same time. The Emperor's brother, Joseph Bonaparte, was then Master of the latter. Freemasonry was under the thumb of the government, just as it was later in the second Empire, when

Origin

According to current understanding, the freemason is the builder responsible for the 'great work', subject to neither feudal, corporatist, nor Church control. Continuing the analogy, the term 'freemason' differs from 'roughmason', just as 'skilled craftsman' differs from 'labourer'.

Napoleon III decreed that grand masters had to be appointed by himself.

In 1877, the convention of the Grand Orient (i.e. its ruling body) decided to end the obligation on lodges to work for the glory of the 'Great Architect of the Universe'. This was of the greatest importance: the main rite was cutting itself free of all spiritual (or traditionalist) obligation and it adopted a more democratic constitution. Most freemasons of the period showed a frankly republican tendency and the Grand Orient was to play a decisive role in the laicization of the state. This involved a certain amount of upheaval: a number of lodges broke away to set up the Scottish Symbolic Grand Lodge, which merged later with the Grand Lodge. Similarly, in 1913 the French National Grand Lodge was founded and recognized by the British. In 1940, freemasonry was banned by Marshal Pétain, but was allowed to reform after the Liberation.

The movement in France

Note the existence of three main strands of freemasonry in France on the one hand, and 'The Rights of Man' and a scattering of unorganized lodges on the other. The first is the French National Grand Lodge, with a minority of members, but recognized by London and claiming to be the only one to maintain 'masonic regularity'. Reference to the Great Architect is evidently compulsory, and in certain temples, postulants must even provide a certificate of baptism. It is perhaps not overtly religious, but after the collection, there is a symbolic allusion to God. This lodge claims 'not to go in for politics' but most of its members are right-wing.

The second is the Grande Loge de France, occupying a position between the former and the Grand Orient, both in terms of numbers and also in terms of philosophy. Reference to the Great Architect is compulsory, but the movement claims not to be dogmatic. The Grand Lodge insists on tolerance and any display of political or religious opinion is forbidden. However, in practice, its members are politically in the centre.

The third is the Grand Orient of France, the most important in France in terms of both numbers and influence. It is placed firmly on the left of the political spectrum. The Grand Orient uses laicization as one of the main ways it roots itself in the profane world. It is anti-racist and aware of all contemporary problems such as underdevelopment, but it lays equal stress on the 'humanizing' influence of the masonic movement.

This division into three main rites tells us a lot about the movement, its limits and its meaning. Is initiation concerned with the human dimension, or more with the spiritual? Every rite has its own answer to this question. Masonry as a body strives, within the modern world, to achieve the fine balance between meditation (or symbolism) and action (or politics). The lodges are of course centres for reflection, where members take stock of themselves, and any action outside the temple depends entirely on the individual. But it would be to miss the point of freemasonry completely if we neglected the psychocultural influence exercised by the movement on society. Alongside the Church, freemasonry provides the impetus for feelings we ignore at our own peril.

From the Zohar

'In every world there shines a triad, commanded by a monad, for it is within this triad that all things have been sown. ... It is the spring of springs, and the womb which contains all things.'

Personal experience of the secret

Why does freemasonry work in secret? In what way is it a secret society? What is the secret, anyway? What do these mysteries mean? It is absurd to claim, as some have, that the secrecy stems from unspeakable practices. Modern religious extremists continue to make this claim, although it is patently untrue. After all, we only have to read the many books about freemasonry, in order to find out all we want to know. Everything is known, except — quite naturally — the personal experience of each mason. The masonic secret, let us be quite plain, has no independent existence; it is reconstituted anew in each masonic meeting. If we accept that the masonic quest is metaphysical (and it might be more accurate to state, as we did previously, that it has a mythological side), this explains why there is so much talk of symbolism and alchemy in the lodges. It is through these mythological references that a scarcely acknowledged psychical and cultural dimension emerges. This is a dimension which influences morality indirectly, but quite tangibly.

Freemasonry is a most unusual institution. It claims to have turned aside from politics and religion, but to say there 'must be no politics' in the lodge entirely misses the point of freemasonry. Masons reject neither politics nor religion. How could they without crippling those within the movement? The motto in the lodge is not 'We have no politics here' but 'We have something more urgent than politics to do'. The lodge is supposed to be the place where the initiate is aware of himself and his relations with others. It is the place where, with all dogma or teaching set aside, the individual is supposed to experience his inner freedom and to see that this freedom ultimately expresses itself in solidarity. This apprenticeship does not lead on to a reality, but to a virtuality, for initiation is concerned with potentiality, not dogma. This explains the banning of freemasonry in communist and fascist countries. However, it is worth noting that a number of Latin American countries have recently tried to revive freemasonry. Perhaps that means it has been robbed of its substance?

Women's lodges

Along with the Grand Orient, the Grand Lodge and the French National Grand Lodge, the minority group, 'Rights of Man', and the adopted lodges (the French Women's Grand Lodge) must be mentioned. These last are respectively the first mixed rite and women's lodges. This is not of merely anecdotal interest, but raises an important problem currently facing freemasonry and the phenomenon of initiation in general — the admission of women. Lodges of the Grand Orient accept Sisters as visitors, and sometimes even initiate them, but there is no general agreement on this point. In fact, the Grand Lodge and the French National Grand Lodge refuse absolutely to do so. The recognition of women remains therefore something foreign to masonic custom. The problem is not as trivial as it might seem, as it is symptomatic of the ability (or inability) to be alive to the age. Initiation, like art, needs to acknowledge tradition and to approach the invisible, without becoming entrenched in modernity.

The three points

The meaning of the mysterious sign of the freemasons is purely numerological, and may come from Pythagorism. The three points, arranged to form an equilateral triangle, are a sign of masonic recognition. The age of the apprentice is three (the journeyman is five and the master seven). From a cosmogonic point of view, 3 is the sign of accomplishment (while 1 represents unity and 2 the division of being). Echoes of this type of speculation are found in Hegel. (See **Numbers and Symbolism**.)

The masonic temple

The masonic temple is not a simple hut, as in some Red Indian initiatory societies, nor a place of worship, as in revealed religion. It is a temple rebuilt each time by those taking part. In other words, for the masonic temple to be built (ie for the universe to be revealed to the initiate) it must be created by a common effort. Brotherhood is spirituality: God, if he exists, can only exist between beings. Spirituality and freedom are two aspects of the same reality, which have wrongly become separated through social alienation. It is therefore understandable that the new initiate should be required, symbolically, to question the existential concepts which hinder him from acquiring the status of 'seeker', i.e. an individual in quest of a reality which appears paradoxical to the profane. The seeker is thus expected to set himself free from his 'metals' or inner misunderstanding.

Gnosticism

Gnosticism is religious existentialism

The Gnostic is in search of the answer to the mystery of existence. His quest is for a fragment of the divine.

Gnosticism has arisen from man's desire to know God, his 'secrets' (as the Cabala puts it) and the mysteries of creation. Gnostics start with the sacred word, the texts of the religion to which they belong, but they decipher these writings as if they were uncovering a hidden message or an esoteric meaning. Gnosticism is therefore a kind of hermetism. Its adepts treat religious language existentially, for they believe that sentences, words, images and the structure of holy texts amount to much more than mere literary figures: correctly interpreted, these texts can reveal the deep meaning of life. They believe that it is enough to strip them of their obscurities to cause the word of God to shine within them. Gnosticism begins by supposing the existence of a shadow, unconsciousness, non-being or lack which must be elucidated to attain truth. This shadow symbolizes evil.

Evil is the root of the problem

As Gnosticism aims to reach the heart of the matter, and to search out fundamental 'roots' and 'secrets', at some point or another it must encounter the problem of evil. Why does evil exist? Has it a function within creation? How can God, who is all goodness, allow its ravages to go on? How can it be avoided, or overcome, or rooted out? This is not simply a theoretical problem, and it is easy to see how the Catharians, living in such troubled times, were worried by it.

We read in the *Zohar* that a king who had fabulous treasures, guarded them with a poisonous serpent. Anyone daring to lay his hand on the coffer ran the risk of being bitten and dying. The king had a friend, to whom he entrusted the secret of how to reach the casket and seize it without coming to any harm. The 'Blessed Holy One', we are told, acted in the same way when he placed a serpent near the sanctuary, revealing only to his friends, the angels and the just, the secret of how to remove the serpent and approach the *Shekinah*. The parable is quite explicit: the serpent is not autonomous but acts as God's agent.

Here is the same idea in a Catharian text: Jean de Lugio, in 'The Book of the Two Principles' asks, 'How could the true creator in this visible world condemn little children without mercy to the most cruel death? Thus, it is necessary to distinguish between the world of the serpent (the visible world) and the kingdom of the just (the invisible). But, as numerous heretics repeated to the Inquisition, 'Even if they were not created by God, visible things nevertheless exist by His consent'. How can this contradiction be accepted? Taking as a first principle the appearance of evil with the creation of the universe, the Catharians attempt to reconcile divine unity and the dispersion of Creation, by trying to re-create a fabric, unified yet changing, which through transitions, discords and harmonies permeates all things to make a cosmic symphony. In a similar way, the Cabala develops its sefirot, divine attributes deployed to make the universe manifest, and its sefirotic tree, which is supposed to be the archetype, according to which everything falls into place. In their turn, the Gnostics of Alexandria refer to

***The conjunction** (man and woman embracing) is effected under the sign of death, which must be overcome. (Wood-engraving taken from* Rationarium Evangelistarum, *published by Georg Simler in 1507. National Library, Paris)*

'aeons', a series of intermediaries between the world above and the world below, the world of good (God) and the world of evil (Satan). These philosophies gave rise to all manner of texts, which deserve much closer study for their at times bewildering portrayal of man's struggle with the problem of evil.

The quest for the light

The Gnostic willingly plunges into darkness to combat the evil he finds within himself and in the world. Elucidation of inner misunderstanding leads the subject on to elucidation of cosmic misunderstanding. An Essenian text speaks of 'the struggle of the sons of light against the sons of darkness'. The struggle goes on in heaven as it does on earth and, pursuing the argument to its logical conclusion, the apocalypse will shake divinity itself. This does not mean, however, that Gnosticism is either puritanical or fanatical. The mystic is looking for the light which, though invisible, is ever present. 'A lighted lamp sheds its shining rays around; if we try to catch hold of them, we only find the lamp' says the Cabala. Most commentators have believed that the Gnostic tries to identify himself with God, and have not perceived that it is only possible to speak of identification if the Gnostic has deviated from the quest. In fact, the mystic only wants to discover the spark of divinity within his own dark recesses. He believes that man is made up of two principles and, to realize his potential, he must seek, in the manner of the fallen angel, to bring about the triumph of God. The Gnostic does not wish to illuminate the mystery of God (for any light shone upon God to illuminate Him would become dark) but seeks rather to illuminate himself. The object of Gnosticism is that this illumination is not purely intellectual, as it is for, say, Descartes, but that it is focused on the existential, on the very body of the mystic, which is thus sanctified.

Freedom is a struggle

As a sort of mystical existentialism, Gnosticism is the mother of freedom. The Gnostic wants to proclaim himself the ally of creative divinity. Evil enters the designs of the Creator, but, to be rid of it, according to Gnosticism, the Creator needs man to overcome his misunderstanding. When men find themselves again, evil will be transcended on earth as well as in heaven. Thus, man-

Quest and revelation

'Gnosticism is a quest for redeeming knowledge and a quest for oneself. More than a doctrine, it is a deeper and deeper revelation of this doctrine. In this sense, it is the historical dimension of the Tradition's cultural figures.'
M. Mirabail, *Les 50 Mots clefs de l'ésotérisme* (The Fifty Key Words of Esoterism)

kind is not the source of evil and is not entirely responsible for its appearance, although it must be held accountable for its existence, arrogance and permanence. Gnosticism is the philosophical foundation of hermetism. It is instituted in the quest for the secret of the universe, it is elaborated in myth, it develops through symbols and swings between love and despair. The distinction between Gnosticism and initiation is precisely this, that the mystic remains one of a group in a community of believers. The Gnostic wants to become the 'Son of God' whereas the alchemist, for example, wants to become the 'son of his own works'. The latter wants to owe everything to himself alone. Initiation is an individualistic form of existentialism; Gnosticism is its collective manifestation.

The origin of Gnosticism

According to Puech, one of the greatest specialists in the subject, Gnosticism is 'originally pagan and impregnated with Iranism'. It first emerged in the Babylonian lowlands, then spread to Asia Minor and Syria. There is also a Jewish element in its make-up: 'The diaspora in Babylon, after the destruction of the temple in Jerusalem, brought Judaism into contact with the Persian culture of Alexandria, Greek syncretism shaped in Egypt and the Judaism of Asia Minor.' According to the same author, certain details prove that the Gnostic holy books must be assigned such an early date that Christianity itself may be seen as no more than a 'branch of Gnosticism'. Certain theories maintain that Jesus was an Essenian initiate, and the Essenes were certainly Gnostics. In their view, the Bible was a coded text, telling of the creation of the world and the coming apocalypse. They developed a cosmogony in which good and evil were in conflict, just as the Manichaeans did, and their 'master of justice' was an enigmatic figure rather like the Gnostics' Jesus — a spirit descended, living in an illusory body.

But Gnosticism could equally be compared to any religion at all. All religious knowledge develops, after all, from an ancient primitive origin, lost in the 'mists of time', and Gnostic procedure is the spontaneous expression of religious feeling. Gnosticism is a constant which reflects man's physical and spiritual history. It sustains and opposes official religion at one and the same time, just as reality is driven hither and thither by poetry or dreams.

The sanctification of matter

In the early stages of the Gnostic quest (although, it must be said, the mystic will not be aware of what leads him on until the end of his quest), one is driven by terrible despair and, at the same time, a powerful upsurge of love. Gnosticism, like initiation, is not a conversion to goodness, but the transmutation of evil into good, and of solipsistic despair into solidarity with one's fellow man. Throughout history, Gnostics have often confused the issue and forgotten that, although spirit can overwhelm the world, it is incapable of stabilizing it. Churches, which have shared power with people in politics, have long understood this but this sharing, or compromise, was seen as another form of evil by the Gnostics. To acquit them of the charge of crazy utopianism, we must recall that reality passes through dream and that it is through myth that the invisible is made present. How is this possible, other than through Gnosticism, where the images, ideas and themes of religion become personal entities on which the mystic sets to work? In this scheme, Satan symbolizes the mystic's lack of inner understanding, Mary his virginity, Eve his femininity, the crucifixion his sadomasochism and so on. The essential drama is that of the soul, fallen and imprisoned in matter. This fall is repeated on the cosmic scale and its function is to sanctify matter, or to make the visible world sensitive to the invisible. The Gnostic quest is to take responsibility for the fall, with a view to preparing for the resurrection.

However, Gnostic philosophy is much more than this. It is a collection of poetic texts of great beauty, impregnated with mystery, in which a real world, a hidden secret world of tears and splendours, can be felt alive within mankind. These texts are full of wisdom. *The Pimander* says, 'God shared wisdom among all men, but not thought'; Gnostic texts bring together poetry and thought.

The Golden Mean

The lost secret of the builders

The golden mean, supposed to have been discovered by Pythagoras, was a secret handed down in ritual.

The golden mean is a manifestation of the invisible, which is derived from a mathematical formula. One may well wonder what link there is between philosophy and mathematics, and how it can be revealed in concrete terms. The answer given by many writers is that the two disciplines, however different, come together in the occult without in any way losing their individual identities. Such writers remind us that every account of Creation presents a mythological picture, in which appear gods, and that every figure may be symbolized by a number, which is his unique cipher or seal. The mythological account is peppered with numbers. So there is a hidden link between statement and number. To convert, or to pass from one to the other, all we need to know are the laws.

The music of the spheres

This hypothetical link has given rise to much speculation and some have sought a sort of Cabala which might produce a total fusion of philosophy, painting, music and so on. However, beyond this type of conjecture, the golden mean can be seen, expressed in physical terms. To take three examples: cathedrals, pyramids and Greek temples are all built according to the principle of the golden mean. These monuments echo, encapsulate and embody the mythological story of the creation of the world, of the coming of a god, or of his death and resurrection.

So, it can be said that art orders chaos. But what precisely is the relation between art and religion? For the Taoist, religious feeling is the raw material which it is the duty of art to surpass. It is the initiatory society (here the corporations of builders) which is the psychocultural medium which enables the conversion or transmutation of the religious into the artistic.

A formula

Number is the key to the universe, and proportion is all. Man, too, is part of the analogy deriving from the order which Fra Luca Pacioli di Borgo, in 1509, called 'divine proportion'. This is the proportion, already known to Pythagoras, considered to express the secret of visual harmony. In geometrical terms, this is a line divided into two parts, so that the proportion of the smaller part to the larger, is the same as that of the larger to the whole line. It can be expressed as the equation, AP: PB =

From Paul Valéry

'What is a poem but an expression of ø, the golden mean! The number must be seen as an instrument which does not render redundant the skill and intelligence of the artist. On the contrary, it must rouse the artist to develop these qualities, and this is where the remarkable properties of the golden mean intervene ... I have long dreamt of making a work of art secretly loaded with well-reasoned conventions, and founded on exact observation of the relationship between language and spirit.' Preface to M. Ghyka, *Le Nombre d'or* (The Golden Mean)

Fra Luca Pacioli di Borgo *is the author of the 'Divine Proportion' (1509). He is seen here accompanied by the Duke of Urbino. Portrait by the Franciscan monk, Luca Pacioli Jacofo Barbari. (Capodimonte Museum, Naples)*

AB: *AP*, where *AB* is the straight line and *P* the point which divides it. Numerically, this golden mean or golden section, is calculated as the ratio 1:ø (ie 1:1.6180339), which is roughly equivalent to the ratio 8:13.

The golden mean has been extensively applied to art and architecture. Leonardo da Vinci used this 'Canon of proportion' in his drawing of 'Vitruvian Man', recalling its use by the Roman architect, Vitruvius Pollio. Widely discussed during the Renaissance, this proportion forms the basis of, for example, Piero della Francesca's 'Baptism of Christ', which can be seen in the National Gallery, London.

However, the formula by itself is obviously not enough, if we wish to avoid a dry, academic approach. The perception of proportion in hermetic thought is, first and foremost, as an aspect of being, rather than as a method of mathematical reasoning. Thanks to the golden mean, the artist can gain direct access to being, and any mathematical explanation is largely superfluous and irrelevant.

The Great Architect of the Universe

A being without any god-like qualities

The demiurge of the builders, or an abstract concept, the Great Architect is an occult principle with no religious dimension.

The Great Architect of the Universe, the demiurge who is said by the builders (that is to say, the masons) to have made the world, may be seen simply as a unifying principle. And yet he seems to be a little more than that, for he is not an organizing principle, such as we meet in mechanics, but something more like the structure underlying a sublime musical work. He is the archetype of archetypes, the ultimate abstraction and, at the same time, the crystallization of the greatest actual riches.

A necessary hypothesis

It is really quite impossible to define the paradoxical reality of the Great Architect, who could just as easily be called the 'Great Conductor of the Universal Orchestra'; the reality reveals itself symbolically in the course of the quest for the invisible. Proudhon, who was a freemason, called God a 'necessary hypothesis'. This is perhaps the best possible definition for the concept of the Great Architect of the universe. A necessary hypothesis is, after all, a working fiction acceptable to atheists and believers alike. A decision on whether or not the concept conceals a reality must be taken by each individual.

St Albert the Great said of the philosopher's stone, 'If it exists, I want to know what it is like. If it does not exist, I would like to understand the meaning of such an illusion'. Between God and the Great Architect of the Universe, between the religious and the invisible, mysticism and inner freedom, there exists the same distinction as between worship and symbolization. Some writers consider that religious feeling is indeed the 'prime matter' or raw material on which the process of initiation acts. Others think that the transmutation which occurs in a person gaining access to the invisible has the effect of converting his religious feeling into poetry.

The response of the initiate is to explore and examine the working fiction. This fiction crystallizes and expresses a dream, not a concrete solution: a dream which looks into the future, a dream not yet freed from the false and the pathetic, but a dream without which people would never achieve enlightenment.

It is surprising to see side by side the two terms **spirituality** and **secularism** which, in their common sense, contradict one another. However, freemasonry was founded to reveal their possible identity, to expose the rending of the human into two constituent aspects (the political and the poetic) and to seek a possible answer to this apparent paradox.

'The very notion of the Divine, in the light of science, takes on a new aspect. It is no exaggeration to say that today Perfection, the Absolute or the Principle to which one aspires — whether we call it God, Reason or the Great Architect of the Universe — comes about in one's progress towards Knowledge. Is this not the object of the Reintegration which the Tradition asks of the initiate?' Paul Naudon, *La Francmaçonnerie* (Freemasonry)

Initiation

The start of the journey

To be initiated is to set off on the trail of an occult truth which not all can perceive. Initiation is a ritually transmitted process.

Put quite simply, to be initiated is to truly begin to live. The neophyte enters a new life and yet, at the same time, he is only, as Goethe put it, 'becoming himself'. The Greek oracle even commanded: 'Become thyself!' — but added 'in order to know the universe and the gods'. Herein lies the first paradox of initiation: it is easy to see the need to become oneself and realize one's potential, but it is hard to see how one is to identify oneself with the universe and the gods. The latter could be seen as an exaltation of the inner self— but what about the universe? How can anyone contain within himself that of which he is but a part? The occult answer is this: that the aim is not complete identification, but an analogy between the microcosm (man) and the macrocosm (the universe). Analogy is the first principle of the quest, and the purpose of the initiation ceremony is to create an awareness of analogy.

The 'straight path'

So, by initiation the mystic (re)discovers his true existential origins, concealed from him until now. He discovers himself, is renewed, re-born and stripped of the misunderstanding which hindered him from becoming his own creator and, in alchemistic terms, the 'son of his works'. As Dante put it, he is now on the 'straight path', that is to say on the way to discovering his uniqueness. It is easy to see how much confusion and fantasy has arisen and been associated with a phenomenon such as this. Renewal has been confused with ascetic purification, and others of a more neurotic nature believed that initiation conferred extraordinary powers, whereas it is simply a poetic function which is normally ignored. The initiate is supposed to discover and enter into the mystery which invented and invests him, and to reveal 'the cruel beauty which runs through him as it runs through the world'.

> '**Initiation** essentially aims to go beyond the possibilities of the individual human state, to make possible the transition to higher states and finally to lead the individual beyond any limitations whatsoever.' R. Guénon, *Aperçus sur l'initiation* (Glimpses of Initiation)

Initiation is identified with the 'original'. The best way of speaking of the original is to consider the process which leads one towards it. Jung took a close interest in this; for him, initiation is the stage leading towards inner freedom. He describes it in terms of a symbolic regression to life inside the womb. In fact, the postulant is led to the 'centre of the earth', into the 'womb of creation', into a cave or a 'room for reflection'. In short, he is led to a space-time where his psyche has yet to discover its identity. According to Jung, this allows him to renew his contact with the collective unconscious. It is only in our modern society that the ceremony has become mere simulation; in 'primitive' or 'traditional' societies, it is something real and effective, because it fulfils a psychocultural function that every-

Meeting of freemasons to receive Masters *'The member elect is stretched out on the coffin which is drawn on the floor of the temple, with his face covered by a linen cloth stained with blood. All those present, having drawn their swords, present them with their points towards his body. To the left, a member elect on whom the Grand Master has not yet conferred the accolade.' (Anonymous 18th century engraving dedicated to Brother Léonard Cabanon, writer of the Freemason's Catechism. National Library, Paris)*

one accepts. In the modern world, psychoanalysis resembles the phenomenon of initiation both in its objectives and in its procedure.

The double dimension

The second paradox of initiation is that it presents two dimensions, which are apparently contradictory: it is concerned with the invisible as much as with the visible. It hinges on the point where these two dimensions meet, the first being perceived through myth, and the second being simply the socio-historic reality of the moment. Initiation in the trade guilds, for example, was only truly dynamic when the art of building still enjoyed its original social function; that is to say when it still had its 'useful value' as well as its 'mystical value' (for the invisible exists beyond any concrete stage, but can only be perceived within a historical dialectic). This mythical exploration is the most characteristic dimension of the practice of initiation. To paraphrase Jung, the function of myth is to accentuate a subliminal reality to enable it to spring forth, but it is necessary thereafter to absorb this reality without giving way to the psychological self-indulgence which it can cause. The exploration of the mythical is a sort of crutch from which one must learn to become independent very soon. However, it is only possible to understand this mythical journey and the activities which accompany it by describing, or better still experiencing, the ceremony of initiation.

We must go back to the very beginning, to the descent to the centre of the earth. The centre of the earth may be compared to the subconscious; for Jung, as we have seen, it symbolized the womb. It is certainly true that the legends of Hiram and Osiris are similar to the legend of Oedipus, the central emblem of psychoanalysis. However, occult philosophers maintain that the unconscious of the psychologists is but a pale reflection of what the initiation ceremony reveals. The descent to the centre of the earth is not, in their view, to be seen as a mere symbol for introspection. It is much more than this, for in the journey the initiate renews his connection with a darkness which may link him with the mysterious.

The initiation ceremony repeats this beginning over and over again. The descent into oneself foreshadows infinity and its aim is the perception of a complex reality which the ceremony reveals stage by stage. Thus, the final stage of 'death to the world', a dramatic metaphor for the murder of the hero around whom the secret society has evolved, is an elaborate repetition of the entry into oneself. 'Descent to the middle of the earth' (the first stage) and 'death to the world' (virtually the last stage) both evoke, in different ways, the phenomenon of the darkness within the mystic himself. However, it is with the second stage that the very heart of this reality is attained, and the ultimate point is reached where, as we shall see, the sign of this reality is transformed into its antithesis. This is the moment when tangible reality opens itself to the invisible. This extreme is like an existential wound which the initiate, rather than staunching, gladly suffers.

Jungian individuation

'Secret societies are but an intermediate stage on the way towards individuation: it is as if one surrendered to a collective organization the duty of differentiating oneself through it, that is to say that the subject has yet to understand that it is the task of an individual to stand on his own feet and to be different from all others ... It is wrong to consider this intermediate step as an obstacle to individuation. On the contrary, it is, and will remain for a long time, the only possible independent existence of the individual who, today more than ever, is threatened with anonymity. Membership of a collective organization is so important nowadays that many people justifiably consider it to be a definitive state, and any attempt to suggest the eventuality of a further step along the road to personal autonomy is considered sheer presumption, defiance, fancy or utter impossibility.' Jung, *My Life*

The ritual of initiation

Many types of ritual are known. Gérard de Nerval tries to romanticize one of them, which recounts the martyrdom of Hiram, the emblematic figure of medieval trade guilds and freemasonry. Here, by way of example, are some extracts from the text where Hiram appears under the name of Adoniram, and Solomon under the same of Soliman:

> 'Adoniram was in the great hall of the temple. The darkness thickened round his lamp and rose in red columns showing the walls of the hall where three doors faced towards the north, the west and the east ...
>
> Adoniram was preparing to leave, when suddenly a human shape stepped out from behind a pilaster, and said fiercely, 'If you wish to go out, give me the password of the masters.'
>
> Adoniram was unarmed; respected by all and accustomed to being obeyed at a sign of command, he did not even think of defending his sacred person.
>
> 'You wretch!' he replied, on recognizing the mason Methusael. 'Get away from me! You will only be received among the masters when treason and crime are honoured. Flee with your accomplices, before the justice of Soliman catches up with you.'
>
> Methusael listened to him, then brought his hammer crashing down on Adoniram's skull. Dazed, the artist staggered and looked instinctively for a means of escape, by the second door facing the north. The Syrian, Phanor, who was standing there said, 'If you want to go out, give me the password of the masters!'
>
> 'You have scarcely spent seven years on the campaign!', replied Adoniram in a fading voice.
>
> 'The password!'
>
> 'Never!'
>
> Phanor, the mason, thrust his chisel into Adoniram's side; but he could not do so a second time, for the architect of the temple, aroused by the pain, flew like an arrow to the east door to escape his assailants.
>
> This is where Amru the Phoenician,

a journeyman among the joiners, was waiting and demanded in his turn, 'If you want to pass, give me the password of the masters!'

'That is not how I gained it,' Adoniram, exhausted, said with difficulty. 'Ask the one who sent you.'

And, as he was attempting to make his way past them, Amru plunged the point of his compasses into his heart.

At this moment the thunderstorm burst with a great clap of thunder.'

The manner in which this simple drama unfolds helps us to understand that the initiate is an actor with a particular part to play and that this is really a spectacle in which the spectator symbolically has an essential role.

The mystic, as we saw earlier, is supposed to renew his connection with an embryonic darkness which is favourable to the invisible. In fact he lives and experiences this ceremony as a dreamer experiences a dream. His guides encourage him to recognize in each of the figures which pass, like shadows, before him, a representation of himself. He identifies himself with Hiram's murderers, who represent inner darkness (some rituals explain that these journeymen symbolize ignorance, fanaticism and tyranny). He accepts the darkness so that spontaneously an inner light, represented by Hiram, wells up within him. The text continues,

'The king of the Hebrews ordered nine masters to prove the death of the artist, by finding his body. Seventeen days had passed; searches in and around the temple had been fruitless and the masters were searching the countryside in vain. One of them, overcome by the heat, took hold of an acacia branch to help him to climb more easily. A strange bird with brilliant plumage had just flown off from this bush. The master was surprised to find that the whole bush gave way as he leant on it, because it was not rooted in the ground; it had been recently planted, and the astonished master called his companions.

Immediately the nine masters began digging with their bare hands, and discovered the shape of a tomb. Then one of them said to his brothers, 'Those who did this are perhaps felons who were wanting to force Adoniram to reveal the password of the masters. In case they succeeded, would it be wiser to change it?'

'If we find our master here,' continued another, 'the first word which one of us says can be our new password.'

They joined hands over the tomb, and then began to dig again with renewed vigour.

When the body was found, one of the masters took hold of a finger and the skin came away in his hand; the same thing happened with a second master; a third took it by the wrist as a master might do to a journeyman and the skin came away again, whereupon they cried out 'Makbenach', meaning, 'The flesh is coming away from the bones.'

Initiation has aims similar to psychoanalysis; the difference is that it is not resolved by a realization of the death of a father or a hero, but by the realization of the death of the mystic himself. This is the death, maturing imperceptibly within each one of us, from which all life seems to arise. This death is not physical death, but the death of the mystic's inertia, unawareness and alienation. The aim of initiation is to kill this death, to uncover the 'true life' buried under old habits. By killing Hiram, the mystic symbolically kills his alienated self, so that he delivers himself from the 'old man'. Finally, let us not forget that, according to hermetic thought, being set free from this death allows the mystic to foresee his own future real death.

However, if the death of the hero is the climax of the initiation ceremony, it does not dominate all of it. The death of the hero corresponds to the process of transmutation supposed to seize the initiate, and so it com-

> 'Rites of entry to a secret society correspond in every detail to tribal initiation: confinement, torture, tests, death and resurrection, imposition of a new name, revelation of a secret doctrine, instruction in a special language, etc.' Mircea Eliade, *Naissances mystiques* (Mystic Birth)

pletes the ceremony. Let us now look at the events which take place from the moment the actor goes down to the 'centre of the earth' and the moment he feigns the wound which snatches him from life to rebirth. The newcomer who is being initiated, in many ceremonies, passes through phases of making contact (or being 'impregnated') with moral and physical realities, and phases of travelling. The moral realities are imparted by solemn precept, painted allegory or enactment; more often, though, it is the physical realities which are stressed. These are the four elements (fire, water, earth and air) on which alchemists work and to which Heraclitus and Aristotle refer. The elements are not simple chemical, but psychophysical compound structures, which express symbolically the ways in which our being is rooted in the world. They refer probably to fundamental kinesthetic sensations such as nausea, anguish and inspiration. The newcomer's passage through the elements is a way of simulating his roots and of his taking charge of his being and of his body in all its fullness and subtlety. But the passage is interrupted by incidents, rather like pilgrimages, which themselves simulate a call from elsewhere (or transcendence). So, this rooting and transcendence are the fundamental double aim of initiation. Initiation is taking responsibility for the whole being, both psychosomatic and cosmic. The elements which make it up also compose the universe, in accordance with the analogy between the microcosm and the macrocosm.

'For Australian aborigines, the main thing was and is the teaching of the name of the *dema* (the term in New Guinea for divine creators and primordial beings who lived in mythical times), the handing on of the *tjurungas* (sacred boards) they left on earth and of the rites attached to these, and finally the moral and social instruction received by the candidate after these rites.' Neverman, Worms & Petri, *Les Religions du Pacifique et d'Australie*

'We commonly find in primitive secret societies a **symbolic interpretation** of rites of initiation in which death and resurrection figure. In Melanesia, the candidate leaving his family for initiation is mourned as if he had died.' A. Métraux, *Encyclopédie française*

An operative simulation

Initiation is distinguished from religious ceremonies by many features; most importantly, at the start the mystic is the spectator of a drama taking place before his eyes — a drama telling of a quest, a death and a resurrection — and he then becomes an actor in this very drama. He sees Hiram lying at his feet, lies down beside him and is identified with the hero. He goes looking for fire, water, earth or air, then makes contact with them, touches them and discovers them just as if they were part of him. He is just like the fire that burns and the water that soaks, but he does not lose himself in them. None satisfies him and all call him to something beyond themselves. The fire and the water, these realities, stand as symbols for the dimensions of an invisible reality which may yet come to touch him. The change of state which initiation is meant to effect is shown in the fact that the newcomer is a spectator at first, but becomes an actor towards the end. The ceremony aims to awaken and bring into play a faculty of 'creative simulation'. It is theatre, but the nearness of death reminds the mystic that life itself is but a dream. The mystic's inner darkness is symbolized in terms of death and, in simulating his own end, he is given a glimpse of the invisible, the hope of inner freedom. Initiation is always virtual; the process is never completed, except when fictitious death becomes real death.

The enigma of initiation can be neatly summed up by the dictum, 'The object of the quest is the very way of the quest.' In other words, the goal of the journey is not the country we are seeking (for it will always remain invisible) but the journey towards it. Initiation is only a symbolic ceremony, which can never replace that which it celebrates, which is the result of a long process of maturation.

Finally, what does it mean to become oneself? There are plenty of answers: entering a secret society, becoming a stone of the temple, occupying a place in the cosmos, finding one's centre and so on. To be an initiate, though, demands this and yet more: it is finding roots in this world and living in the invisible. It is truly becoming a microcosm in the image of the macrocosm that is the universe.

The Invisible

Fact or fancy?

Is the invisible something suppressed or some super-reality?

The occult sciences act on an invisible reality, which may be either an invisible history into which the individual enters (by initiation) or invisible entities and psychic forces which the operator manipulates (by magic). In occultism, there is a parallel and invisible world alongside our known world. This world is only invisible because it is necessary to possess certain powers in order to perceive it or, more accurately, to make it manifest rather than virtual. For the rationalist, there is only a plethora of chimeras and deceptions and the conviction that the invisible world is a product of the observer's imagination. A view occupying the middle ground between current rationalism and occultism is that we are dealing here with fantasies and appearances which, nonetheless, share an inner truth. Psychoanalysis has taught us to decipher the hidden meaning of the incongruous.

The infiltration of dreams

We are told, in hermetism, that the souls of the dead sleep in the invisible, and that unsuspected forces and magic powers lie there. To put this another way, the notion of the invisible comes from an unexpressed, undeveloped dimension of the psyche, which crystallizes a fundamental dream. Or, yet again, the invisible might be merely dreams filling the gaps in the real world.

According to hermetism, religion reveals the invisible only in a confused way. The invisible of religion, then, is the raw material which has yet to be refined; it has the same relationship to the invisible, as sentimentalism has to poetry. This perhaps explains why so many poets have been interested in magic and alchemy. It explains also why occultism is so often failed art: the magician confuses symbol and reality, forgetting that the Word is effective only in the invisible (or the poetic).

In the end, the notion of the invisible leads on to the notion of atheistic spirituality, or religion without God. So perhaps it is ultimately philosophy, in the primary sense of the word. Hermetism does, after all, run through the works of Heraclitus, Empedocles and the pre-Socratic philosophers, where concepts such as the four elements and the cosmos are found.

Invisible History

Another, secret, history

Alongside the history we know, hermetism affirms the existence of a subconscious history and attempts to grasp it.

Occultists, magi and initiates often speak of a history which runs parallel to the 'real' history we know and record. Whether or not this means that 'secret powers' are involved, some go so far as to speak of 'unknown superiors' and to believe that the fate of the world is directly under the influence of secret societies. True, historiography has often neglected this phenomenon; true, Sufism is a problem nowadays in the Soviet Union, just as Catharism in the Middle Ages was the vehicle for a revolutionary movement which came close to destroying both the Church and feudalism. Nonetheless it would be wrong, even unhealthy, to explain everything by means of secret societies.

The founding event

So-called invisible history is bound openly to a founding event — the death of a god or a hero under whose sign the group is formed, such as Master James for certain journeymen. Its method is not chronological, but epiphanic; it is not causal but symbolic. The founding event has an extra-historical origin with the structure of a myth (e.g. the death of Osiris). Without going into theoretical analysis, it is possible to say that with invisible history, the important point is not to comprehend the succession of events, fix and date them, but to reveal their meaning. However, it is not true to say this is the same as Hegel's philosophy of history; for him, history ultimately 'realizes' itself and reabsorbs its meaning. This is not so in invisible history. The stage of invisible history is always elsewhere — the Catharians kept reiterating that it was not of the world. So where is it? Everywhere and nowhere. More precisely, invisible history constitutes a virtual history, relating to visible history rather as Freud's unconscious does to the conscious. Initiating ceremonies, like psychoanalysis, serve to increase the sensitivity of the subject.

Another dimension
Invisible history, according to certain modern hermetists, stands in the same relation to ordinary history as Lobachevskian geometry does to Euclidean. It is another world, or rather a world of another dimension.

An original made actual

Mircea Eliade pointed out that mention of invisible history is a repetition of the message of the founding myth: initiating ceremonies re-create this history and magic conjures it up in order to imbue itself with its substance. This is an essential point: invisible history manifests itself only through and in an endlessly repeated quest for the original. But Eliade forgets this does not mean that the event happens once and for all, as is the case with dogma. The difference between the death of Christ for Christians and Catharians is therefore this: for the former it is a fixed event, whereas for the latter it goes on manifesting itself.

For Catholics, the death of Christ on the cross is an exterior reference, whereas for Catharians what counts is the death-of-Christ-in-us which must endlessly be rediscovered by any 'good Christian'. This means that Christ was not killed by the Jews but by all mankind. Moreover, this death is not an oddity which slams the door of history shut on a collective blame, but is on the contrary a mystery which opens up this door, offering the possibility of transmutation. By dying to our sins, we create the beauties of the world.

So invisible history enhances the value of the original, the beginning of history. It raises it up by dressing it in colourful fables, whereas profane history gradually reduces it into a series of causes and effects.

A symbolic field

Invisible history is not historiography; it is the ceremonial evocation of a legendary past so that it can be relived. The aim is to abolish the distance between past and present. Obviously, this only works in a symbolic way. The mystic acts as if he were Osiris, magically assuming the being of Osiris for as long as it takes to reveal his own being. So it is probably more accurate to speak of 'invisible reality' rather than 'invisible history', a rather clumsy expression only intended to draw our attention to the fact that the original is invisible.

Therefore, invisible reality is of necessity bound up with the theme of the original. Correctly understood, the occult sciences seek to call up this original which profane science can only set to one side. (Physics would, after all, never have become an exact, operative science if it had remained concerned with cosmogony.)

Is the original, then, an 'absolute'? To say so would be to identify it with the 'efficient cause' of the scholastics, that is to say, God. As far as hermetic philosophy is concerned, the absolute does not exist in itself; all there is, each and every time, is an absolute which is relative to the event taking place. The original constantly overwhelms us: it is not a point in space and its epiphanies are many and charged with meaning.

> An initiatory society is an irreplaceable framework for ripening certain ideas in the dark and then distilling them into the fabric of society.

The Lost Speech

The secret of initiation is a 'lost speech'

> *Whether this speech was ever given in the beginning or is a working fiction, the main thing is the coincidence of speech and being.*

Lost speech relates to the myth of origins and refers to the world in a 'psychocosmic' state where being coincides with knowing and words with the things they describe. In the Garden of Eden, before the Fall, Adam named things and animals in the sense of touching their very essence.

The Word is the reason behind the universe

This lost speech is not only the unifying principle, as, say, Eros was for some of the pre-Socratic philosophers, but in the end it is 'us' and even science itself. To name, to feel the true pulse and to control are one and the same thing. Some people even talk of the 'language of the birds', by which they mean that this lost speech sang in perfect harmony with the universe. To know this language is to penetrate the inner heart of creation. Like Orpheus, we can then charm the animals and speak to them.

Lost speech symbolizes the invisible. It expresses and makes the invisible present, but itself remains a myth, almost a fiction, free of the constraints of any syntax. The initiate in quest of it can 'neither read nor write'; he can only 'spell'. Lost speech is the source of hermetic philosophy, which develops as it loses itself in the world and then bursts forth from its own darkness. The techniques of esoterism try to rediscover, in the various ways, the original state described in the myth: magic through provocation and initiation through symbolism. Lost speech may even have been a form of telepathy, an archaic means of communication such as Freud described in his writings on parapsychology.

Literal meaning and mystical meaning

'You can see that I am now showing you a mystical meaning in the same words where, previously, I showed you a literal meaning. Just as before, there is neither addition nor subtraction: all the written words are necessary and not a single letter can be added or taken away.' *Zohar*

Speech — total, not totalitarian

It is futile to speculate about whether this lost speech was reality or fancy; it is better to try to discover what underlies it. It is a sort of total, all-embracing speech, but it is most important to remember that it is not totalitarian in nature: it holds the secret of the world, but it results from an existential conquest and an opening out.

Lost speech is a form of Gnosticism, which reveals itself in snatches, in a sort of sacred trance, when the universe bursts into our being. It is only original in that it slumbers within us from our own beginning, and is only lost because our own inner darkness obscures it.

Macrocosm and Microcosm

The founding text of occultism

The Emerald Table, which expresses the analogy between the macrocosm (M) and the microcosm (m), is the key text of occultism.

In hermetism, the microcosm (m) is man and the macrocosm (M) is the universe. This definition also occurs in a different form in science. The distinction between macrocosm and microcosm is made, for example, in modern physics, but here M is the world of men and m is the world within the atom. However, like esoterism, physics has to postulate the unity of its object. Thus, m and M are only modes of matter, or 'levels', which alter according to the position taken up by the observer.

The search for the right relationship

Every human activity starts with a break between the human and the world — it is necessary to have an object at the outset as well as a subject — but the result is always to go far beyond this break, so that in the end the subject comes to know the object. The main thing is that there should be a good relationship between subject and object, so that there is effect or real experience. Obviously, the scientific relationship is not the same as the hermetic one; the terms m and M are not the same realities in the two approaches. Science seeks to establish cause and effect relationships, occultism analogies.

The 'Emerald Table'

The importance of analogy in hermetism is illustrated by the following extract from one of its central texts, the 'Emerald Table', attributed to the legendary Hermes Trismegistos:

> 'All that is above is like that which is below, and all that is below is like that which is above. It is thus in order to bring about the miracle of one single thing, from which everything else derives in an unchanging way.
> Its father is the sun, its mother the moon, the wind bore it in its womb and the earth is its nurse.
> This is the talismanic father of the whole world, whose strength is entire and must be transformed into earth. You shall separate earth from fire and the subtle from the substantial, gently and with understanding.
> It will rise from the earth to heaven and will descend again to earth to receive the strength of both higher and lower things.

The image of God
'All worlds, both above and below, are included in the image of God.'

The unity of the cosmos
'Between heaven and earth, there is a unity reflected, on the one hand, in the real or supposed influence of the sun, stars and planets on the life of plants, animals and men and on the medicines derived from them; and, on the other hand, in the repetition of the structures from which sprang the notions of macrocosm and microcosm.' Paracelsus

In this way, you shall have the glory and fame of the whole world.
Thanks to this, all darkness will flee from you. This is the strength of all strength. It will overcome every subtle thing and penetrate every solid thing.
It is in this way that this world is made. Such are the wonderful arrangements which I am evoking.
This is why I am called Hermes. I hold the wisdom of the three modes of cosmos.'

In this text we recognize the quest for the philosopher's stone, upon which all esoteric research is founded. This text contains the axiom on which hermetism rests, that analogy, or equivalence, is the unifying principle of the whole universe, man included.

Analogy

But how can the microcosm — this cheese-mite, as Pascal put it — be in analogy with the universe? What is the common measure?

The function of analogy is to establish a rapprochement between the microcosm and the macrocosm, but it does not stop here, for this would be mere comparison. Its aim is to reveal, as if in passing, possible conjunctions between the self and the universe. Everything is based on the understanding that the universe is both around us and within us; is both transcendence (other) and ourselves (self).

Such ideas may at first seem incongruous, but they were common coin to the pre-Socratic philosophers, and they will become familiar to anyone taking an interest in hermetism. But are they relevant today, or merely historical or philosophical curiosities? Perhaps, if in the past they were capable of rising above religious obscurantism, they will be able to free us today from the tyranny of the scientific myth. But, a word of warning. These ideas must be probed, without abandoning oneself to the type of wild interpretation which proves not that the time of the metaphysicians is past, but rather that the time has come to free ourselves from the shackles of collective beliefs.

Relative notions

The notions of macrocosm and microcosm are relative to one another. In terms of the absolute, M is the universe and m is man, but we must remember that the absolute is only a theoretical model. Take, for example, the microcosm (man). The microcosm (m) that is the body of man is itself made up of various organs and, in the relationship of each organ to the body, the former plays the part of m, and the latter that of M. The main thing is therefore the relationship discerned when these notions come into play; being unable to describe objective realities, they have the curious status of being only operative concepts.

The image of the All

'The Holy one, blessed be He, made man by printing the image of the kingdom of heaven within him, which is the image of the All. It is this image that the Holy one, blessed be He, beheld when He made the world and all the creatures of the world. This image is the synthesis of all creatures above and all creatures below, with no separation; it is the synthesis of all the sefirot, all their names, all their epithets and all their denominations.'
Zohar

Magic

Magic will never be rooted out

There is magic in all behaviour, however apparently rational. The problem is how to be aware of this without yielding to it.

The magician lives, or believes he lives, in a world inhabited by spirits over which he has power. This power is initiated by ritual and by spells: a word correctly spoken becomes more than itself, expressing physically the being, or essence, of the thing it describes.

The Word (logos), it must be remembered, is the reason behind the cosmos. Coextensive with being, it becomes a science too. 'Magic is the science of the Word,' wrote the occultist, Piobb, earlier this century. But how can this be possible? According to the *Keys of Solomon*, an old book of spells:

> God wanted to perfect His works by making a creature which was half divine and half earthly: this is man whose body is coarse and earthly, while his soul is spiritual and heavenly. He set the earth and all its creatures below man, and gave him the means of drawing close to the angels, who are there, some of them to control the movement of the stars, and others to live in the elements. You can therefore recognize many of them by their signs or their characters and make them familiar and compliant.

At the heart of things

Conventional analysis, such as the positivism of Auguste Comte, supposes that magic was a sort of fanciful forerunner of science. The magician replies, however, that the methods, fields of influence and objectives of the two are quite different, even if they sometimes cross. Magic is the putting into practice of an analogical system in which plants, metals, perfumes, planets and so on communicate; it therefore reaches the living heart of beings and things, whereas science works only on appearances or externals and deals only with symptoms. This, it seems, is what gives the magician his power. It is manifested in bewitchment, exorcism, invocation and many other ways. Another book of spells, 'The Little Albert', gives the following spell to guard against unfaithfulness on the part of the magician's wife: 'Take the tip of a wolf's penis, some hair from near his eyes

The four operations of magic

'The main operations of high magic can be reduced to four fundamental types. By **consecration**, objects or gods are given powers. **Execration**, common to all forms of exorcism and by means of which demons are driven out, is the action resulting in the withdrawal of evil forces attached to things or beings. **Invocation** concerns the ritual chants and spells by which contact is made, and a request is addressed to, a superior or benevolent spirit. Finally, **evocation** is an invitation or command for a creature to show itself. In all these cases, the magic operation is prepared in minutest detail, from the arrangement of the place, especially the magic circle drawn on the ground, to the magician's equipment.' Michel Mirabail, *Les 50 Mots clefs de l'ésotérisme* (The 50 Key Words of Esoterism)

and some of the whiskers on his muzzle. Reduce it to a powder by heating it and get your wife to swallow it without knowing. You are then assured of her faithfulness.'

The science of the invisible

It is the invisible with which the magician is concerned. He believes he can affect the invisible, or essence, and bend it to his will. True magic works by ritualizing the space around the magician, within which the 'powers' are to appear or to work.

The difference between this and other rituals such as initiation or even religion, is that the words are drawn out into incantations and curses and the symbols are supposed to condense physical and cosmic energies. Using astrology, the auspicious moment is pinpointed for the appearance of a particular spirit, angel, archangel or demon (for they are all 'specialized'). The magician is barefoot so that he is in contact with earth forces, and then he draws his circle. Note that magic can act for good or for evil: the former is called 'love magic' or 'white magic' and the latter 'black magic', which aims to enslave its victim or do him harm.

Magic pentacle *'The secret of secrets, otherwise known as the Key of Solomon or the true book of spells' (17th century manuscript, Arsenal Library, Paris)*

Dealings with the supernatural

It is interesting to mention the Martinists (followers of Martines de Pasqually) briefly at this point, because they stand at the border between initiation and magic. They seem to want 'to enter into relations with the invisible', to touch it, make it material and even use it. Joseph de Maistre says that 'supernatural knowledge is the great aim of their work and their hope. They have no doubt that man can communicate with the spirit world, have dealings with spirits and thus discover the rarest mysteries. Invariably, they give extraordinary names to the most everyday objects.'

But the magician goes further still. He seeks not only to join with spirits and collaborate in the divine work, but also to act on his own account and pursue his personal designs. Prospero in Shakespeare's *The Tempest* is a good example of this. The scientist may be said to be free and independent, too, but the difference, once again, is that science is not concerned with the invisible, and acts not through the word, but by tech-

> 'Magic considered as a **science** is the knowledge of the principles and the way, by means of which the omniscience and omnipotence of the Spirit and its control over the forces of Nature can be acquired by the individual, even though he is still within his own body. Considered as an art, magic is the application of this knowledge to practice.'
> Helena Petrovna Blavatsky, *Isis Unveiled*, 1877

> '**Nature** performs in a natural way the things that the magician achieves by his art.'
> Pico della Mirandola, *Conclusiones philosophicae, cabbalisticae et theologicae*, 1486

niques; science is impersonal, whereas, to succeed, the magician must be entirely involved in the operation. Here the coincidence between microcosm (man) and macrocosm (universe) is no longer symbolic but must be real and effective.

The two moments of magic

Agrippa von Nettesheim (qv) explains in his book *Ceremonial Magic* that,

> Sacred ceremonies and the rite surrounding them have such virtue that even if they are not understood or scrupulously observed, they are nonetheless effective and clothe us in divine power if they are carried out with faith. Initiation in the mysteries of religion indeed confers dignity and by this dignity you can bring all magic gifts to life.

But his *Celestial Magic* begins with these words: 'Mathematics are indispensable to magic and have many connections with it; so much so that a person studying the latter without relying on the former will never reach his goal.' The text continues:

> If it is desired to bind and cast a spell by using the influence of the sun or any one of the planets, neither the sun nor the planet which is invoked to help accomplish the work can hear the prayers addressed to them, but they are moved by a sort of natural link which ensures that all parts of the world communicate with one another and form one whole. In the human body, a limb is caused to move by the movement of another; in the harp, a string which is touched vibrates and makes others vibrate.

Agrippa von Nettesheim carefully distinguishes between magic and science, but stresses their complementary natures. Furthermore, he was writing at a time when a new spirit of rationalism and secularism was in the air, and which threatened to sweep away everything in its path. His works are a fascinating point of contact between the ancient and the modern world.

Eliphas Lévi

A few centuries later, magic rediscovered its autonomy. It no longer cared about science, and this may perhaps be seen as a reaction against the prevailing scientific mood of the time. In the work of Eliphas Lévi in the 19th century, we find the same ideas as in Agrippa: the same unitary, living picture of the world; the same analogical causality, but in a less orderly manner. Agrippa's work is almost rationalist, whereas Lévi is flamboyant. Lévi claims that 'the original alliance of Christianity and the science of the Magi' is essential. Everything is explained in terms of occult philosophy. 'Dislike is purely and simply the suspicion that a spell is being cast.' 'According to the great masters of astrology, comets are the stars of exceptional heroes and return to earth only to announce great changes.'

Lévi even tells us that one day Cambriel, another 19th century alchemist, saw in his crucible 'the figure of God, incandescent like the sun, transparent as crystal'. A little further on he states that 'the resurrection of a dead person is the highest achievement in magnetism because, to bring it about, a sort of sympathetic omnipotence must be exercised. This is possible in cases of death from apoplexy, stroke, decline and hysteria . . . Sometimes all that is necessary is to take the person by the hand, raise them quickly and call them in a loud voice.'

If this does not work, the author also describes the preparation of philtres and talismans. Here, as we can see, the balance between science and magic is lost; the world has had enough of being stifled by science.

'Magic is, above all, the **divine art** of making contact with the universal Spirit.' E. Canseliet, *La Tour Saint-Jacques* (St James's Tower), No. 11–12, 1957

'1. Magic is the **mother of eternity**, and of the essence of all essences, for it makes itself by itself and is understood in the desire. 2. It is nothing in itself but a will. . . . 5. Magic is spirit, and being is its body . . . 6. Magic is the most secret thing.' Jakob Böhme, *Base des six points thésophiques*, 1620

Lévi feels able to express, wildly and without circumspection, the unmentionable parts of the quest for knowledge. But, if magic cannot be dissociated from human life, then we must learn to decipher it, to find what it conceals. We must search for the grain of truth hidden behind the extravagant flourish which, though almost always obscure, contains occasionally flashes of insight. Lévi does not ask himself any questions, though; he does not seek. He is happy simply to set out his ideas, without realizing that magic can no longer dispense with science.

A wild causality

Science, we are often told, is an ascetic expression of causality; magic, on the other hand, adopts a frenzied approach to it. It is said that, paradoxically, it is this asceticism that permits scientists to act on reality, whereas the profusion of magic only serves to lead the experimenter astray. But is this true?

The trouble here is that between out-and-out occultists and strict scientists there is utter polarization. The former believe that the 'Little Albert' — or, indeed, any book of spells, provided it is dusty and written in old-fashioned language — contains practical truths; the latter put their trust in dry equations, diagrams and plans. However, even for the most sceptical scientist, there remains the intriguing possibility that some magical practices *might just* work, operating on the invisible as science does on the visible, but without the need for the scientist's complex technical equipment.

> **'Natural magic** or physical magic is nothing other than the deepest knowledge of the secrets of nature.' Del Rio, *Disquisitiones Magicae*, 1606

Magnetism

The glory-hole of occultism

Practically everything can be put down to magnetism, a notion that evolved into a scientific concept.

In the scientific sense, magnetism may be defined as the phenomena connected with magnets: attraction and orientation. The magnetic field of the Earth has also been defined, stretching from north to south some 65 000 km out around the Earth. The two characteristics of magnets led occultists to believe that, by studying magnetism, they could directly observe a mysterious phenomenon, which was revealed in a concrete way. Here was the model of universal sympathy: according to them, the thing that unites all things and raises them up. In this way, magnetism virtually became the manifestation of Eros, the god believed to give the universe its cohesion. Further evidence of the link between magnetism and occultism is provided by Needham, who states that 'the discovery of magnetism in China was not unconnected with research into alchemy and magic, with Shamanism and Taoism'.

Animal magnetism

This expression dates from 1775 and Mesmer described it in his 'Memoir on the Discovery of Animal Magnetism' (1799). He thought there was a universal magnetism (or 'fluid') circulating in the substance of the nerves which made the human body analogous with a magnet. Thus the ancient analogy of hermetism, that of macrocosm and microcosm, was replaced by the correspondence between the body and the magnet. Mesmer added that, 'if this fluid was controlled, nervous illnesses could be cured directly, and others indirectly'.

Vital magnetism

Boirac, in 1908, brought the idea of 'vital magnetism' or 'psychodynamics' back into fashion. This included all those phenomena which can apparently be explained by physical or animal magnetism: dowsing (the art of detecting underground water by means of a pendulum or a stick); radiesthesia (a way of treating illness by manipulating radiation from the body); and secondary psychotic states such as hypnosis, suggestion, catalepsy and sleep-walking.

Thaumaturgism, or miracle-working, as practised by Cagliostro and the Count of Saint-Germain amongst others, derives partly from vital magnetism. Apart from occult remedies, the notion of 'spiritual ambience' also comes into play. At first, it was the notion of touching that was important. It was believed that St Louis could cure scrofula by touching those suffering from it. King Francis I tried it in December 1515 in the chapel of the Palace of the Popes. It was Robert the Pious who introduced the practice to France in 987 and Henry I who introduced it to England around 1100.

The Martial Arts

A warrior may become an initiate

Martial arts are not simply techniques for fighting; they have a spiritual dimension.

The East, and Japan in particular, has led us to accept the idea that a technique for fighting can become an art and even a form of initiation. In Japan, almost anything can become a pretext for, or an aid towards meditation, or initiation: for example, a few stones artistically arranged on sand in a garden, or a tea ceremony.

How to be both the arrow and the target

Nothing is more foreign to initiation and spirituality than war, aggression or fighting. And yet, there exist the martial arts! The philosophy underlying these teaches that by freeing himself of his enemy, the initiate frees himself every time from himself. He does not simply kill an enemy, but at the same time destroys a dark area within himself. We become aware of the truth of this only by practising one of these disciplines for ourselves. Archery is one such technique which has nothing to do with the archery that we know in the profane world. The important thing is not to hit the centre of the target, but to hit 'something' within both oneself and the world in so doing. This is not simply a pretence, but an emotion, something real and evident that can only be talked about once experienced.

From Lao Tzu

'The gentlest thing in the world will always win over the most solid. That-which-has-not penetrates that-which-has-no-gaps. In this way, we learn the advantage of inaction.'

'There is nothing in the world weaker, yet more supple, than water. But to attack the strong, who will ever be as effective as water? The void within it gives it the power to transform.'

The dialectic argument between full and empty

There are various arts such as judo, ju-jitsu, karate, kung fu and tae kwon do. These are all fighting arts, but also contain a spiritual element. The principle on which they are based — often corrupted nowadays under the pressure of competition or spectacle — is a dialectic argument between full and empty. In boxing, one opposes one's adversary, tries to thwart his movements and pits one's strength against his. This is the reflex of the uninitiated — to meet strength with strength. In judo, on the other hand, one steps aside, and tempts one's opponent to go to the limit of his movement in order to throw him off balance. In other words, far from opposing his strength, one uses it to send him in a different direction. One removes oneself in order to confront one's opponent with the disorder which he is creating in the world. Applied to popular mass movements, this echoes the non-violence preached by Gandhi.

But if archery is an ancient discipline of Zen, the martial arts proper are relatively recent (less than 300 years old). Zen arose in 800 and developed until the 12th century. It follows the principle that each one of us carries Buddha within himself and that he must discover, by one means or another, this 'Buddha-ness' under the layers of his own ignorance. Is this not the very principle of initiation?

The Masonic Lodge

A place of initiation

The masonic lodge is the basic cell of freemasonry. It crystallizes a procedure which is essential in occultism.

Whether theocratic, democratic or mixed, whatever the form of their organization, the lowest basic level of the masonic orders is the lodge. These lodges (or workshops or temples) are the places where the real work of the masons is carried out. The representative court of the institution — in the case of the Grand Lodge, for example, it is the 'federal council' — has its own necessary function, but is quite different: it is concerned with logistics (buildings, administration, etc.) and with the links between the order and the profane world.

Children of the light

The masonic lodge symbolizes the universe, and frequent reference is made to the sun in particular: the ritual journey in the lodge follows the progress of the sun, and masonic work begins at midday and ends at midnight. It is plain that freemasons desire to be the 'children of the light'.

The Worshipful Master, or Chairman, stands in the east, where the sun rises. The brothers, according to their degrees, are arranged along the columns, in the lateral bays, to the north and south. Entry to the lodge is from the west, after making the appropriate signs. It is the Tyler who ensures that those who are seeking entry to the temple are brothers of the lodge or known visitors. This is because the temple must remain hidden and set aside from the profane world.

The Worshipful Master directs the lodge, but other dignitaries (wardens, for example) help him in this task. Numerous symbols adorn the walls: the sun and the moon, the star in flames and the luminous delta which, more or less obviously, refers to the 'Great Architect of the Universe'. The brothers are adorned with aprons, medals and crossbelts. The masonic temple could even be said to be a conglomeration of signs, the meaning of which is often lost. Nevertheless, it is important not to lose sight of the fact that they are dealing with a symbolic system. Masons are in agreement that the meaning of the constituent elements of the lodge is not given once and for all, as is the case in religion or in revelation; their significance is revealed in the course of the work itself. Taking this to extremes, certain lodges — a minority, it is true — make a point of only revealing this meaning through magic.

The brother who is speaking stands by the Chair, his hand on his neck. All signs and gestures are intended to help the postulant to integrate himself into the lodge (or to become a stone of the temple). The object of the ritualization is to make him realize that the work of the masons proceeds simultaneously on two levels: in the lodge itself and elsewhere or, in esoteric terms, within both the visible and the invisible.

'**The Reception Ceremony** is valid only in so far as it sets the scene for a programme, which the new recruit must follow through, in order to enter into full possession of all faculties.'
Instruction manual, Grande Loge de France

So, the initiate finds himself faced with a strange world which is based partly on mythological readings. This underlines the rather ridiculous appearance of masonic ritual. Some writers have even called it theatrical, implying that 'symbolic stimulation' is taking place, or that the initiation only works if a 'creative imagination' takes part.

The hierachy

So, the lodge creates above all a state of mind. Its decor, and the network of symbols arranged within it, are there to help this state of mind (sometimes called 'egregor') to emerge. The ritual which opens and closes the masonic meeting is in particular a sort of handbook of discipline which contributes towards this end by cutting the mason off from the profane world and making him explore the mystery of initiation. In strict lodges, every gesture made and every word spoken is supposed to have been codified.

What exactly goes on in a masonic lodge? After the opening ritual, followed by the reading of the minutes of the previous meeting and any news about a particular brother or a particular problem or obedience in general, a speaker deals with a specific question which everyone discusses afterwards. (Certain lodges refuse to recognize this type of work and prefer simply to open and close the meeting according to ritual.) The problem discussed can be of two sorts, symbolic or profane. The liveliest lodges are those which maintain a balance between the two. Apprentices, whose symbolic age is three, are not normally allowed to speak. Their work is to dress the rough stone of which they are made, so they must assume their symbolic state by merely listening. Freemasonry is a quest for the *lost speech*, and so apprentices are there to rid themselves of their lack of intimate understanding, in order to find within themselves the place where this true speech is born. The search for dialogue is more important than what is said: the mason is supposed to have rid himself of 'profane rumours or opinions.' He is attempting to place himself at the source of being and has set off in search of truth which, although transcendental, is born from him, or more precisely within him, at the moment when he meets other brothers.

The lodge is a hierarchy: there are apprentices, journeymen and masters, who are initiated or raised to their respective degrees in particular ceremonies. But make no mistake; there is no military discipline and no elitism. We are dealing with a symbolic hierarchy and 'competencies acquired by work and continually open to challenge'. In a minority of lodges, the masters, after a certain time, put on the apprentice's apron again.

'**The method of initiation,** as we can see, is an essentially intuitive way. This is the reason why freemasonry uses symbols to provoke that understanding which comes through analogy.'
P. Naudon, *La Francmaçonnerie* (Freemasonry)

Egregor
According to the Book of Enoch, a Gnostic writing of the second century, the Egregor is an angel who is in charge of one of the six cosmic directions. Nowadays, the term refers to the common consciousness of a group gathered with an initiatory or magical purpose. The poet Max Jacob writes: 'The Egregors are beings from heaven or elsewhere, more material than the gestures we make in dreams and more immaterial than protozoa.'

The building of a temple

Goethe, who was a freemason, said of initiation that it was what enabled individuals to become themselves, and that it was always virtual. Masons build a temple which is never completed. This puts them on their guard against becoming puffed up, proud and unjust, and it underlines the fact that the state of being an initiate is never completely acquired. (Some authors, on the other hand, among them René Guénon, believe that the ceremony of initiation leaves indelible traces, appearing almost to confuse it with baptism.) Whatever the case may be, its precarious nature brings it even closer to the ephemeral art of the theatre, and we should note that alchemy is very much in favour in most lodges. Whether or not the lodge is strict, it is the place where the mason reveals and assumes a part of his intimate nature, the part on which his spiritual freedom is founded. But the lodge is only an instrument; it can lose its way — there are lodges which exist purely for the material benefit of the members — and it is always relative to its sociological surroundings. Many writers contend that the freedom which freemasonry holds in trust is always relative to this environment and to the 'seekers' who make it up.

The centre of the union

One of the founding texts of modern freemasonry, *The Anderson Constitutions*, published in 1723, says:

> A Mason is oblig'd, by his Tenure, to obey the moral Law; and if he rightly understands the Art, he will never be a stupid Atheist, nor an irreligious Libertine. But though in ancient Times Masons were charg'd in every Country to be of the religion of that Country or Nation, whatever it was, yet 'tis now thought more expedient only to oblige them to that Religion in which all Men agree, leaving their particular Opinions to themselves; that is to be *good Men and true*, or Men of Honour and Honesty, by whatever Denominations or Persuasions they may be distinguish'd, whereby Masonry becomes the *Centre* of *Union*, and the Means of conciliating true Friendship among Persons who must have remain'd at a perpetual Distance.

The text is clear and is very appropriate even today. Freemasonry is a 'centre of union' where individuals, who would otherwise not have known one another, come to meet. This does not mean that the initiates must adopt the same political opinions, but simply that they seek to find points of contact at the human level. Are we, then, talking only of friendship? Do masons go to the lodge only to socialize, or to cultivate their minds? The answer is obviously no. The person who goes to the lodge feels, without being able to put this into words, that something is lacking in his life. The compassion of the lodge helps define this lack. The initiate will find out that initiation is the coincidence of spirituality and humanism. Through the works of the freemasons, he will come to understand that the true 'art', to use Anderson's words, the quality which the ancients sought when they spoke of 'religion', is not revealed in heaven but in the course of meeting other people. Spirituality, then, is not obedience to a moral law, but that which is revealed when one person meets another in love or in friendship.

Acacia

Not to be confused with the *Robinia*, which grows widely in Europe, the acacia, which flourished on the tomb of Hiram, is a symbol of renewal. Thanks to the acacia, the master masons found the place where Hiram had been buried. Nowadays, the acacia is a most important symbol of the craft.

Metapsychics

God, Devil or matter?

Originating in the 19th century, metapsychics seeks to explain the world of the paranormal.

'Metapsychics' is a term coined by Charles Richet, who defined it as 'the science concerned with all phenomena appearing due to unknown intelligent forces, including the astonishing intellectual phenomena of our subconscious'. Synonyms for the expression include F.Clare 'psychotronics', J. André's 'transphysics', J.W. Campbell's 'epsionics' and, of course, 'parapsychology'.

Metapsychical phenomena may be explained in terms of: God or the Devil; energetics, whereby 'psychic forces' act on matter (as Crookes postulates); spiritualism (or the presence of the dead); superstition, error or sheer trickery (as the Rationalist Union claims); and modern physics (as Costa de Beauregard argues).

Unverifiable hypotheses

'Metapsychical hypotheses ... cannot be varied (unlike Freudian hypotheses, for example) and so are incapable of being repeated or checked ... So they immediately lose their value of rigour and are reduced to the same level as convenient, spiritualist theory.'

Yvonne Catellan, *Le Spiritisme*

Various domains

Metapsychics, which has had a profound influence on spiritualism, dates from the time of Mesmer and his theory of animal magnetism. Sir William Crookes attempted to make it experimental or scientific, but its objective period starts in 1934, when Rhine introduced the discipline of statistics to the subject. This is really the point when metapsychics became parapsychology. The fields covered by metapsychics include metapsychology (eg telepathy, clairvoyance, split personality, hypnotism and table-turning) and metapsychophysics (eg ectoplasm and telekinesis, or the ability to move a remote object).

So, as we have seen, metapsychics lies at the point where spiritualism, or communication with the supernatural or the beyond, gives way to parapsychology, which is subject to scientific asceticism. Metapsychics, however, avoids the fault of parapsychology, the loss of contact with its object, which, of course, renders it unmeasurable. Metapsychics is purely phenomenological and seeks to classify.

It is important, though, not to view metapsychics in terms of hermetism. Certainly, a number of esoterists have provided glimpses of paranormal phenomena; and it is true that metapsychics confirms the reality of the invisible. However, the aim of these two disciplines remains fundamentally irreconcilable.

Music

The celestial and the earthly

Occultism has often drawn on music. Some musical masterpieces are owed to initiation ceremonies.

Without going right back to the theories of Pythagoras, who read the universe like a musical score, and putting to one side the influence, theoretical or otherwise, he had on a number of 18th century musicians like the French composer, Rameau, we shall concentrate on the music of the freemasons, the best known music of initiation. Before we come to Mozart, we can point out a whole host of musicians, among them François Giroust (1738–99), Friedrich Heinrich Himmel (1765–1814) and Henry Joseph Taskin (1779–1852), who were all fully initiated masons and composed ceremonial music, such as funeral works and songs, for their lodges. It seems very unlikely that Beethoven was a mason, but a number of his melodies were inserted later, with his agreement, into ritual texts by his friend Wegeler. His seventh quartet bears the curious inscription, 'an acacia branch on my brother's tomb' and the acacia is, of course, the symbol of the master mason. The musicologist Roger Cotte states categorically that the March in B flat is absolutely characteristic of masonic works of the period.

Mozart as a mason

The greatest and most famous freemason musician, who even dedicated some of his masterpieces to freemasonry, remains Wolfgang Amadeus Mozart (1756–91). It is well known that he was an active mason and that he took his father and Haydn to initiation. He composed masonic marches and chants, a magnificent funeral lament for the ceremony of elevation to the degree of master (a lament because it refers to the killing of Hiram) and his marvellous opera, *The Magic Flute*. This last would never have seen the light of day had it not been for the librettist, brother Emmanuel Schikanader, who commissioned it from an impoverished Mozart.

Intellectual and popular, and revolutionary in both the aesthetic and the political sense, *The Magic Flute* is a masterpiece which has caused a lot of ink to flow. Whether or not it is a 'masonically composed' opera, it is nonetheless certain that the sensitivity expressed through the mythological curiosities of the libretto clearly illustrates the masonic preoccupations of the period: how to bring together the most exalted spirituality and the most overwhelming tenderness in love; the serious and the comical; happiness and humanism. The ideal would certainly have remained an idea if Mozart's genius had not illustrated it in a work capable of reaching all classes of society. Freemasonry did not make Mozart but, on the contrary, it would have lost something without his contribution. Freemasonry provided him with the purpose which crystallized his inspiration.

Debussy
'Music is a mysterious form of mathematics, whose elements partake of the infinite.'

Myth

It is always necessary to explore myth

Occult operations are achieved through an exploration of myth.

Exploring myth, or validating the present in terms of a founding legend, has the effect, as Jung points out, of accentuating the subliminal impulses which act on the mystic's unconscious. Thus, the myth reveals what was hidden; it brings about transcendence; it enriches the subject's relationship with the world; it reveals a stage on which the subject is about to become an actor; it uncovers an unknown dimension, so fabulous it seems the origin from which all things sprang. And is it not this sense, of being present at the origin, that gives existence its full meaning? However, Jung goes on to warn that this accentuation of the mythological can deform the personality with a concomitant psychological 'inflation': the subject now tends to identify himself with supernatural forces and consider himself a type of magician. It is only the 'sacrifice' of the self or ego — the 'death to the world' of the initiation ceremonies — which allows the mystic to feel intuitively the nothingness within him (the 'void' of Taoism). This nothingness paradoxically engulfs the invisible for the good reason that the symbolic relationship between self and universe springs up at that very moment.

Myths and numbers

But, if mythology and its emergence are indispensable for magic or initiation, is it possible to make sense of its various figures? Hermetic philosophy has certainly attempted to assimilate aspects of mythology into its work. The same is true of magic, and of alchemy, where every operation corresponds to a mythological sequence: Jupiter is tin, Minerva is sublimated mercury, and so forth. The following is an extract from the writings of Agrippa von Nettesheim:

> Unity appropriate for the Sun, which is the king of the stars ... This ideal or spiritual force, also called the primary cause, has been attributed to Jupiter, head and father of the gods, unique principle and origin of numbers. Duality has been attributed to the Moon, second luminary, symbol of the soul of the world ... The number three is given to Diana, that virgin said to be powerful in heaven and in hell.

A number can therefore be attributed to each god, symbolizing a natural element. We can see, then, that the knowledge of such 'numbers' confers mastery over the invisible, and enables miracles to be performed, within the natural as well as the human world.

> **'Every plan for remythicization,** however rough, and every contact with the universe of archetypes and gods, however distant, automatically opens up possibilities of stimulating enlightenment.' G. Durand, *Science humaine et tradition* (Human Science and Tradition)

Numbers and Symbolism

The mystery of numbers

In occultism, the number is the sign of a god; for the philosophers, it represents a mode of being.

Numbers have a symbolic function which does not come from arithmetic, but from arithmology, a metaphysical form of mathematics. The aim of arithmology is not to count or enumerate, but to unveil the structure of the cosmos.

One and multiples

According to Schuré, 'Number was not considered as an abstract quantity, but as the intrinsic virtue of the supreme One, of God, who is the source of universal harmony. The science of numbers was the science of living forces, of divine faculties in action in the world and in man, in the macrocosm and in the microcosm.' 'One' (the first unity) symbolizes and, at the same time, manifests what occultists call the 'First One', the fire of Heraclitus, the Spirit uncreated, the indivisible, the unmanifest, the unchangeable which is hidden beneath the multiple. 'The true essence of things is hidden from man,' says the philosopher Philolaus, who continues:

> He only knows the things of this world, where the finite is combined with the infinite. How can he then know essence? By virtue of the fact that there is between him and things a harmony, or a relation, or a common principle. This principle is given to all things by the One who bestows on them their measure and their intelligibility along with their essence. He is the common measure between subject and object, the means by which the soul shares in the reason behind the One.

How is it that the world is intelligible, so that the subject knows the object? This is so because there is a 'common principle' between the observer and the universe; this 'principle' or 'measure' reveals itself in various modes, according to the position in the universe occupied by the observer at any particular moment, and these modes are indicated by numbers. The guiding principle is to know the One: the primordial unity; the essence of One, containing the infinite, and rich with all manifestations and possibilities; the essence yet to be defined, for its manifestations are ever virtual. Jakob Böhme put it neatly when he said that unity was, paradoxically, the same as nothingness. Schuré described the concept thus:

> 'The infinite is shown as a circle, or a snake biting its tail, representing infinity moving itself. As soon as infinity is defined, it produces all the numbers it contains in its great unity and governs in perfect harmony. This is the meaning of the first problem, the reason why the Great Monad contains all smaller numbers and why all numbers spring from the great unity in movement.'

'When the **genetics of numbers** becomes a sure technique, certain transliterations from one language to another, when universal numerical values are applied, will allow the identity of gods and key words to be recognized, and the movement and vicissitudes of civilizations to be followed closely.' R. Abellio, *La Bible, document chiffré* (The Bible, a Coded Document)

A creative dimension

The Pythagoreans said that the 'Great Monad', or Unity, was like a creative dyad in its action. From the moment it became manifest, the primordial principle became double: an indivisible essence or inexhaustible infinity on the one hand; and divisible, manifest substance on the other. The monad is the essence, while the dyad is the ability to reproduce, and to bring about creation. The ancient philosophers made the idea comprehensible by assigning a sex to each of the two: they said that the One was the masculine principle and the Two, the feminine, meaning that the One stands for activity, and the Two the object on which the activity is exercised eg matter, nature or even the soul of the world. To recap: One is the primordial principle (Being) and Two is the principle through which Being manifests itself, a principle combining active and passive. Finally, the product of this dialectic between active and passive, which introduces a rupture into the fullness of being, concludes with a manifestation: the world has created itself. The creation is represented as a trinity: 1 = Being; 2 = the process of manifestation; 3 = the result. (Note that manifestation, epiphany and creation are all synonymous here.)

The triad or law of three is therefore the founding law of all things in the world. An oracle of Zoroaster said, 'The number 3 reigns throughout the world and the monad is its principle.' This is the key to the analogy of macrocosm (universe) and microcosm (man) for, just as man is made up of three distinct but unified elements (body, soul and spirit), the universe is divided into three spheres (the natural world, the human world and the world of transcendence).

Hermetic thought assumes not only that each number reveals a cosmogonic structure but also that the sequence of numbers which, taken together, are the manifestation of the universe, also has a meaning. So, according to numerologists, 4 or quaternity symbolizes the trinity epitomized by the monad, for the number 7, as the sum of 3 and 4, in turn symbolizes the union of man and transcendence. Finally, the number 10, formed by adding the first four numbers together, is the perfect number, the sacred *tetraktys* of the Pythagoreans; it represents a new unity.

An operative system

So, as we have seen, the symbolism of numbers is not mere counting, but an operative mysticism. Perhaps we might say that, where ordinary arithmetic makes things objective, enabling them to be counted, arithmology makes them subjective. This may, however, be an over-simplification. The arithmology of Plato, Pythagoras or the Cabala, does not come from any desire to merge with the rest of existence; the aim is not to replace a clear, distinct idea with some strange hotchpotch. Arithmology is rather a form of metaphysics, a reflection on the creation of the world. Obviously, such reflection has given rise to many superstitions and encouraged charlatans. Nevertheless, the symbolism of numbers is a metaphysical problem with which modern philosophy must grapple and strip of its wild fancies.

Occult Geometry

A different sort of geometry

Occult geometry is symbolic. It has no practical use, except in magic.

Every gesture, and thus every rite eg prostration, genuflexion and the sign of the cross, refers to an implicit 'bodily scheme', or to a geometry of 'living'. There must be an unexplained significance in the geometric figures drawn superstitiously on talismans, walls or the floors of temples. However, even superstition may derive from a degraded form of ancient knowledge.

The importance of the circle

In magic, the most important figure is the circle: it stands for unity, and for the number 10. Agrippa von Nettesheim says that 'unity is the centre and the circumference of all things'. The drawing of a circle by a magician, or in the Catholic rite of *circumitio*, draws upon the person doing it, by analogy, the influence of the sun or the moon (for the sun is a complete circle). Jung discovered that, in his patients' dreams, a circle symbolized the self, that is, the whole person. According to the occult philosopher Malfatti, this is the 'inclusion of the ideal in the real, the conception of the spiritual and corporal in man, as in the whole of nature'. Note, finally, that the squaring of the circle – the supposed coincidence of the square and the circle – is the emblem of the philosopher's stone, or of spiritual freedom.

Circle and infinity

'The circle can be said to be an endless line, without any part which could be called beginning or end, and yet with the beginning and end at every point. This is why it is also said that circular movement is infinite, not with regard to time but with regard to place. The round figure is therefore considered the greatest and most perfect of all, and the most suitable for ligatures and exorcisms, which is why those conjuring up evil spirits generally enclose themselves within a circle.' Agrippa von Nettesheim

The cross

Even before the dawn of Christianity, the cross was a symbol of fundamental importance. According to the occult philosopher, Piobb, the Latin cross alone 'is the key to the metaphysical doctrines of Christianity; not because it stands for Christ's suffering and death, but because it stands for adept's death to his own death.'

The cross symbolizes life. On its Y-axis, the top represents transcendence and the bottom the unconscious. Elucidating the latter, by shining a light on it from above, has the effect of opening a person's being to the universe, and giving him the values of the X-axis which, with the other, makes him complete; this enables him to find firm root in his own centre, for the junction of the two axes is an 'earthmoving coincidence'.

The pentagram

The pentagram symbolizes the coincidence of microcosm and macrocosm; it is the image of man who, standing with arms and legs outstretched, fits it perfectly. In magic, it is believed to condense magnetic forces.

The triangle

The triangle symbolizes the great Architect in occult tradition. The list of figures quoted here is far from exhaustive. Finally, it is worth noting that these figures are all perhaps archetypes in the Jungian sense of the term.

The Operative Masons' Lodge

The lodge, built alongside the cathedral

It is in the lodge that the journeymen ritually hand on the secrets of building.

The term 'trade guild' conjures up pictures of the great cathedral builders. It is true that the guild in its most ancient form — the roman *collegia*, for example — is concerned with the building of palaces and temples, and the meaning of the symbolism, practised in its activities and ceremonies, only becomes evident when we remember this. The object is to make the earth habitable by putting up buildings which are capable, at one and the same time, of rooting human beings on the earth and opening up horizons which lie far beyond this world. The symbolic object was to show that the inhabitant of one particular place was also a citizen of the universe. However, in the course of history, the trade guilds extended their activities to embrace guilds of coopers, printers, plasterers, and many more. Should this be seen as a deviation, or a natural evolution? Opinions vary, but everybody agrees that the lodges of the cathedral builders are the original, and most authentic, expression of the trade guilds. This is where spiritual life is most vibrant and where knowledge is handed on. This is where the invisible is made manifest.

On the road

Journeymen used to go all round the country; they went from town to town and spoke of going 'on the road'. Every journeyman had to present himself at the lodge of the town in which he arrived. In early times, these lodges were inns kept by a 'father' and 'mother', where everybody met after the day's work. We are told that a guild's headquarters had to include an inn (with bedrooms, dining-rooms, kitchen and common-room), professional facilities (such as a room to examine masterpieces, a meeting room, library and records office) and a trade facility (with workshops for training and producing masterpieces, and offices for allied trades).

The 'mother' received trainees and qualified journeymen — the guild usually only recognizes these two grades. She washed their clothes, looked after them when they were ill and, in short, provided some sort of family life. The 'father' was in charge of discipline and, if a journeyman was guilty of some misdemeanour, he would pay a fine to the common fund. The job of the 'fixer' was to find a place of work for newcomers, for the journeymen in work remained under the authority of the guild. Travellers always carried a pass or letter of introduction which went under a variety of names, such as 'the horse' or 'the ship'. Travelling had two functions in training: the professional and the psychological. It was also a form of initiation, because the initiate set off, at one

Educators for life

'You can stay a simple workman and yet be a great workman. In this way, I have known some journeymen and some workmen who had not completed their tests, who were in my eyes masters and teachers of the trade, for they loved the trade with all their heart. They were also teachers of life, for they loved their fellow man, doubtless without even being aware of it. That is how they came to have the gift of teaching and handing on.' La Volonté de Vouvray, journeyman and the same time, to find himself and to see the world. George Sand, in her book *Le Compagnon du tour de France* (The Journeyman on the Tour of France), says:

> The tour around France is the poetic time in the journeyman's life, when he becomes an adventurous pilgrim, a kind of knight errant. With neither house nor belongings, he sets off along the highways and byways under the protection of an adoptive family, which will never abandon him either in this life or the next. Even the man who wants to have a safe and honourable place in his home town will go off in the full vigour of his youth to enjoy the heady delights of an active life.

The length of time journeymen spent touring the country varied, but was usually between three and five years, this period ending when the journeyman married or settled down in one particular town.

Initiation, masterpiece and ritual

The guild also conducts reception ceremonies. With his eyes blindfold, the newcomer is subjected to a sort of ragging; he is jostled and sometimes even bundled into a hole, then his eyes are uncovered and he finds himself in the 'thinking room'. This symbolizes the centre of the earth (in alchemy, the womb from which everything springs). The newcomer is stripped of any jewellery, his watch, tie and so on, and is told:

> My country is the symbol of a new life. For you are going to receive a new name, which will be blessed and purified by water and fire. You are going to make a new family for yourself. You are entering a new world. For us, you are a newborn baby, making its entry among us, stripped of all the things invented by human vanity, which you leave at the door of this temple. For God made us all equal, and gold, jewels and clothes only serve to hide our faults and the good heart of a man must never be judged by trinkets or outward show, but by his actions. (quoted by Jean-Pierre Bayard in *Le Compagnonnage en France* (The Guild in France)

Another document, cited by Luc Benoist in his book *Le Compagnonnage et les métiers* (Guilds and Crafts), adds some interesting information:

> Records do not lay down the order of events in an initiation, but they list the items necessary to carry out these ceremonies ... In the guild of hatters, there were two rooms. One was used for reception or initiation, and the other for festivals. There was an ante-chamber outside the reception room, where the newcomer, accompanied by the 'fixer', waited and knocked three times for admittance. The three leading journeymen in the town's guild would be waiting for the newcomer in this room. There was a table representing the holy sepulchre, covered with a white cloth (the holy shroud), on which there was placed a big cross (to represent Christ's passion). In the middle of the cross there was a crown of thorns. On the two arms of the cross there were two plates, each with a lighted candle, representing the sun and the moon. Three knives on each arm of the cross represented the nails in Christ's hands and feet and a piece of wood, Longinus' lance. Ropes symbolized the scourge, a table napkin folded in two represented the tongs and a salt-cellar stood for the pillar where Judas threw his 30 pieces of silver. ...

Duty

For us, Duty has a special meaning: we extend it to include not only all the duties of an honourable man or a good workman, but also those of the journeyman who is entrusted with a particular task of a more social nature.'We also identify it with our rule. For us, duty calls up ideas of the whole range of our customs and our rules, our houses and our order. It is the motto of our tradition, as well as our rallying call and our family name.' Jean Bernard, *Le Compagnonnage, rencontre de la jeunesse et de la tradition* (The Guild as a Meeting Place for Youth and Tradition)

> In the same room there was a casket representing Noah's ark (symbolizing a second birth after the ordeal by water of the Flood). ... Finally, there was a fireplace with a fire lit in it to represent, as in all mysteries, the mouth of Hell.

The initiate took a new name and, in this way, the apprentice began his life as a journeyman. The crowning moment of the initiation was the making of a masterpiece, that is to say a remarkable piece of work, by which the journeyman proved his competence.

Ritualization had a bearing in all sorts of ways on daily life. Quite apart from the reception ceremony, or initiation, there were secret signs given on meeting, ceremonies to receive newcomers, the fraternal embrace, the farewell to a journeyman travelling away from the area, patronal festivals, funeral rites, and so on. Furthermore, every journeyman had his own mark to put on the stones he worked, seen to this day in old churches, for example.

The Orgy

A love-offering

Orgies have — occasionally — been a means of spiritual research.

Gnosticism has rather a bad reputation. The Church, which overcame it, attempted to reduce it, at one and the same time, to a doctrine of extreme austerity and one of immoral sexual indulgence. Indeed, this may even have been true in some cases.

Carnal pleasures

The followers of certain Gnostic and occult tendencies have always made frequent reference to the principle of Hermes, 'If you hate your body, my child, you cannot love yourself' (*Corpus Hermeticum*). This belief in achieving salvation through pleasure is held by both the Ophites (worshippers of the snake) and the Marcionites. As for the Carpocratians, their belief was that the soul was reincarnated as long as it had not exhausted the pleasures of the flesh. While, by making love, the Barbelognostics sought to help Barbelo, the divine mother, to gather the seed she needed to produce universal energy.

The Cainites went even further. They believed that the true friends of Sophia (qv) were all those who had rebelled against Jehovah, so they admired Cain and the citizens of Sodom and Gomorrah. They had a 'Gospel of Judas' and preached sexuality as a revolt against a cruel God.

Like the others, the Cainites indulged in orgies. The proceedings began with a banquet, at the end of which the men present invited their wives to 'be charitable with a brother'. After orgasm, they collected the sperm in their hands and, holding it up towards heaven, chanted, 'We offer you this gift, the body of Christ.'

Jesus's answer

The apostle Thomas asked Jesus, 'We have heard that there are men on this earth who take the sperm of men and the menstrual fluids of women, put them in lentils and eat them, saying, 'We believe in Esau and Jacob.' Is that allowable or not?' Jesus was angry and said, 'Truly I say, this sin is worse than all other sins and iniquities.' *Pistis Sophia*

Towards other shores

Ritual orgies are also found in Asiatic Tantrism — indeed, in one form or another, they have existed at all times. A psychoanalyst might offer the explanation that this collective exchange, fusion, or loss of individuality helps to overcome sexual fear; in a group we can do what we dare not do alone.

If there is a basic fear, it is due to the opposition of sexuality (Eros) and death (Thanatos). Real freedom is delivery from disease and death, and the physical starting-point for this process is sexuality. Besides the group, the orgy may well include the idea of fusion and loss of personality, but it also includes the notion of exchange. The exchange of partners expresses, in a debased form, the desire in the couple for exchange. So we must conclude that the ritual orgy distorts a real need for loving tenderness, just as eroticism follows in the wake of sacred feeling.

Parapsychology

Measuring the occult

Parapsychology is an attempt to satisfy scientific criteria.

Parapsychology must not be confused with metapsychics: The latter is phenomenological, while the former is statistical. Parapsychology is materialist, even scientific, whereas the latter is spiritualist. However, the object of their study is the same.

The experimental procedure of parapsychology, a discipline inaugurated by Rhine in 1927, is taken from science and involves laboratories, instruments and repeated experiments.

The simplest experiments are done with Zenner's packs of cards (cards bearing simple geometric figures), which are systematically shuffled by apparatus. An experimenter then draws a series and tries to guess the drawings on them. The experiment shows that the experimenter guesses correctly more often than the laws of chance would lead us to expect. This 'proves' the existence of the supposed psychic phenomena. But is it really necessary to 'prove' this? We can certainly have premonitions, but is it not absurd to wish to show this, especially as the scope of the experiments is considerably reduced by their being carried out in laboratory, rather than real-life, conditions? Experiments in telekinesis (see **metapsychics**) are more interesting because, if they can be verified, they would prove the action of the spirit on matter.

ESP

'Rhine's idea, which he explored in his experiments, was simply to try to find out if there was the possibility, hitherto uninvestigated by scientific instruments, to experience events other than through our five senses or, rather, what we know of the five senses. This attitude, so limited according to spiritualists, so crazy according to rationalists, is what allowed him to obtain results which are still intriguing today. He called this possibility Extra-Sensory Perception (ESP in short), the most general description possible.' Pierre Vigne, *Lumières sur l'après-vie* (Light on the Hereafter)

Astonishing experiments

Experiments in parapsychology are currently being carried out in universities throughout the world and, recently, the so-called 'out-of-body experience' seems to have been recorded for the first time. The experiment centred on a person who claimed to be able to leave his body and go, at a pre-arranged time, to a given room. This room contained nothing but an apparatus sensitive enough to record the slightest presence and, at the given time, it did indeed record a 'presence'. If the experiment was conducted in truly rigorous conditions, it may well prove the possibility of out-of-body experiences. However, it could equally well indicate the phenomenon of telekinesis, with the subject influencing the apparatus from a distance.

It is difficult to know just what to make of this experiment (a full account of which may be read in the report on the parapsychology convention held in 1973 at Charlottesville in Virginia, USA). The strangest point about it is that very little has been heard of it since. Was it then a hoax? Whatever the case, whether it is a hallucination or partly real, the phenomenon of out-of-body experiences is also found in psychology — admittedly in a less spectacular form — where it is known as autoscopy.

Psychoanalysis

A link with hermetism?

Like occultism, psychoanalysis links up with pre-Aristotelian thought; this gives a fleeting resemblance to the two techniques.

Psychoanalysis and hermetism, at first glance, could not possibly agree: the former shuns all obscurity and claims to be rational; the latter in its exuberance seems to welcome confusion. Freud told Jung to avoid the 'muddy water of occultism' and René Guénon went so far as to say of psychoanalysis that it was, like Einstein's relativity, a product of the *Kali-Yuga*, the present age of utter degeneration of truth.

However, on closer examination, the two disciplines are not so far removed from one another. To see this, all we have to do is look closely at Jung's idea of a collective unconscious, which seems very close to the 'truth' of the Tradition. We might also examine, as David Bakan did, the influence of Jewish thought, and the Cabala in particular, on Freud's work.

Analogical causality

However, there are even deeper resemblances between psychoanalysis and hermetism. Even without putting forward the hypothesis that the inner freedom reached by the patient at the end of his cure resembles that conferred by initiation, nor comparing on the other hand the different moments of alchemy with those of psychoanalysis (black = making contact with the unconscious; white = exaltation and free interpretation; red = revelation of consciousness), we cannot help but be aware that psychoanalysis itself is built around mythology — why else is there the central allusion to Oedipus? Psychoanalysis certainly uses, and even abuses, symbols, albeit in a restrained way. In psychoanalysis, as in hermetism, analogy is the means by which causality is demonstrated: the causality of dreams, not of physics.

All of this encourages the profane to place psychoanalysis somewhere between science and magic. This is not so short of the mark if we remember that what is usually meant by magic is a sort of poetry of the universe. And is not psychoanalysis a form of inner poetry, and alchemy a way of showing how inner poetry and poetry of the universe are related?

Jewish mysticism
'In trying to interpret the development of psychoanalysis as an expression of Jewish mysticism, we have sought to highlight the mystical as well as the Jewish element. Jewish mysticism was undoubtedly an important means of transmission. Perhaps it acted by developing in Freud a certain perceptive and affective receptivity, and by defining certain reactions to the problems he faced.' D. Bakan, *Freud et la tradition mystique Juive* (Freud and the Jewish Mystical Tradition)

Reincarnation

Living again in another shape

Whether metempsychosis or reincarnation, the theories of life after death always begin the same way.

It is a truism to state that, for mankind, death is the ultimate mystery. It is easy to understand the temptation to identify death and the invisible world. However, if initiation includes some such assimilation, it does it in a symbolic way, aware that it is a simulation. The sense of the mystery leads, by anology, to death; that of initiation to immortality; and that of rebirth to reincarnation. Approaching reincarnation as a psycho-spiritual reality, and accepting that the soul after death enters a new body, is a very commonly shared belief.

As René Guénon writes, 'An indefinite series of changes of state in a being may be taken for a succession of lives on earth. Each being has its own characteristic conditions different from all others; this constitutes a cycle of existence for the being through which he can pass once only.'

Metempsychosis

This is reincarnation extended to all of nature and includes a moral notion of cosmic destiny (the Hindu *karma*). It states, for example, that a human being who has lived like a pig or a snake in this life will be reincarnated as a pig or a snake. 'Those who have lived in evil and impiety will not only be refused entry to heaven but will also be condemned to go through a shameful migration, unworthy of the holiness of the spirit, into the body of another species' (*Corpus Hermeticum*). The person who has behaved well becomes a sage when he returns to earth and, in the end, the fortunate break the cycle of reincarnation and become part of the cosmos.

A philosophical belief

Theories of reincarnation are based on: experimental fact (memories of earlier existences, regressive hypnosis, seances, etc); textual authority (eg Matthew II, 13–16, Matthew XVI, 13–15 and Luke I, 15–17); beliefs like *karma*, where the fruits of an earlier life are carried on to the next; or on the spiritualist separation of body and soul.

Orpheus, Pythagoras, Plato and certain Gnostics and Cabalists explicitly referred to reincarnation, but did so in more philosophical terms than modern believers in reincarnation. In Tibet, where the belief is central to dogma, it takes on two dimensions, the exoteric and the esoteric; the *Bardo Thödol*, or Tibetan 'Book of the Dead', takes account of the esoteric dimension.

Ritual

A discipline to reach the invisible

All initiatory societies and all occult procedures emerge through ritual.

All initiatory societies work through symbols and rituals. These vary according to the society, within a society according to the branch, and within the branch according to the temple or lodge. This diversity causes much confusion, especially when politics come into play and each organization claims to be the most 'regular', or truest, and to identify its own particular ritual with the rite.

Existential sacralization

Firstly, a definition. It can be said of rite that it is on the level of the archetype, whereas ritual is on that of the manifestation. Rite is therefore inaccessible and revealed — always uniquely — in and through rituals. Note, however, that the archetype is neither model, nor pattern, nor an *en-soi*! Initiatory transcendence is not the same as religious transcendence, for the former always concentrates on its manifestations.

Ritualization — activation of a ritual or, to others, 'existential sacralization' — is carried out by bringing into play the elements of a symbolic reality. For the mystic it is indeed a case of identifying with what is revealed to him, all the while knowing that he is taking part in a creative simulation. Ritual opens up a mythological reality; there is no question of forgetting that its lights reveal deep darkness. (As René Char puts it, 'I love that which dazzles me and then accentuates the darkness within me.')

Whether in American Indian secret societies, medieval trade-guilds, freemasonry or yet other groups, ritual gives dynamism to symbols which pass, as the philosophers put it, from *en-soi* to *pour soi*. Once dusty emblems, they become the characters in a play which is acted out before the eyes of the mystic himself. Fire, air, earth and water, formerly abstract notions or concepts, become for the time of the dogma concrete realities with which the postulant believes he is in contact. Ritual is a play acted out by the spectators themselves, recounting, through archaic details, important events such as the death of Christ, which can only be reconstructed through mythology. Ritual, in short, is a 'handbook of discipline', as the Essenes would have it, whose task is to unite a community and put it, symbolically, in harmony with one of its founding myths.

We should not lose sight of the fact that in the trade-guilds the ritual varied not only from one branch to another, but even from one trade to another. For example, the admission ceremony for stonemasons was not the same as that for the shoemakers. The same is true for the freemasons; there are different rituals according to the rite the lodge observes. Freemasonry can be defined as a federation of rites, but each branch has its dominant ritual.

Rite and ritual

The difference between rite and ritual is not easy to define. However, it seems that the rite is the archetype for any possible ritualization and the ritual is the concrete, local experience of the rite. In this way, the need to formulate the rite is avoided, but it is considered to be the force behind all efforts to formulate it.

Doctor Faustus *calling up the Devil goes through an extremely complex ritual. (Frontispiece of* Doctor Faustus *by Christopher Marlowe (1564–93). Wood-engraving from the London edition of 1631.)*

The three sources of freemasonry

The first cultural source of freemasonry is the philosophy underlying the work and humanism. Proudhon points this out when he writes, 'In the archives of the human mind there is something which dates from before all signs, of which all signs were copies and which was the first matter human intelligence worked on. This . . . we can call equally well rudiments of knowledge or rudiments of work.' An excellent definition of the tools of masonry. The second source is Christian esoterism, rejected by the Church although the Gospel of St John is steeped in it and certain lodges call themselves 'lodges of St John'. The third source is the Gnostic tradition, Pythagorism, the Cabala, alchemy and so on, and this is obviously the most mysterious of all.

The United Grand Lodge of England works according to the 'Emulation' rite; it states that 'true freemasonry is a cult to sustain and spread belief in the existence of God'. Freemasonry in Latin countries and the Grand Orient and the Grand Lodge follow mainly the 'Ancient and Accepted Scottish Rite' and the 'French Rite'. Alongside these, there exist also: the 'Corrected Scottish Rite' (with its founding ritual referring to the Templars); that of the Elect of Coen, founded by Martines de Pasqually under the influence of Swedenborg; an Egyptian rite founded by Cagliostro, etc. Before we leave the freemasons, we should note that the 'blue lodges' — those which deal with the initiation of the first three degrees, of apprentice, fellowcraft and master — are paralleled by higher grade lodges, leading right on to the 33rd degree, all with their own particular rituals.

However, from the point of view of initiation, these ceremonies are only repetitions of those carried out for the lower degrees.

Ritual is also a sign of recognition. Thanks to ritual, it is possible to know both who one is (what position to take up in relation to the profane world or to the lodges which follow other rituals) and where one is (in what sort of temple and what one is supposed to do there). Ritual, therefore, fulfils the same function as medieval coats-of-arms and, because of that, it gives rise to quarrels which are quite impenetrable to the profane. The modification of a single word or phrase can reflect quite decisive intentions. For example, the consequences of the omission of the traditional reference to the Great Architect of the Universe were incalculable for the Grand Orient.

Symbolic simulation

However, we should seek to avoid getting lost in details and disputes which are largely academic, without any meaning other than that of enabling the protagonists to be placed within the whole phenomenon of initiation and showing whether they lean more towards humanism or rather towards the spiritual dimension; it is better to try to see how ritual works, or rather how to be aware of its effect. A ritual which works well unfolds rather like a dream: every figure appearing is a particular aspect of the dreamer himself. Thus, the killing of Hiram by the three bad journeymen is told in the masonic ceremony for initiation to the degree of master and is the image of the initiate's own ambivalence. The three journeymen represent the initiate's inner darkness and the passions he has not yet taken upon himself. Hiram is his ego, or his super-ego; in any case, he symbolizes the man who is 'building himself'. Initiation is the conquest of man's innate ambivalence, enabling him to pass to the creative stage where there is no longer any contradiction. There are three bad journeymen, and this number is also the sign of the apprentice. These bad journeymen symbolize the darkness of the mystic and the three dimensions of the unconscious which, according to esoterism, emerge during the process of interpretation.

The man undergoing initiation is, at one and the same time and successively, Hiram and the murderers, the process being, as we saw in the article, **Initiation**, the killing of his darker parts, experienced as murder and death-to-the-world. However, the play must be acted out with the figures on the stage, and the initiate must identify with them, without becoming fascinated by them. In order for the creative simulation to work, the characters must remain at a

The 33 Degrees of Freemasons

There are 33 degrees as set out below. (Those in italics require a special initiation; the others are merely conferred.)

1. *Entered Apprentice*
2. *Fellow Craft*
3. *Master Mason*
4. *Secret Master*
5. Perfect Master
6. Intimate Secretary
7. Provost and Judge
8. Superintendent of the Building or Master in Israel
9. *Master Elect of the Nine*
10. Illustrious Elect of the Fifteen
11. Sublime Knight or Chevalier Elect
12. *Great Master Architect*
13. *Royal Arch*
14. *Grand Scottish Chevalier of the Heavenly Vault*
15. Chevalier of the East or of the Sword
16. Prince of Jerusalem
17. Chevalier of the East or of the West
18. *Sovereign Prince Rose-Cross*
19. Grand Pontiff
20. Venerable Grand Master
21. Noachite or Prussian Knight
22. *Royal Hatchet or Prince of Libanus*
23. Chief of the Tabernacle
24. Prince of the Tabernacle
25. Chevalier of the Brazen Serpent
26. Scotch Trinitarian or Prince of Mercy
27. Grand Commander of the Temple
28. Chevalier of the Sun or Prince Adept
29. *Grand Chevalier of St Andrew of Scotland*
30. *Chevalier Ka Dosch*
31. *Grand Inspector Inquisitor Commander*
32. *Sublime Prince of the Royal Secret*
33. *Sovereign Grand Inspector General*

distance: they must be strange without being strangers. The initiate must play his part sincerely in this symbolic simulation; he must accept all the conventions. The work of initiation is impossible without absolute respect for this.

The paradox of the work of initiation is that it begins with an act of faith, while claiming to free us from our inner darkness and to transmute our unconscious religious feelings. This is not, however, surprising: psychoanalysis teaches us that freedom is achieved by overcoming alienation. Ritual roots (or recentres) the initiate in the visible, real world only to open him out to invisible, mythological reality. But, like a good director, ritual disappears as soon as the show comes to life, as soon as the miraculous conjunction of dream and reality comes about. These are rare moments, almost imperceptible, and it is only the light shed by them that suggests they are more than illusion.

Rite and structure

The rite gives structure to the initiatory group. It is simultaneously the badge by which the group affirms its uniqueness, and the reflection of its inner organization. It is easy to see why it remains mysterious.

The rite of freemasonry is remarkable from this point of view. It has penetrated European history and been a driving force within it.

The value of rites

Contemporary ethnology tends to distinguish between: (a) behavioural rites (rites of passage, taboos, etc); (b) magical rites (spells, etc); and (c) religious rites (offerings, prayers and sacrifices). Marcel Mauss distinguished between negative rites (taboos) and positive rites (propitiation).

Rites of passage have been those most closely studied. They are mainly concerned with puberty, marriage and death. Their aim is to integrate the individual into the group or tribe. Everyday rites, such as meals, are similar to mere habits.

Rosicrucianism

The most mysterious secret society

The mystery of Rosicrucianism has never been penetrated; legend mingles closely with historical truth.

The Rosicrucians are a brotherhood of scholars, alchemists and esoteric researchers who appeared in the 17th century. Adepts were bound to one another very informally, but the legend which surrounded them was (and remains) tenacious. What are we to make of the posters which appeared in Paris in 1622, proclaiming 'We, deputies of the principal college of the brothers of the Rose-Cross, are making our stay both visible and invisible in this town ... in order to draw men, our equals, from deadly error'? Was this the work of political agitators, or merely of hoaxers?

Whatever the case, the history of Rosicrucianism can be summed up as follows. Around 1615, there appeared three successive manifestos: 'Echoes of the Fraternity of the Most Praiseworthy Order of Rosicrucians'; 'Confessions of the Enigmatic Brotherhood of the Most Honourable Rose-Cross'; and, especially, 'The Chemical Wedding of Christian Rosenkreuz'. Around 1710, Samuel Richter organized the first fraternity of Golden Rosicrucians; then, in the 19th and 20th centuries, Rosicrucian societies arose in great numbers, among them Stanislas de Guaïta's Cabalistic Order of the Rose-Cross.

Posters

'We deputies of the principal college of the brothers of the Rose-Cross are making our stay both visible and invisible in this town, by the grace of the All-High to whom the hearts of all just men turn, in order to draw men, our equals, from deadly error.' (Taken from posters which appeared in Paris in 1622.)

Humanism before its time

The origin of the brotherhood is the subject of much confusion. We are told, on the one hand, that Robert Fludd was one of the 'inventors' of Rosicrucianism. He wrote, 'Elijah hears the voice of God as the Rosicrucians only see the treasure at break of day ... All the mysteries of nature are open to them ...' (*Tractatus apologeticus integritatem societatis Rosae Crucis defendens*, 1616). On the other hand, the *Fama Fraternitatis*, first published in 1614, and its accompanying *Confessio* recount the life of Christian Rosenkreuz, viewed by some as the actual, and by others as the mythical, founder of the Rosicrucians. The myth of Rosenkreuz tells how his tomb was discovered by a great master 120 years after his death. The tomb 'occupies the house of the Holy Ghost. It has seven sides, each five feet wide and eight feet high. It is constantly lit by inextinguishable lights. In the middle, a cylindrical altar bears the inscription, 'I have made for myself this sepulchre which will be a summary of the universe for the living.'

The symbol of the order is a rose with seven petals and a cross, usually black. The rose represents secrecy and evolution, while the cross symbolizes difficulties, the sorrows of life and karma, according to the Rosicrucian manual. Legend claims that Rosicrucians are 'unknown higher beings' who live in the invisible and manage the world.

Rosicrucianism preaches 'humility, justice, truth and chastity', according to Irénée Agnostus (in *Fons Gratine*, 1619) and calls on its adepts to 'cure all ills' of both body and soul. The order is opposed to the papacy and to Muhammad, and aims to be truly Christian. Its ritual is composed of prayers, meditations and ceremonies.

German Rosicrucian engraving of the early 17th century, showing the oratory (Ergon) which, as in alchemy, is also a laboratory (Paregon). (National Library, Paris)

The Sacred

'Sacred' does not mean 'religious'

'Sacred' and 'religious' are distinct in occult thought. The latter is a debased form of the first.

Every temple and every ceremony, whether magical or initiatory, requires a sacred space. This is often in the image of the universe. Those officiating are cut off from their visible, day-to-day surroundings solely in order to reveal a richer relationship to the world. The walls do not exist in order to shelter the mystic but, on the contrary, to expose him to the universe and its storms. However, it is impossible to mention the idea of the sacred without thinking at some point or another of God. The paradox is that, more often than not, initiates or adepts claim to be agnostic, and this has given rise to a great deal of contention throughout the whole history of occultism and of secret societies. Perhaps we can put this into some kind of perspective if we note that God, as revealed in religion, is an en-soi of God, whereas the God of the sacred is a God-among-men. The sacred, however, does not so much deify humanism, as 'realize' divinity. God, for His part, is no chimera, but humanity in its virtual state, about to be made manifest.

The unity of God
'The gods of mythology, with their character and their psychology, are but personifications of the sacred, just as the names of God are so many attributes. It is impossible to mention the unity of God without unfolding His essence during the initiatory experience of consciousness.' M. Mirabail, *Les 50 Mots clefs de l'ésotérisme* (Fifty Key Words in Esoterism)

Transmutation

Speaking in profane terms, we might say that occultism holds that humanity is only revealed to itself by transcendence. To paraphrase Feuerbach, the sacred is revealed as an attribute of man of which he has allowed himself to be dispossessed. The terror provoked by this statement is a measure of its social danger, and further explains why the adherents of this belief must take refuge in secret societies. Nonetheless, the idea cannot simply be dismissed. In hermetism, religious feeling is a necessary part of humanity, with the important provision that this religious feeling is the 'raw material' on which the initiate works in order to experience glimpses of the sacred, borne within him and all mankind. This transmutation of the religious into the sacred is the very object of the occult sciences and, especially, of initiation. Modern freemasonry, for example, considers that the sacred is revealed whenever two human beings enter a relationship with one another (thus, a meeting is the best possible setting for a manifestation). Such a relationship reveals not only the richness of the human condition, but also the invisible. To be aware of this, it is necessary to explore myth, either through initiation or magic. Therefore, to sum up, hermetism is an exhaustive form of humanism since it transmutes religious feeling (or makes it whole), instead of putting it to one side, as tends to happen in everyday life and within religious organizations.

Secrecy

Is the secret fact or fancy?

If the secret exists, what is it? And if it does not, what does this tell us?

Esoteric knowledge must be kept secret. The adept passing on his knowledge to a disciple or the secret society carrying out an initiation ceremony both demand, under pain of retribution, — and they often seal the promise with the swearing of a solemn oath — that nothing of what is learnt will be revealed to the profane. The punishment nowadays is symbolic, but was sometimes real in the past; there were even cases of indiscreet initiates being murdered.

The reasons for secrecy

There are several reasons for secrecy, one of which is not to 'cast pearls before swine'. This means not to give knowledge to a person who is not prepared for receiving it (ie initiated) and who, by misunderstanding it, might degrade or denigrate it. Some occultists, especially adepts of magic, say it can be extremely dangerous to give these 'pearls' to 'swine', as forces, even if only psychic, can turn upon the person manipulating them. Unveiling the secret and putting it in the public domain drains 'force and vigour' from the hermetic ceremony in progress and from the initiating group the person belongs to. However, whatever the reason advanced, it is important to realize that secrecy is an essential part of hermetism and of the functioning of the occult sciences. Even today, when there is so much easily accessible information on all subjects, secrecy performs its essential role, rendering it indissociable from initiation, magic and the sacred.

To name a thing is to destroy it

More profoundly, secrecy is a fundamental part of hermetism because the initiate has set off in quest of a mystery. To say, or be able to say, what it is all about, and to name this 'thing', is the same as destroying it. Secrecy encompasses the seeker and anything that the seeker might say of his secret, using everyday language, would be a mere husk, and, quite simply, the alienation of any meaning at all. It is not so much a question of not revealing to the profane what goes on in the temple, as of realizing that what might be revealed would entail the destruction of the secret. Hermetism only dissembles in order to attain that which cannot be put into words. Secrecy is not only an objective secret (even a technical one, like the golden mean), it is also an existential secret. It is the secret of one's own intimate self, real and stripped of pretence. The Cabalists wanted to be 'secret masters', that is masters capable of playing with the mystery of the world; they believed it was enough to be consumed by their own secret.

Personal secrecy

'Just as the initiate, thanks to the secret of his society, is incapable of deviation to a less differentiated society, even so the solitary individual, to make his way alone, needs a secret which he must not and can never give up. A secret like this makes him withdraw into his own individual secret . . . Only a secret which cannot be betrayed, that is to say a secret which inspires fear or which cannot be put into words . . . can keep us from inevitably sliding back into the collective . . . A significant example is the story of Jacob wrestling with the Angel: he got away with a dislocated hip and because of it did not commit a murder.' Jung, *My Life*

The Shaman

A doctor-priest

The shaman is a healer, seer and intermediary between man and the spirit-world.

The Tungus word 'shaman' describes a man or woman who goes into a trance, or a state of ecstasy, in order to enter the spiritual dimension, thereby attaining powers of healing, divination and clairvoyance. Shamanism is thought to have originated in South Asia, and it is possible that the word 'shaman' derives ultimately from the Pali word *samana*. Today it exists in various forms throughout the world, in areas as diverse as Africa, North America, Australia and the Arctic.

The shaman has the central role of healer within his own community. Such societies place great emphasis on the interdependence of the body and the soul, and perceive physical illness as the loss of the soul. There is a common belief that the human soul has the ability to leave the body; it may be enticed away by same malevolent spirit, or stolen by demons. The shaman alone has the power, while within a trance, to enter the spirit-world, capture the wandering soul and restore it to the body of the sick person. After a person's death, the shaman's function is no less vital, for he is also psychopomp, the conductor of souls to the other world.

Initiation, once again, plays an essential role. A shaman may inherit his profession through birth, or gain it by election, but only achieves true recognition after taking instruction from qualified masters and successfully performing initiatory trials, involving his symbolic death and resurrection.

Sophia

Did God have a wife?

As the feminine dimension of divinity, Sophia has occupied a central position in Gnosticism and occultism.

Even if we set to one side the socio historical significance of the replacement of fertility goddesses by male gods, it is impossible to ignore the resulting loss of sensitivity. This suppression of the feminine seems to have gone hand in hand with urbanization and to have been exacerbated, first by feudalism and then by industrialization.

Fall and resurrection

The *Pistis Sophia* is a famous Gnostic text which tells how the 'Virgin of Light' judges the soul of a dead person. It is Sophia who decides whether the soul is to live in the light or return for reincarnation. However, there is more: this central act of the cosmic drama took place because Sophia, the wife and companion of God, was overcome with pity for fallen souls. Drawn by this pity, she herself now suffers grievously. In the end Sophia will rise again to heaven, but only after a struggle which will bring all the forces of Creation into play.

The introduction of the idea of Sophia obviously enables a completely original philosophy to be developed, fundamental to Gnosticism as well as its derivative, hermetism. Here the Creator himself fights side by side with mankind, whom he needs in order to perfect his work, which cannot be other than good.

Sophia brings a complementary sentiment to the essentially masculine, and abstract, figure of divinity. In the Old Testament she is not named but appears fleetingly as Wisdom and it seems that the temple of Solomon was originally meant for her. The Christian Gnostics ultimately made Sophia into a sort of Christianized Isis.

Just as Gnosticism, like hermetism, referred to the principle of Hermes, that 'all that is below is like all that is above', so Gnostic groups distinguished between the Sophia above, the heavenly mother, and the one below, for example, Sophia Prounicos (or 'the Wanton'). Here it is worth noting that, occasionally, the figure of Sophia has negative connotations; this is the case with, for example, Sophia Barbelo, who hated her son for stealing her 'dew of light'.

In occultism, Sophia remains a central, if less conspicuous, figure. She is to be found, among others, as the 'soul of the world' in magic or alchemy, as well as in the philosophy of Jakob Böhme.

Earthly Sophias

Ptolemy dedicated his *Letter to Fora* to a Roman lady, Zozima, the author of several fine works on alchemy; in these, Zozima left her secrets to another woman, Theosobia. The Marcionite Apella drew inspiration from a female adviser, a mysterious virgin called Philumenia. Marcos, who began his preaching in Palestine about AD 180, had a high regard for the power of feminine intuition. Eventually he went to Rome, where he was able to persuade the most beautiful women to leave their families and follow him. He preached Grace, a divine inspiration he claimed to have received, and initiated women by giving them this 'seed of light'; they were then supposed to have the gift of prophecy.

Spiritualism

Are the dead amongst us?

Spiritualist communication may well have concrete effects, but it does not necessarily prove there is a hereafter.

Spiritualism was born in the late 19th century and flourished in the early 20th century; it had many followers, including the writers Victor Hugo, Sir Arthur Conan Doyle and Rosamond Lehmann and the criminologist, Cesare Lombroso.

Communication with the dead

Spiritualists believe it is possible to communicate with the dead. 'It is a doctrine founded on existence, manifestation and the teaching of the spirits [or disembodied souls],' according to the leader of spiritualism, Allan Kardec.

Seances are held in darkness or semi-darkness and those present concentrate and place their hands on the table, with fingers touching. In the group there are always one or more mediums (or 'good conductors') who can contact the 'souls of the dead'. The latter manifest themselves, sometimes by knocking on the table. The code might be one knock for the letter A, two for B, three for C and so on, and this is how the spirits 'write' their messages.

The medium is a 'living subject, man or animal, who produces, or helps to produce, metapsychic phenomena'. Some, such as Daniel Douglas Home, Doris Stokes and Eusappia Pallado, achieved great fame, but most have been exposed as frauds.

A definition of spiritualism
'The principles of the doctrine of the immortality of the soul, the nature of Spirits and their relations with men, the moral laws, this present life, the life hereafter and the future of humanity, according to the teaching given by the higher Spirits, with the help of various mediums.' Allan Kardec, *Le Livre des esprits* (The Book of the Spirits)

A strange phenomenon

What are we, then, to make of all this? It has been shown that paranormal phenomena, such as knocking or table-turning, do occur; it is the interpretation of these occurrences which can be fanciful. Spiritualism too readily identifies spiritualist phenomena — mediumship, table-turning, talking in tongues etc — and gives them spiritualist interpretations, such as the survival of the soul, the existence of the perispirit or communication between a disembodied soul and a living being. Paranormal phenomena have undoubtedly occurred, but they do not necessarily have to be attributed to the dead.

The practice of spiritualism goes back to earliest antiquity, and is related to animism and shamanism (see **The Shaman**). In the Bible, Saul asked a witch to call up the souls of the dead for him. The doctrine of spiritualism was founded by the Frenchman H. L. Rivail (1804–69) who adopted the name Allan Kardec. It was Kardec who created the discipline of metapsychics, later to become modern parapsychology.

The Subtle Body

An immaterial body surrounds us

According to occultism, the physical body is enveloped in a less material body called the subtle body. This is what connects us to the cosmos.

According to hermetism, the human being is composed of three parts — body, soul and spirit. In this threefold arrangement, the soul plays a mediating role, that is to say, it is the 'common measure' which serves to maintain the relationship between the spirit and the body. In music, the soul's equivalent would be the middle note of a chord.

Gnostic thought, on the other hand, suggests that the spirit has been captured by the body, that it is incarcerated in the 'prison of the flesh'. The spirit suffers because it has fallen, but it retains one chance of escape — 'rising to join the Father'. The soul is therefore both the cause of the fall and the hope of resurrection. If the soul did not exist, and if it had not been tempted by matter, then the spirit, which is its source, would never have fallen; on the other hand, if the soul did not exist, matter would not have been tempted by the spirit to transmute itself.

Nothing is more foreign to hermetism than the contempt for the body sometimes found in religion. The initiate wants, simultaneously, to spiritualize the material body and to corporealize the spirit. He is trying to gain a 'body of light' in this life, without prejudging the other or the possibility of a life after death. In other words, he seeks immortality, in spite of all the ties which bind him.

Shakra

'Shakra' is a Sanskrit word meaning 'wheel'. In the mystical physiology of yoga, shakras are the centres (or knots) of psychic forces situated along the vertebral column and in certain parts of the body such as the head, chest and penis. Their function is to maintain the communication between the individual and the cosmos. Often shown in pictures as revolving flowers, they are the salient points of the subtle body.

From St Paul

'If there is such a thing as a physical body, there is also a spiritual body. Thus it is written, 'The first man, Adam, became a living being', whereas the last Adam became a life-giving spirit. Observe, the spiritual does not come first; the physical comes first, and then the spiritual. The first man was made 'of the dust of the earth'; the second man is from heaven.' (I Corinthians 15, 45–47)

Continuous refinement

The aim of the occult sciences is to refine the body of the mystic or operator, so that he can acquire the 'subtle body' which can receive the spirit. The object is, therefore, to rid the body of its 'scoria', in order to make it sensitive to the analogy of the microcosm and the macrocosm, or to make it aware of the light which lies within it. It is this light which recentres the mystic, enables him to coincide with his source, and sometimes confers magical powers upon him.

Symbolism

Symbolism leads to the invisible

The symbol in occultism is more than a mnemonic; it reveals a super-reality.

For hermetism, a symbol is not a simple convention as is the case in mathematics. Symbolism is not a language, but a way of speaking; it is much more than a collection of signs. A true symbol always designates the being-in-the-world, whereas an ordinary sign refers to either the being or the world. The sign appears to be objective but is in fact only superficial; the symbol includes the observer and its truth comes from the awareness born of personal experience. If we reduce symbolism to the equation, signifier=signified, we miss the whole point — a living symbol is never given, but always re-created.

> 'Symbolic forms exist to let us move on from the form of a manifestation to its spiritual content. Koranic exegesis involves *zāhir* (the exoteric meaning), *bātin* (the esoteric meaning), *tafsīr* (the literal interpretation) and *ta'wīl* (the spiritual interpretation). Knowledge is symbolically represented in terms of water: true knowledge as pure water; eternal truths as water springing from the ground; and inspired knowledge as water falling from above.' Sadrā Shīzāzi, *Shart*

A symbol expresses or reveals an analogy between an element of order A, representing the current state of the observer, and an element of order B, representing the state which this observer can see or must achieve. It indicates the way towards a transcendence, which is why it is so significant.

Christ said in Matthew X, 16 'Behold, I send you out like sheep among wolves; be wary as serpents, innocent as doves.' The serpent stands for cunning and the dove for simplicity. The symbols illuminate a shadowy, grey area — here, the fact that we cannot come to terms with the world without losing our souls — and show, by analogy, what must be done. We are not told to be serpents or doves, but to act as serpents or doves. The ultimate exposition of symbolism occurs when the subject discovers his own emptiness and he is invested with being. There is a sort of psychological crystallization which brings about a tenuous relationship with the world, in which consciousness itself is perhaps only of a symbolic nature.

The maieutics of symbolism

The hermetic quest, whether initiatory or magical, philosophical or practical — this tuning in to the hidden and the secret — revolves around symbols, which lead on to the invisible. However, although they act rather like midwives, assisting in the 'birth' of meaning, symbols are not to be deci-

The uroboros

The 'serpent biting its tail' is the symbol for the circle of interpretation in alchemy, which aims to approach the fundamental, eternal and infinite unity of matter and the universe. This symbol illustrates the axiom that 'All is in One'. The uroboros expresses the fact that, in achieving the philosopher's stone, the adept has won not only his inner freedom, but also his true relationship to the world.

phered like a coded message, but engage the individual in a spiritual adventure. The great cosmological symbols are the links between different chapters in a mythological story and give it its meaning. Ultimately, any mythological account, like any initiatory or magical ceremony, is the repetition and deepening of a symbolic urge. The symbol glints like a secret jewel lying within the dark folds of the story.

The same myths and symbols recur in civilizations the world over. This surely shows that something of the universe is in all of us. Intriguingly, a *symbolon*, or pledge of recognition, is something cut in two, of which two individuals each hold one part. In alchemy, the first half of the symbolon is the part of the universe we know and recognize, while the second is the part of being we seek to conquer; it is understood that this conquest will, through the emergence of awareness, 'complete nature' or realize the cosmos.

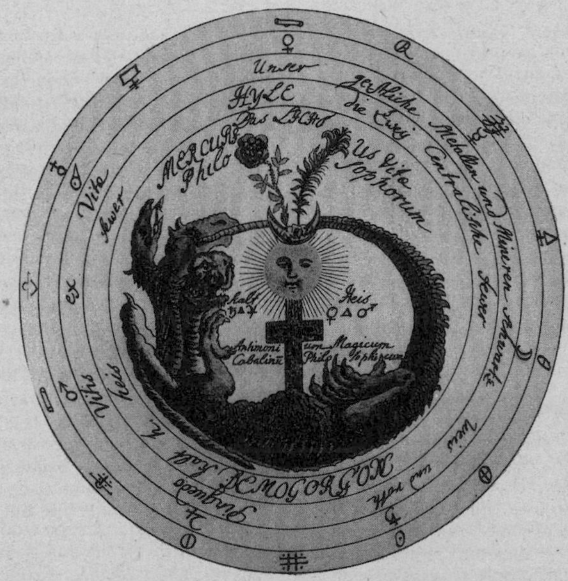

The dragon of chaos *The cross of Christ with the sun divides chaos into four elements, depicted as concentric circles; such a division does not hinder the turning of the world. In the centre of the circle there is a three-headed dragon whose heads symbolize ignorance, superstition and fear or, in another interpretation, evil thought, evil feeling and evil actions. The dragon has its tail in its mouth to symbolize the eternity or chaos from which came the dark womb of the cosmos or of order. The cross, the full moon and the crescent moon together form the symbol of Mercury, the perfect hermetic symbol for adepts or for man in all his perfection. The rose of Sharon and the lily of the valley rise from the crescent moon. Here the rose symbolizes the red tincture, the elixir of life and the lily of the valley, the white tincture which transmutes metals. The whole is a Rosicrucian rebus. (National Library, Paris)*

Tantrism

An initiatory quest through eroticism

The ways of initiation are many;
sexuality is one.

The most ancient Tantric writings date from the 6th century BC; the most recent from the 19th century AD. The ritual manifestation of Tantrism is a particular form of yoga with its own religious ceremonies and sexual practices; its aim is to transform, or transmute, the mystic. All Tantric procedures are strictly codified and must take the place of the devotee's daily routine. Tantrism, then, is a quest for spiritual development through existential development. However, God is not to be found by shutting oneself away from the world, but through the pleasures of making love.

Sexual cosmogony

Tantrism is a sexual cosmogony. Mahakala is the masculine great All and Kali is his consort; together, they make up the creative functions of Brahma (the supreme Truth) who encloses and projects all that exists in constellations 'as numerous as the sands of the Ganges'. The process of creation is represented by *yantras*, images loaded with sexual symbolism.

The principal object of devotion is a goddess mad with love, who dances and lets down her hair in order to create worlds. The goddess is, however, ambivalent for she also causes disease and war. The act of love between man and woman, conducted according to the rules of art, comes close to the *hieros gamos* (or divine intercourse) from which the world came. Some sexual rituals are carried out in a cemetery and their aim is to 'desubstantialize', or vampirize, the woman by terrorizing her. In every case, the woman stands for the 'force of dissolution', although this does not mean she is a force of evil or an inferior being. Mircea Eliade writes:

> Any naked woman incarnates *pakriti* (or neutrality). She is to be regarded with the same admiration and detachment as one would bring to the consideration of the unfathomable secret of nature. The ritual nakedness of the yogini has an intrinsic mystical value. If a man does not discover in his deepest being the same terrifying emotion before a naked woman as before the revelation of cosmic mystery, it is not a rite but merely a profane act.

Schools of Tantrism

Alongside Buddhist Tantrism, there exist (among others); the form of Tantrism founded on the cult of Shiva and Shakti; a form centred on the consort of Shiva, in which the original ritual was accompanied by blood sacrifices; and the syncretic Tantrism of Vishnu.

Taoism

A whirling cosmos

According to Taoism, human beings are borne along by the cosmic storm which rages through the universe.

The *Tao-te-ching* is a collection of 1465 different texts published in the mid-15th century. However, Taoist thought and practice seem to go back to a much more distant period.

Yes, the supreme Tao is vast;
Author of itself, acting through
  inaction,
Beginning and end of all ages,
Born before Heaven and Earth,
Silently embracing the whole of Time,
Endlessly passing through the continuity
  of the centuries,
In the West, it instructed the great
  Confucius,
In the east, it converted the Man of
  gold.
The model of a hundred kings,
Handed down by generations of wise
  men,
It is the ancestor of all doctrines
And the mystery above all mysteries.

The **elements of Taoism** are earth, wood, fire, metal and water; they can be seen in terms of the space they occupy, or of their trigrams. Other associations are also possible, notably with the organs of the human body and in the ritual exercises of Taoism.

Taoist art is not limited to mere visual effects. It brings into play the whole range of feelings to enable adepts to become imbued with the currents, lines of force and cosmic whirlwinds of Taoism.' P. Rawson and L. Legeza, *Tao*

A philosophy of yin and yang

The world-view of Taoism is radically different from any Western vision. It refutes the Cartesian idea of a reality built up from clear, distinct ideas and states that the essential element is a numen which eludes any attempt to grasp it. However, unlike the Kantian conception of the numen as a dimension beyond our reach, Taoism seeks development through reflection. Taoism has two guiding principles: no event ever recurs in exactly the same way; and the universe — Taoism's 'womb of time' — never changes in any way. It is the great All, which contains 'the endless duration and infinite change of infinite space'.

The universe is made up of cosmic whirlwinds, and works of art help us to relate to them. Tao, or Being, results from the complementary contradiction of yin and yang, symbols of the two polarities, male and female, of energy. Yang is masculine, brilliant, heavenly and active; yin is feminine, dark, earthly and passive. The whole universe can be explained in terms of the balance of these two forces. For example, in the dragon, mountains and the season of summer, it is yang that dominates; in fish, valleys and winter, it is yin. However, this is no division or sharing fixed for all time: every being, every single thing is a combination of yin and yang around a dominant force. The aim is to harmonize the two; this harmonization brings peace and concord with the universe. In Taoism, as in all hermetic thought, the individual is the microcosm and the universe is the macrocosm. Taoism is not merely speculation, mysticism or magical practices, though; it comprises the set of rules for living on which Chinese society has always sought to base itself.

Cosmic cycles

Taoist metaphysics is expounded in the ancient *I Ching* ('The Book of Oracles [or Changes]'), which sets out cyclical models of human history. The book is based on a series of eight trigrams composed of solid or broken lines representing different patterns of change. The unbroken lines are yang and the broken ones yin. Every figure has a symbolic meaning, deriving on the one hand from its position in the circle in which all the figures are arranged and, on the other hand, from its own balance of yin and yang.

The *I Ching* is an oracle consulted using yarrow stalks, which are manipulated in order to identify the particular trigrams which will give guidance. However, apart from this divinatory function, the figures and their interpretation are probably the only attempts ever made by human thought to define categories of movement in terms of uninterrupted duration. The *I Ching* does not describe change in abstract terms, but by analog with natural cycles of day and night, summer and winter, etc it is a very particular kind of physics. The world revealed by it is no longer the object of one's actions — the world of which one is 'master and possessor' — it is the world of one's absence, or inaction. So this world is not something objective, but wells up from a kind of symbolization of self-in-the-universe. This symbolization is regarded as divinatory because it proceeds by way of intuition, as does art.

Trigrams of *I Ching*

☰ Heaven, creative energy, conflict, strength, jade, ice.

☴ Wind, wood, gentleness, cockerel.

☵ Moon, water, abyss, labour, ear, pig.

☶ Serenity, beginnings and endings, birth and death, mountains, hand, dog.

Erotic rituals

Taoist ritual accords great importance to art and eroticism. Texts describe various methods of sexual intercourse and embrace, such as 'the flight of seagulls over the cliff', 'the ram butting the tree' and 'the cat and the mouse in its hole'. The positions have names like, 'opening the oyster to find the pearl', and 'the brave soldier fighting his way through the enemy ranks'.

The cult of eroticism is a quest for long life in which the couple making love share in the motion of the universe. The sexual quest ultimately awakens a 'subtle body', or rids the body of its psychosomatic darkness; in the language of initiation, it opens up the body to the invisible.

The Tarot

A mysterious reflection of the world

A simple pack of cards — a powerful tool for divination.

The tarot pack is made up of 78 cards, called 'Arcana'; there are 22 major cards and 56 minor ones. The mysteries are decorated with symbolic drawings: the 'Fool' reminds us of the 'Return of the Prodigal Son' by Hieronymus Bosch; the 'Wheel of Fortune' is purely an allegory of chance; the 'Death card' needs no comment; and the 'Star' can be seen as a symbol of love.

Unlimited combinations

Every one of the cards has been the basis of endless speculation. In esoteric circles, it is claimed that the cards operate on different levels, and thus allow numerous interpretations — initiatory, magical, Cabalistic, alchemical and so on. It is traditional to say that they constitute a totality or sum, even a picture of the world. It is perhaps interesting to note, in passing, that the number of major cards is exactly the same as the letters in the Hebrew alphabet, and to recall in turn the practice of gematria in Cabalistic thought (see **The Cabala**).

A paradox

'The originality, advantage and, at the same time, the paradox of using a pack of cards as an aid to divination is this: the limitlessness of life, with all its possible accidents, is made to depend on the visible presence and finite number of combinations of a few traditional symbols; moreover, the meaning of these is enshrined in the most banal language.' Roger Caillois, in the preface to O. Wirth's *Les Tarots*

However, the main fascination of the tarot cards is the fact that they are arranged like a game, to that they can seem to reflect the game of life. The cards are, however, not rigid concepts; their strength lies in the combinations they reveal.

A well-kept secret

The tarot cards are especially well-known as a tool for fortune-telling — a Western *I Ching*. There are numerous methods, but none is definitive. The cards are always dealt in a particular way so as to give a significant series and, with the help of chance, a message; all that then remains is to decode it. The cards are laid out in configurations of 3, 2 and 4 cards, and the principle is to reveal affirmation and negation, then synthesis and solution. The tarot cards are therefore a support to help the clairvoyant to do his job. He is helped in this by the fact that every card, despite its various possible interpretations, is summed up in an accessible, everyday word, such as 'death', 'the devil' or 'love'.

The tarot cards can be read at various levels. However, like astrology, the haphazard truth of the cards arises from a dialectic between meaning and chance. The shuffling and dealing of the cards reflect the chance which put us in the world; their interpretation is an attempt to see a meaning in the cards and, equally, ourselves.

Etymology

The origin of the word 'tarot' is obscure. It first appears in the 15th century and occultists believe it comes from the Latin word *rota* ('wheel').

Teaching

Occult teaching is handed down

But how is it handed down? Perhaps the true 'secret' of hermetism is to be found here.

How and where is esoteric teaching undertaken? This is indeed a problem, because, not only is hermetism centred around a secret, but also this teaching engages the whole being, aiming, as it does, to kill the 'old man' within; in other words, it aims to initiate the pupil into the invisible, liberate him from his lack of understanding, and bring his whole subtle body to life.

Collective teaching

This is the practice in both Gnosticism and initiation proper (see **Initiation**). In the first case, there will be a community of believers; in the second, a lodge or some such meeting-place. In both cases, teaching is dispensed by means of an 'egregor' (see **The Masonic Lodge**). However, initiatory teaching is distinguished by seeking to stress the individuality of the initiate, whereas Gnosticism tends to stress his solidarity with the group. The members of the craft-guilds knew that they belonged to a particular social group, whereas the Gnostics formed a 'party', hoping to become all humanity after the apocalypse.

From master to pupil

This approach is typical of the martial arts. Note, however, that even in masonic initiation and Gnosticism, fully initiated members — the Grand Master in the case of the masons, or the *perfecti* in the Catharian Church — are expected to transmit their knowledge to newcomers.

Individual teaching

This is the method favoured by alchemy today. From this point of view, the difference between freemasonry and alchemy is that the knowledge of the masons is handed down through ritual (in the temple, through symbols, etc), whereas the alchemist works alone with his retorts and his furnace. It might be said that the alchemist, like the magus, is privately repeating a ritual. If this is true, then the ritual is only a step away from becoming merely a technique.

According to the writer, Peter Handke, esoteric teaching is the handing down, from generation to generation, not of a 'sacred trust' fixed for all time, but of an 'inheritance without instructions'. It is therefore an event which is, at one and the same time, mysterious and banal. It is mysterious because it cannot be summed up in one technique (the technique is necessary, but it remains merely a support); it is banal because it goes on every day in all realms of cultural life (education, professional training, etc). Finally, esoteric teaching is problematic only in so far as it symbolizes the mystery of all transmission of knowledge.

The living root

'To attain complete and holy initiation, there is no mystery other than to plunge deeper and deeper into the depths of our being, and not to let go until we have managed to extract from it the living and vital root. For then, all the fruits which we are to bear, according to our species, are produced naturally in us and from us, as happens in the case of trees, because they cling to their own root, and never stop drawing sap through it.' Claude de Saint-Martin

The Temple

The temple simulates the cosmos

The temple symbolizes the universe in hermetism and many religions.

Certainly the religious buildings of the past — medieval churches, for example — are built according to plans which give them an esoteric meaning. Nobody knows whether the Church sought thereby to hold on to the memory of the mysterious religions which preceded it, or whether the builders and journeymen were merely making use of pagan models. However, it is quite impossible simply to gloss over the fact that the masonic lodge, certain Amerindian secret societies and the medieval Church present curious analogies.

The temple is made in the image of Creation. As far as the mystic is concerned, to walk into the temple, or to be admitted to it, is to relate to the universe, that is to enter into a relationship with the symbolic whole of life, transcendence included. The temple defines a significant space, in the same way as the world brings meaning to the original chaos of Creation.

The space-time of initiation

The plan for building a temple — whether real, as in the case of a church, or fictitious, as in the case of a masonic lodge — follows a mysterious technique, a secret handed down from generation to generation: the golden mean. The golden mean is found in all the proportions of the temple — be it the temple of Solomon, a Greek or Egyptian temple or a Christian church. The golden mean inscribes the sacred in stone; it makes the stone sing. Such buildings are also oriented in a particular way, to allow the ambulations to 'follow the day'. It seems unlikely, though, that this represents the survival of a form of sun-worship because the initiate does not adopt a position of prayer, but one of symbolic simulation. Through this simulation, the universe becomes immediately accessible to him, while maintaining its transcendence.

The initiate acts as if the cosmos were contained within the temple and initiation consists in learning this almost theatrical game. Invisible reality, the focus of hermetic study, hinges at the meeting-point of the cosmos and history, to which the temple bears witness. The temple of initiation, of course, always remains symbolically incomplete and this distinguishes it from a religious temple. Its ultimate meaning derives from an operation, such as initiation, carried out by the mystic himself. At the outset, the mystic is chaos; in the end he becomes an actor by taking up his part in a play which was, until then, being acted without him. In short, the temple makes manifest the stage of the invisible.

Templum
The world 'temple' derives from the Latin *templum*, which refers to a zone of the sky or the earth marked out by the augur or soothsayer, using spells, as a suitable place in which to take auspices. The augur would observe the flight and the cries of birds within the *templum*, and draw omens from these signs.

The Temple of Solomon is a concrete expression of the alliance of the Jewish people and their God. It symbolizes that founding moment in Western history when the Jews, nomadic until then, settled in one land. They established a bond with one land, not founded on blood, but open to transcendence.

Theosophy

Between spiritualism and initiation

The Theosophical Society has numbered eminent people among its leaders, and has been influential in the history of occultism.

Two colourful figures founded the Theosophical Society: Helena Blavatsky (1831–91) and Colonel H. S. Olcott (1832–1907). Coming respectively from the Russian nobility and the American army (Olcott fought in the Civil War) both became passionately interested in the occult. In fact, it appears that Helena Blavatsky was endowed with 'paranormal powers'. Both were great travellers, especially Blavatsky, and they met in 1874 in the USA, where Olcott was researching into the spiritualist phenomena of materialization. They founded the Theosophical Society in New York in 1875 and, from then on, devoted themselves to occultism.

In 1879, Blavatsky and Olcott travelled to India. Commissioned by Rutherford Hayes, then president of the USA, to open up new commercial markets there, they received an enthusiastic welcome, especially among Indian nationalists, such as the Maharaja of Benares, who subsidized the Society. It is even said that lectures given by the two travellers played a part in encouraging the Indian people to seek independence from Britain.

'**The Theosophical Society** nowadays preaches an eclectic approach to philosophy and religion. Nevertheless, it carries on the traditions of its founders, to whom we owe in great part the introduction of Buddhist philosophy and various forms of yoga to the West.' *Dictionnaire des sociétés secrètes*

Besant, Leadbeater, Krishnamurti

On the death of the founders, the succession passed to two equally flamboyant characters, Annie Besant and the clergyman, C. W. Leadbeater. Influenced by spiritualism, Leadbeater (1847–1934) believed that numerous psychic faculties lie dormant within each of us, merely waiting to be awakened. Annie Besant (1847–1933) was initiated by Helena Blavatsky and it was she who discovered Krishnamurti, and claimed he was the reincarnation of Krishna and Christ. Krishnamurti himself denounced this in later life, and went on to preach a truly philosophical theosophy and acquire a well-deserved international reputation.

Krishnamurti's philosophy rejected all unthinking religious feeling; he considered that religions all became 'obstacles preventing spiritual self-fulfilment, for they are mere refuges'. There was no need for a Messiah — which was why he refused the part he was expected to play — and no need for dogma. It was possible, he maintained, indeed necessary, to become one's own 'incarnation of truth'.

The Theosophical Society continues to exercise a certain influence. It has spread worldwide and exists on the fringes of spiritualism, initiation and spiritual quest.

A truism

Jiddu Krishnamurti contrasted the great technical and material progress of humanity with its spiritual barbarity. This declaration is accepted today as a truism.

Time

Is there anything to say other than trivialities?

The intriguing hermetic conception of time.

There are three sorts of time: scientific, Galilean time (clock time); time lived (such as Bergson speaks of); and hermetic time. The Catharians concentrated on the last, saying that it was 'not of this world', and the second, which they did not distinguish from profane time, was as nothing to them. In other words, hermetic time remains something apart from concrete time, as the source of a river is considered to be apart from the river (just as the gushing spring is not to be confused with the flow).

The fixation with origins

It is common practice to become fixated with origins, to try to give them an absolute value (see **Tradition**) and to believe that human history (see **Invisible History**) is running on a downward path because it is, inevitably, moving further and further away from its origin. With Jaurès, we could respond by saying that the river remains faithful to its source by running to the sea. Origins can (and indeed must) be made actual. That is the whole point of initiation ceremonies, as it is of hermetic philosophy.

Making origins actual means restoring intensity and vividness to the present by imbuing it with poetic inspiration, or, to put it another way, restoring to it a dimension which is continually suppressed and which only an acausal relationship (see **Analogy**) can unveil. At the level of mythology, time moves in a circular fashion (see **The Ages of the Earth**); it moves in a sequential fashion at the historical level.

Where is the Golden Age, to speak in mythical terms? There are several answers: pessimists, like René Guénon, say it is lost in an inaccessible past; optimists, like the poet Rimbaud or the surrealists, say it will arise in the future. Yet again, ritual places the Golden Age at the point where past and future meet. All this can be said to be theory, but is it not theory which clarifies and then decants the pathos without which we would be unaware of the passage of time?

An intense virtual presence

Initiation ceremonies, magic and hermetic philosophy each allude, in their own way, to a fabulous origin. The origin can be seen in various ways; it can influence the art of building, as with the guilds (see **Hiram**), or be concerned with matter, as in alchemy. This origin is thought to symbolize a beginning of the invisible, but it is essential to note that the origin is to be perceived only through a project, whether existential or political, which gives it form. Notice, finally, that the original and the symbolic tend ultimately to become identical, that is, the origin, whatever form it takes, symbolizes in essence the entire history of the universe — or rather, the most intense form of its virtual presence.

Trade Guilds

Initiation through work

Initiatory associations of builders have been influential throughout history.

From the earliest times right down to the Renaissance, work constituted a mystery, and the fact that it was seen to be in part holy is stressed by anthropologists. Quite naturally, the legends of the guilds contain allusions to a mythical — that is to say mysterious or holy — origin. In history, from the earliest times, professional groupings are known; far from being mere pressure groups, these usually group round a patron god. Thus, the Greeks had associations of builders (the *Hetairies*) and in Rome, about 715 BC, King Numa codified the rules for the *collegia* ('colleges') of craftsmen such as the *tignarii*, who were carpenters and builders.

From the *collegia* to the guilds

Every *collegium*, or 'college', had a house where it held the *agapae*, or brotherly feasts, presided over by the *magister cenae*, and the ceremonies dedicated to the tutelary god. The *collegium* was the guardian of professional secrets and, in a way, these were its capital. The members made ritual use of gestures, signs and touches which, quite apart from their religious meaning, enabled the initiates of different colleges to recognize one another and to establish common solidarity. The Roman *collegia* were influenced by the Greeks who, in their turn, had been influenced by the Egyptians, Persians, Syrians and Jews. They followed in the footsteps of the legions, growing as the empire expanded. Evidence of the existence of these *collegia* can be found in towns throughout Europe.

When the empire collapsed, they disappeared from northern Gaul and from Britain, but they remained in the Eastern Empire and in parts of Italy which were attached to it; here they became *scolae*. In France, the continued existence of the *collegia* to the south of the Loire is shown by the buildings of the fifth and sixth centuries. However, since the developing feudal society had no use for them, the *scolae* became absorbed by monasteries, so that from the sixth century onwards monastic associations arose as guardians of the secrets of the builders. The most famous architects of the period therefore were clerics: Leo and Gregory, bishops of Tours; Ferreole, Bishop of Limoges; Fructueux in Spain and so on. In the 11th and 12th centuries, though, brotherhoods began to be established outside monasteries. At the same time as the influence of Gothic art was being felt, this new secularism grew in the free town. Famous French lay builders of the period were architects such as Villard d'Honnecourt, Jean d'Orbais and Pierre de Corbie. This, too, is the period of the *Bauhütte* in Germany — the federation of the guilds of stone carvers in the Holy Roman Empire.

The 'challenge'

Ritual questions and answers, accompanied by ritual gestures, allowed a guild member to know whether or not the person to whom he was speaking was a fellow member. A special kiss was a way of recognizing another initiate, and a ritual greeting.

'The genius of the trade guilds going round the globe.' (*Lithograph by Granger, 1848. National Library, Paris*)

This growing lay influence led to the replacement of the religious associations by genuine trade organizations. These were the crafts regulated by the free towns or the lords. The Templars were particularly important; each commandery had its own architect, and in Paris, for example, where the mother-house occupied a third of the surface area of the town, the freedom of the city was accorded to the craftsmen towards the end of the 12th century.

How are we, then, to understand these different types of organization? Paul Naudon explains that:

> The terminology demands some explanation. When the craft was being organized, the orginal word used to describe it in France was *confrérie* ('brotherhood'). Later on, the brotherhood in its religious and social sense, was distinguished from the craft as a purely professional organization. However, the two always existed together. Later on, the craft became known as the 'craft community', and finally in 18th century France it became the 'corporation'. In Great Britain, there was first of all the general term 'guild', then 'company' and then 'brotherhood'; we hear of the company of masons of London in 1376, and of the brotherhood of masons in 1742. In Germany, the word used is *Brüderschaft*, or 'brotherhood'. As for 'companionship' (the French *compagnonnage*), this is an incorrect term as the *compagnonnage* did not appear until the 16th century. As the name shows, they only included journeymen and workmen (from the French *compagnon*, 'journeyman'); these were essentially associations which defended the interests of their members. The birth of freemasonry owes nothing to them, although they both arose from a common origin.

Differences of vocabulary are of little importance. The essential point is this, that from earliest antiquity right down to the Renaissance, a desire to stress the sacred nature of work can be identified in most of these spiritual movements. This is a type of holiness which, far from being concerned with religious devotion, transcends it. The religious dimension is quite exoteric; the heart of the member, esoteric. He gives his heart not in prayer alone, but essentially through his work, in a welling-up of the self and the universe which is the stage for his 'praxis'. This is all revealed through ceremonies incorporating myths, the handing down of secrets and the work on the raw material.

Secret and praxis

We have already discovered that the secret comprised a certain skill and we have already said that this, in a certain way, constituted the capital of the society. As far as building work is concerned, this was basically a technique founded on the golden mean (see **The Golden Mean**). The golden mean is not a simple formula which, when applied, produces a work of art; it is merely a tool, and a tool without inspiration is nothing at all. The golden mean only works when used by true artists. We shall not concern ourselves here with the question of whether the skill is only available to those who have been initiated. We must note, however, that the brotherhood was historically the first — and probably the only — society to produce a collective work of art (in the Middle Ages, people were probably less self-conscious in producing 'art' in the sense in which we understand the word).

According to Mircea Eliade, all ceremonies restate a founding myth. This is true of both the reception and initiation ceremonies for example. The guild in Christian times evidently saw the world in terms of a biblical mythology. The legend of Hiram, architect of King Solomon and builder of the temple in Jerusalem, dates back a very long time and is still its emblem. Some writers, such as Guénon and Corbin, finding themselves unable to date the origin of the guild, have proposed a 'primitive tradition', whose initiates handed down the sacred trust through the ages. Without

The Passport
The letter of introduction carried by guild members went under all sorts of different names. On death, it was burnt on his coffin.

accepting this theory, which turns the mythological side of the phenomenon into a dogma, it is possible to state that the origin of the guild constitutes a mystery which can be explained through its practice, which 're-creates' it by making it visible in ceremonies. In its moments of glory, the guild was an institution where the worker rediscovered his place in the universe. It is easy to see how, in such a framework, the question of history, in the modern sense of the word, just does not arise; history is no longer a chronology, but becomes an insight into something much more profound.

The secret of the guilds is, then, a skill, but this only comes through practice. As he worked to fashion a stone, the guild member was working on a fragment of the universe to fit it into the designs of God; art, according to the alchemists, was the way of perfecting Nature. The task of workers in the Middle Ages — a tiny minority of the population, it must be remembered — was not merely to contemplate God; they were making Him visible to all. This is why the trade-guilds were impregnated with mystic knowledge. This explains the human phenomenon and the role of man in the creation of the world; according to the Gnostics, the demiurge is an artist and the faithful, that is to say the workers, have their part to play in the creation of the world.

From the Renaissance to modern times

At the Council of Avignon in 1326, in the pontificate of John XXII, the banning of the builders' guilds was reaffirmed; they had already been banned at the Council of Rouen in 1189 because of their secret language and customs. There is supposed to have been a huge gathering of builders' guilds from all over Europe around the cathedral at Strasbourg at Ascension in the year 1315; it should be noted, however, that this is the same date given for the symbolic founding of modern freemasonry.

A social power

The guild movement also had a purely social side. The various chapters were, at one and the same time, trade unions, recruitment agencies and the forerunners of the modern employment exchange. Initiation remained at the heart of the secret societies but we must not forget that the guild was able to call strikes, that it was frequently persecuted by the public authorities, that it was a vehicle for an opposing culture and was also a potential power throughout Europe. The trade guilds clashed not only with feudal overlords, but also with the bourgeoisie. Their whole history is a struggle to free themselves from oppression and to declare their autonomy.

Have the trade-guilds, then, been overtaken by modern developments, such as microtechnology and mass production? Or are they simply lying dormant? Luc Benoist states that 'the new humanism, to which everyone aspires, will not be reached through intense production and competition, but by the work of an artist, such as the craft guilds fostered.' Perhaps this might mean that the spirit of the craft guild might arise, once again, from its ashes.

Compasses
Compasses are the 'Lord's tool' but, when opened to 90°, they become a 'false square'. Using compasses, the worker can carry out nearly all the operations of his trade.

The Companions of the Duty of Freedom
The Companions of the Duty of Freedom sign their membership with their own blood. Nowadays, they do so symbolically, pricking themselves with a quill.

Tradition

Does tradition come from the mists of time?

Some would say not; the musician Varèse said that every ring of tradition was forged by a revolutionary.

Tradition is often wrongly confused with lost speech (see **Lost Speech**). There are those who claim that the history of mankind becomes increasingly debased, so that we are now in a dark age (the 'Kali-Yuga' of Hinduism) at the end of a cycle. At the end of this cycle, the universe will reabsorb itself, like a star in a black hole, to be reformed in a new way. Tradition was given to man in the beginning by God — or by an extra-human presence — and has been handed down from generation to generation, but in the process has become darkened. It is therefore 'lost' and must be found again.

Progress or decadence?

Although this school of thought smacks of transcendentalism, it is in fact the most historically based of all. It accepts the myth of the ages of humanity (Golden Age, Silver Age, etc) but becomes bogged down, instead of deciphering its symbolic meaning. Just like Stalinist Marxism, which it attacks for its materialism, it restricts itself to a rigid, and in this case, apocalyptic interpretation of history. Similarly, this school forgets that it is not enough simply to point to decadence in order to to escape it, as the observer is inevitably a part of what he describes. Extreme theories of history tend to champion either the view of progress or that of decadence. They are politically opposed, but their effects are remarkably similar.

If the initiate is not, as the traditionalists would have it, the defender of tradition, he nevertheless seems to be its recipient. He is part of a long chain of initiates in time and space, the repository of the sacred flame. Modern initiates tend to think, on the one hand, that the mystic is not, ipso facto, the repository of a truth, and that he only discovers this is so when he comes face to face with the universe and himself. On the other hand, they would maintain that tradition, if we still use this word in spite of its profane connotations, exists here and now, in the present. Lost speech is only found again at a time of creation.

Re-creation

Thus, to resume, this initiatory handing on of the tradition of the invisible is not done according to a historical sequence, but in a

Deviation
'We have pointed to the essentially traditional character of all Oriental civilizations; the lack of an effective attachment to tradition is at the root of Western deviation.' René Guénon, *Introduction générale à l'étude des doctrines hindoues* (General Introduction to the Study of Hindu Doctrines)

In a closely related area, Gide was right to say how long it takes to become an **atheist**. That is, to absorb and harmonize the creativity from which one has resigned in the name of a false spirituality.

discontinuity. The fabric of the visible world tears each time, only to be formed anew. If the Cabala was given to Moses on Mount Sinai, this does not stop Cabalists from actualizing this moment and seeing it as an eternal present. Tradition which represents a return to the past, though — any research which cannot bring itself to burn the boats of its past — only wins 'empty shells' or 'a dark sleep', that is merely the exoteric.

The true secret lives only in the present. Time is an illusion, said the Catharians. Future and past, or progress and decadence, are a part of the invisible which drifts towards fabulous shores or nightmare. Initiation ceremonies, then, must inevitably pass through history and its myths. Tradition, in this way, ultimately becomes the raw material which must be overcome; to fail to do so, is to fall at the first hurdle on the path of hermetism.

'An inheritance adrift'

The problem of tradition is of particular interest to occultism. What is it? How does it manifest itself?

In all spheres — take, for example, law or education — there is an element of tradition, something which is handed on and/or re-created orally. Simply because of the human involvement, there is a sort of contract or agreement between the parties involved. Culture, for example, comprises knowledge and experience, but it includes learning, and even then something more which is not concrete at all, a very mysterious 'something more' when all is said and done.

This same 'something' crops up in psychoanalysis, in the final moments of transference. It surpasses words although, paradoxically, it relies on them. Jung, in his *Psychology and Alchemy*, compared transference to an alchemical process.

Forced to choose between the two alternatives of a handing down or of a re-creation, the 'handing down' of tradition is achieved through an inheritance in the widest possible sense of the word. When we speak of an inheritance, though, we must be clear that we are using it in the same sense as Peter Handke in his *Beyond the Villages*.

An inheritance, as a rule, is something inert and passive, mere reproduction, 'a need for dogged perseverance'. Its inner meaning is reduced to little more than nothing. However, Handke's 'inheritance adrift' presupposes renewed life. Land, for example, is not handed down to demonstrate the permanence of a family line, or even a particular philosophy, but so that it will continue to bring forth fruit. By working the land, the heir also 'works' on himself and thus enriches mankind.

Tradition, therefore, exists, but if it becomes fossilized, it has the effect of distorting and paralysing. Of course, this is not to deny the many benefits that tradition has also brought us, such as Roman law. The essential point to remember is that there is a balance to be found, and it cannot be found as long as the actor, or heir, refuses to act creatively. Occultism confronts this problem of tradition, whereas the profane world buries it away beneath conventional words and phrases.

The Tree

A fundamental symbol

The tree symbolizes both growth and the axis of the world.

The tree is a symbol of growth. All mythologies speak of the 'tree of the world'. The importance of the oak tree for the Druids is well known. The 'cosmic tree' is the pillar which holds up the sky and permits communication between the world above and the world below. The Christmas tree, too, is part of this tradition of archaic symbolism which has been assimilated into Christianity.

The tree epitomizes the plan of Creation: it is pivot, axis and sphere. It represents the being, his roots and his development. Through its roots, it is attached to the nourishing earth, and through its leaves it opens to the light. It is the Tree of Life, the tree of all knowledge. The tree of the Cabala encapsulates this symbolism and develops it in a mystical manner. In alchemistic engravings, the tree is sometimes identified with the penis. There is also a relationship between the tree and the symbolism of the shamans.

'Man is an **inverted tree**; his roots are in Heaven.' (Traditional saying)

The Masters of Occultism

The great men of occultism, or of hermetism, have been great initiates, legendary characters, eccentrics — and sometimes even charlatans. Mesmer, who was all of these rolled into one, is a good example of an occult figure.

Such men are to be found in all periods of history, and it would be quite impossible to draw up a roll of honour, or a comprehensive list of them; perhaps the most influential will never be known. As René Char said, like poets, initiates leave no proof, only traces.

The initiate loses himself in his work. That is not to say that he becomes alienated and sinks his identity into it, but that he, symbolically, 'sacrifices' his life so that his work can appear. The word 'sacrifice' is, however, not to be taken in the religious sense; that would be quite wrong. This sacrifice is part of the secret of occultism, a procedure in which the hermetic work can be equated with a work of art.

We can, of course, only follow in the footsteps of those masters who lived in times when writing was known. Other earlier masters, if there were any, left nothing behind. Was Hermes, for example, only a legend? And was Hiram, the central figure of freemasonry, of whom we read in the Bible, merely a historical character? This must, alas, remain mere speculation.

Among those men whose work is known, revolt against the Church or forms of established power is a general tendency. Eliphas Lévi, for example, was not on good terms with the Church and, if the synagogue had held any temporal power, a number of Cabalists would certainly have gone to the stake. It cannot be repeated often enough that, although hermetism works on some religious 'raw material', it is nevertheless linked with Gnosticism, which always adopts a heretical stance towards established religion — perhaps only because it refuses to conform with dogmatism. This is why nearly all of the figures in this book were, to a greater or lesser degree, despite their protestations of respect for established authority, revolutionaries in their day. However, this situation began to change in the 19th century with the triumph of rationalism, to which hermetism eventually gave birth, after many centuries.

At the beginning of the 20th century, after the death of Eliphas Lévi, esoterism moved further and further towards the political right. Julius Evola, whose position moved from the most extreme modernism to the staunchest defence of tradition, is a good example of this changing mood. It is also worth noting that Nazism was only able to erect some semblance of ideology through constant reference to occultism. The great irony of this is that occultism claims to throw light on original darkness, whereas racialism obscures it further.

Contemporary humanism rejects occult thinking for the very reason that it could be dangerous to look too closely. Meanwhile, the darkness remains and it becomes increasingly urgent to throw some light on it. This can only be achieved by a vigorous brand of humanism, which will confront the shadows of history. Perhaps this is the crux of the spiritual crisis of our times.

Abellio, Raymond

1907–86

Where esoterism rubs shoulders with the extreme right

Abellio strove for resolute modernism, while defending tradition. Perhaps he was confusing politics and esoterism.

Raymond Abellio's real name was Georges Soulès. A former revolutionary socialist, he became a militant in the Popular Front, and deputy secretary of the SFIO (the former French socialist party) in 1932. By 1941, he was a member of the (fascist) Revolutionary Social Movement of Deloncle and, in 1944, he was hunted at the time of the liberation of France. In 1951, he returned to Paris, where he set up an engineering consultancy business.

Guided syncretism

Raymond Abellio developed a syncretic philosophy which involved a synthesis of the Cabala, the phenomenology of Husserl, the thinking of Guénon and an early form of structuralism. His thinking ran along two parallel lines which he often confused — the metaphysical and the political. He maintained not only that the West could reverse its decline, but also that it was its duty to do so; this would happen only when 'warriors became priests'. He wrote novels, such as *La Fosse de Babal*, and essays including *La Bible, document chiffré* and *La Structure absolue*. Raymond Abellio's outlook is typical of a right wing, even extreme right wing, form of esoterism which seeks to 'renew the tradition of the West'.

Rene Guénon's aim was simply to rediscover this tradition; Abellio was determined to renew it. He wanted to abolish the slogan 'Liberty, Equality, Fraternity' and replace it with 'Prayer, War, Work'. Abellio dreamt of a mythical time when the king was also priest, and of a society founded on an absolute hierarchy. His thinking aimed to be total but it was in fact totalitarian.

An interesting new method

However, we cannot simply dismiss Abellio. He has many followers and some of his methodological innovations stand up well to examination. One such is the suggestion that texts with a reputation for obscurity, such as the *Zohar*, might repay renewed study. He considered their value lay, paradoxically, in their ability to be interpreted in a number of different ways, and was an enthusiastic exponent of the 'revelation of their more or less deliberate cryptographic nature'. In this way, he was flying in the face of the spirit dominating late 19th century occultism which, always seeking 'scientific justification', ultimately became distorted. Abellio urged hermetism to reverse its decline and rediscover its identity or, as it is often put, to reclaim and mark out its legitimate field of activity.

The new Gnostics

'By new Gnostics, I mean those who live out to the full the postulate of universal interdependence with all its metaphysical and ethical consequences, in order to revise all those naive concepts still held about freedom and individual responsibility.'

Scorn

'May I say that I would despise myself if I reacted to so-called great events. All the more, if I reacted to little everyday flutters, the food of the butterfly mentality ...'

Abulafia, Abraham ben Samuel

1240–92

The man who wanted to be his own Messiah

Abulafia maintained that a Cabalist, because he possessed the secret of 'primordial language', knew the ultimate meaning of history. He could become his own Messiah.

Born in Saragossa, Abulafia travelled widely and appears to have met and been influenced by Sufis. In 1271, he claimed he had received the spirit of prophecy. In 1280, he set off for Rome to convince Pope Nicholas III of the occult unity of religions. He was thrown into prison and owed his survival solely to the sudden death of Nicholas III.

Letters of the alphabet
'Everyone knows that the letters of our alphabet can be classified as individuals, species and genera . . . Every letter is affected by accidents arising from either matter or form. The scribe is the agent for he writes or draws them on a medium; in this way, he imparts a variable form to the matter of the ink, which is the raw material and the most accessible matter of all letters.'

Practical Cabala
Abulafia is a good example of a practitioner of practical Cabala, or speculation about language. As Hebrew was the sacred language (since God created the world with the Hebrew alphabet), every word of the language holds a mystery which can be revealed by a numerical equivalence. To every letter corresponds a number. True Cabalistic speculation works on the linguistic comparisons permitted by this method.

The Creation: divine writing

According to Abulafia, the speculation of those who went before him was only intended to prepare the way for the prophetic Cabala he was inaugurating. In his 'Letter of the Seven Veils', he explains that Creation is the result of divine writing, in the course of which God works His Word into all things. Abulafia held that writing was the matter of Creation. Divine inspiration moved this matter and was imparted to man through revelation and prophecy.

The ordinary man, the non-initiate, is cut off from the divine flux; it is as if he were asleep. Abulafia sought to 'unseal the soul, to undo the knots which bind it'. This is possible, according to him, by meditating on the hidden name of God, which expresses the totality of the cosmos and of history. Abulafia taught a particular discipline, *hokmat ha-tseruf*, or combination of Hebrew letters, which enabled him to achieve a state of ecstasy. The Cabalist would reach 'consonance' in this way with his spiritual guide, the angel Metatron. In this way, Abulafia strove to decode the secret of his biography and his place in the world; he became able to achieve for himself what the Messiah would achieve one day for all humanity.

Posterity after all

Abulafia's Messianic claims provoked the hostility of the orthodox Jewish community, who believed the Messiah could not be human. Nevertheless, he had his followers, the most gifted of whom was Joseph Gitalilia (1248–1325), who wrote *The Walnut Orchard*; he also influenced Moses of Léon, the presumed author of the *Zohar*.

Agrippa von Nettesheim, Henricus Cornelius

1486–1535

Agrippa, 'Prince of Magicians'

Behind the legend, we see a man in love with independence and a scholar who wanted to unify the learning of his time without harming the faith.

Agrippa von Nettesheim is considered to be one of the founding fathers of occult philosophy; it would be more accurate to say that he brought its presentation up to date. He was a Master of Arts at 20, after studying law, medicine, philosophy and languages, and then went as a soldier to Spain. He travelled to Dole in France in 1509, where he tried to teach sacred literature. However, his time there was cut short as the Franciscans drove him out for preaching the free examination of texts.

Harried by enemies

He moved next to London, where he wrote his commentaries on Paul's Epistles. Later, he taught theology in Cologne and then lived seven years in Lombardy in the service of the emperor Maximilian. In 1519, he was in Metz where he attracted the hatred of the Church for opposing the Dominicans when they wanted to burn a peasant woman at the stake for witchcraft. He secured the freedom of the woman, but was forced to leave the town with his wife and son.

'**Words** express the particular individual virtue of things and are its carriers. They have the strength given them by the virtue of Him who ordered them in sentences and who pronounces them.'

Agrippa von Nettesheim was a doctor in Freiburg in 1523. His growing reputation and the recommendation of the Bishop of Bazas led to him going to France a year later, where he became doctor and astrologer to the mother of François I. In 1527, he wrote 'On the Uncertainty and Vanity of Science and the Arts' in which he denounced the contemporary 'intellectual terrorism' exercised by grammarians, doctors and other pressure groups. His work was confiscated and burned by order of the Faculty of Divinity of Paris. In 1532, Agrippa von Nettesheim went to Bonn, where he published *De Occulta Philosophia Libri Tres*, an encyclopedia of magic he had compiled earlier and given to his master John Trithemius to read. He died three years later, rapidly attaining legendary status. He was reputed to have been followed everywhere by a black dog called Monsieur, who was none other than the Devil.

The occult virtues of things

In his key work, *De Occulta*, Agrippa, who was widely-read, attempted to reconcile scripture with the sacred texts of other religions. He believed in the 'unity of all traditions'. He declared from the outset that anyone taking up magic must have a thorough knowledge of theology, physics and mathematics. There was for him no contradiction between these domains — on the contrary, they complemented and reinforced one another. In 'Natural Magic', the first part of the work, Agrippa von Nettesheim presented three worlds: the elemental, the celestial and the intellectual. Each one of these worlds is controlled by its superior and obeys its influence. He revealed the 'occult virtues of things', as

Supposed portrait of the 'Prince of Magicians' *(anonymous engraving in the National Library, Paris)*

distinct from their elementary or immediately perceptible qualities. He examined how these virtues arose from ideas such as the 'Soul of the World' and planetary influence, and also how they attracted or repelled different species of the animal, vegetable or mineral world.

The second part of the work deals with numbers. It sets out their 'magic powers' and also the 'secrets' of cosmic harmony. The last part, on ceremonial magic, presents the hierarchy of angels and demons. We are offered here an astonishing synthesis of the teachings of Christ, Moses, Orpheus, and so on. Agrippa von Nettesheim also reveals rites leading to purification and ecstasy.

Suppressed truth

'I do not give you these facts as truths, but as hypotheses coming near to truth. The lesson we must learn is how to derive good from evil and how to keep all things on the straight path.' Agrippa von Nettesheim's methodology is startlingly modern: he deciphers phantasmagorical figures to reveal suppressed truth. However, it is a long way from act to intention and he is often taken in by the tricks he reports. For example, to cure a fever he recommends wearing around the neck the magic word 'abracadabra', written out ten times.

Nevertheless, Jean Servier wrote of the theories Agrippa von Nettesheim put forward about 'planetary signatures', 'Doubtless they had their excesses and their absurdities, but what research hypothesis, pursued too single-mindedly, has not resulted occasionally in deadlock or error.' For Servier, this theory, like many others developed by Agrippa von Nettesheim, was a rich source of hypotheses for research.

> **'Firm, constant faith** works wonders even in the course of a flawed operation, whereas mistrust and hesitation in the soul of the worker, who holds himself aloof from all excess, lead to dissipated effort and ruin.'

Andreae, Johann Valentin

1586–1654

The greatest enigma of occultism

Was Andreae the writer of the founding text of the Rosicrucian order? Was the order a secret historical reality? Nobody knows.

Andreae came of a very distinguished Swabian family; his paternal grandfather was one of those who, in 1580, drew up the *Concord* which aimed at a reconciliation between Lutherans and Calvinists. In his autobiography, which lay in the archives of his benefactor, Duke Augustus of Brunswick-Lüneburg, until 1799, he confessed to being the author of 'The Chemical Wedding of Christian Rosenkreuz', the novel telling how the eponymous hero found the philosopher's stone. He claimed he had written it for fun at the age of 17.

Accused of heresy

Andreae was still a divinity student at Tübingen when he met Tobias Hess, reputedly an organizer of secret societies, in 1608. In 1610, Andreae successfully presented his doctoral thesis and thereafter practised as a Protestant minister. He described 1611 as the year in which calumny was unleashed against him, referring to the widespread suspicion that he had written the founding texts of the Rosicrucians, such as *Fama Fraternitatis*. He was accused of heresy and subversion. He then published 'The Twenty-Four Labours of the Christian Hercules' in order to distance himself from the 'jests of a certain Rosicrucian brotherhood'.

In 1620, he became superintendent in Württemberg, where he founded a number of charitable societies and, in 1650, he was made Abbot of Babenhausen in Bavaria, where the Duke of Brunswick built a house for him.

The birth of a founding myth
Quite apart from the effect this 'hoax' had on the history of occultism (freemasonry refers to it as its symbolic origin), it enables us to see a clear example of the metamorphosis of literary text into myth. However, this might not have been possible unless the text contained something which destined it to play that role.

'**The supreme science** is to know nothing.'

The author behind the mask

Historical criticism has long debated whether or not Andreae was the true author of 'The Chemical Wedding' and whether he was involved in Rosicrucianism or was simply a hoaxer. Current thinking holds that the answer to the first question is yes.

Apart from his own admission, there are a number of clues pointing in this direction. Firstly, Andreae's family coat of arms, like Luther's, included the double motif of the rose and the cross. Secondly, other writings by Andreae, such as 'Christianopolis' (1619), contain ideas close to those found in Rosicrucianism, even if they reject its subversive side. Finally, Andreae was a talented author, and his style often shows through in 'The Chemical Wedding'.

Ashmole, Elias

1617–92

The first known speculative mason

Ashmole was one of the first intellectuals to be admitted to a masonic lodge. His biography allows us to observe the transition from operative to speculative masonry.

Ashmole was an alchemist. He published the *Theatrum Chimicum Britannicum* and studied the royal art with three Rosicrucians, John Moor, John Booker and William Lilly, along with whom he founded a 'Society of Antiquarians', which corresponded with other learned societies in Europe. The *Theatrum* was influenced by the work of Robert Fludd (see **Fludd**). In Ashmole's diary, there is the following entry for 16 October 1646, 'Today, at half past four in the afternoon, I was made a freemason at Warrington in Lancashire.'

A liegeman

There are those who have asked whether Ashmole, when he entered the masonic lodge, was not commissioned by the Rosicrucians to hide their mysteries in the comforting shadow of the lodges. 'He might have been using the lodges as a sort of crypt where Truth might hide and await less troubled times,' (*Dictionnaire des sociétés secrètes en Occident*). The hypothesis is certainly plausible. However, it is equally probable that Ashmole simply wished to perfect his symbolic culture within this society.

Ashmole was, therefore, one of the first 'accepted' masons, that is, builders, men of culture rather than to whom masonic initiation was given. These men of culture were mainly intellectuals and artists, who were resolutely modern but, at the same time, devoted to the 'knowledge of the ancients'.

Past and future

Ashmole in this way established the direct line of descent between operative and speculative freemasonry. This direct line — for it is highly unlikely that Ashmole was the only intellectual to be admitted into a lodge of builders — does by no means prove, however, a 'transmission' of a secret from ancient to modern times, piously handed down from generation to generation. Quite the contrary, in fact, for here we have the living proof of what Varèse meant when he said, 'Every link in the chain was forged by a revolutionary.' Ashmole and the other creative intellectuals of the period went to the lodge because they had foreseen the role which the 'manual arts' were going to play, and they wanted to forge a link between the future and a distant, neglected past which the present was about to sweep aside.

The Ashmolean Museum

Ashmole's library was destroyed by fire in 1679, along with his collection of nine thousand medals. On his death, he left a historical museum to the University of Oxford, the first of its kind in England, and still in existence today.

Bacon, Roger

1214–92

An alchemist who championed experience

Roger Bacon is counted among the founders of the experimental method. He was also an alchemist.

Roger Bacon was born at Ilchester in Somerset into a well-to-do family which had been ruined by politics. He studied Greek and then entered the Franciscan order. In Paris, where he pursued his studies from 1234 to 1250, he became the pupil of Pierre de Maricourt, the author of one of the first treatises on the magnet, whom he dubbed the 'master of experience'. In 1257, he retreated from the world and remained in seclusion for the next ten years; in 1277, as a result of an argument with his superiors, he was imprisoned for 14 years.

Operative and speculative alchemy

Roger Bacon was an enthusiast of the concrete and of empiricism, while remaining convinced that the Bible contained all knowledge. Although he favoured an experimental approach, this was only in order to reveal the knowledge contained in the scriptures. He still acknowledged the supremacy of 'spiritual' illumination.

> **A forerunner**
> Roger Bacon anticipated many inventions of the future — boats with neither oars nor sails, the bathyscaphe, optical lenses, etc. G. Sarton, in his *Introduction to the History of Science* (Baltimore, 1927–1948), makes the point that not one of these prophecies, taken on its own, would be worth reporting. However, it is extremely impressive to find such a great number of predictions combined in the intellectual work of one mind.

If Bacon is considered one of the founders of the experimental method by the profane world, for occultism he remains an alchemist. He distinguished between 'practical' (or 'operative') and 'speculative' alchemy. This is an important distinction which occurs again later between 'assistants' and 'adepts', developed in a passage by Bacon which is worth quoting:

> [Speculative alchemy] describes the generation of things from elements or from anything which is inanimate: simple and compound humours, common and precious stones, marble, gold and other metals, sulphurs, salts and tinctures, lapis lazuli, minium and other colours, oils, burning bitumen and infinite other things not mentioned by Aristotle, the natural philosophers or by any of the Latin authors. This science is unknown by most scholars.
>
> However, alongside this speculative form of alchemy, there is another which teaches how to make noble metals, colours and many other things by Art, better or more abundantly than they are produced by nature. Such a science has the advantage over all those that went before, for its results are of great usefulness ... Its work confirms theoretical alchemy and, consequently, the natural philosophy of medicine.

Roger Bacon minimizes the importance of the 'prime matter', so dear to many alchemists, but he accentuates that of the four elements. He borrows from Avicenna the theory of the primordial pairing of sulphur and mercury. He seems, according to E. J. Holmyard, to have cherished the idea that alchemy was perhaps the meeting-point of Aristotle's physics and biology.

Böhme, Jakob

1575–1624

The 'cobbler of Görlitz' was a thinker of genius

Böhme's work defies classification. It contains mystical, philosophical and esoteric elements. Hegel was strongly influenced by this thinker.

The theosophist Jakob Böhme fits into the line of mystics born between the Rhine and the Danube in the 16th and 17th centuries. He remains an intriguing enigma — how was this uneducated cobbler able to familiarize himself so thoroughly with Gnosticism and the works of Philo of Alexandria, Joachim de Flore and many others? Böhme himself supplies an answer: 'God gave me the knowledge. It is not I who am myself, who knows these things, but God who knows them in me ... Since it is God who creates them, it is not me myself making them, but God in me; it is as if I were dead during this birth of sublime wisdom.' As a thinker of genius, he influenced, among others, Swedenborg, Leibniz, Hegel and Berdyaev.

Divine uniqueness

According to the 'cobbler of Görlitz', as Böhme was called, there exists a divine uniqueness, whose modes are of three orders (the Trinity). This does not, however, stop him from making the point clearly that 'talk of the birth of God is, quite literally, to use the language of the Devil. For it means that the eternal light sprang out of darkness and that God had a beginning ... But darkness is not only the absence of light, but the fear caused by the brilliance of the light'. So, divine uniqueness is not something created in time, but a virtual reality 'actualized' in humanity. The role or function of the Son cannot be dissociated from the person of the Father. This function is divine uniqueness tending towards actualization. Evil, on the other hand, is an absolutely essential principle; humanity cannot define it, the world is born from it. (Here Böhme is using the language of the Catharians.) Freedom

References
The main works of Böhme are *Aurora* (1612), *De Triplicata Vita* (1620), *De Signatura Rerum* (1620) and *Mysterium Magnum* (1623).

The inspiration of Böhme
Böhme's first inspiration came in 1600. He felt a giddiness throughout his whole being while looking at a pewter vase on which the sun was playing. 'He felt that man, despite his opacity, could shine with the same brilliance in the light of God' (Alexandrian, *Histoire de la philosophie occulte*). He went walking in the countryside while still in this state of mind and understood then some of the mysteries of creation. His full illumination did not come until twelve years later, though. 'In the light, my spirit immediately saw through all things, and recognized in all creatures, in plants and in grass, what God is, and what He is like and what is His will.' He then published *Aurora* (1612) which caused an uproar. However, when summoned by the theologians, he was examined and found innocent. He nevertheless lived like an outcast, supported by a circle of disciples.

appears as the ultimate mystery. This freedom is like Sartre's freedom, but with a more cosmic dimension, and creates meaning and sense ('Freedom is the cause of light').

God is nothing

Böhme was also a dialectician of genius. His arguments — his manipulation of opposites to make Being spring into life — relate to pre-Aristotelian thought, but are contained within a clearly Christian framework in which value is ascribed to the individual. He wrote, 'God is a mystery, by which I mean He is nothing.' For us, God is the absolute void and at the very heart of this void, our longing for God is 'the cause of the darkness'. Any image of God, and any longing man feels for God, is the work of the flesh.

How, then, did Böhme make sense of the endless contradictions of human life? He saw sin as the loss of an original hermaphroditism; the individual has lost the 'Eternal Virgin' (Sophia), who has taken refuge in Heaven. The feminine dimension, separated from man, has become alien to him and the object of all sins.

Böhme's philosophy is infinitely more complex and rich than these few lines might suggest. He is invaluable especially for building bridges between profane psychology and esoterism. He speaks, for example, of Anguish, Compulsion, Bitterness, Sweetness, Light and so on. In his

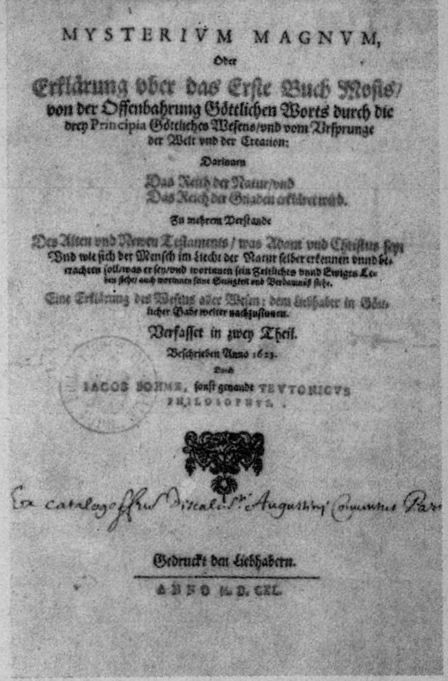

MYSTERIVM MAGNVM,
Oder
Erklärung über das Erste Buch Mosis/
von der Offenbahrung Göttlichen Worts durch die
drey Principia Göttliches Wesens/vnd vom Vrsprunge
der Welt vnd der Creation:
Darinnen
Das Reich der Natur/vnd
Das Reich der Gnaden erkläret wird.
Zu mehrern Verstande
Des Alten vnd Newen Testaments / was Adam vnd Christus sey:
Vnd wie sich der Mensch im Liecht der Natur selber erkennen vnnd betrachten soll/was er sey/vnd worinnen sein Zeitliches vnnd Ewiges Leben stehe/ auch worinnen seine Seeligkeit vnd Verdamnüß stehe.
Eine Erklärung des Wesens aller Wesen: dem Liebhaber in Göttlicher Gabe weiter nachzusinnen.
Verfasset in zwey Theil.
Beschrieben Anno 1623.
Durch
IACOB BÖHME, sonst genandt TEVTONICVS PHILOSOPHVS.
Gedruckt den Liebhabern.
ANNO M.DC.XL.

Title page *of the Mysterium Magnum, 1640 edition (National Library, Paris)*

work these elements are 'affects' and, at the same time, alchemical or Cabalistic concepts. Böhme makes occult mythology operational.

In a way, Böhme inaugurated 'negative theology'. For him, just as for Jung and others, care must be taken to distinguish between God and images of God. God is inaccessible, and all the pictures we have of Him are but falsehood; we can only approach transcendence by burning them.

> **'The visible world** is a symbol of the invisible world.' (Mysterium Magnum)

Boullan, Joseph

d.1893

A scatological priest

Half-understood occult thought does damage.

Joseph Boullan belonged to the congregation of the Precious Blood of Albanos and received his doctorate in divinity in Rome. A few years later, in 1856, he met a 'miraculous nun' at Notre-Dame de la Salette. This nun, Adèle Chevalier, claimed to be in contact with the Blessed Virgin.

Curing 'devilish illnesses'

Having 'recognized' each other as kindred spirits, Boullan and Adèle together founded the 'Society for the Separation of Souls' with a view to 'curing devilish illnesses'. Adèle heard a voice which dictated the rules of the order to her, and they set up their society at Belleville. Rumours of this reached the Bishop of Versailles and, in 1865, Boullan was sent to prison for three years. At his trial it came out that one of the cures prescribed by the society consisted of getting the 'possessed' patient to drink the urine of Boullan mixed with that of Adèle. Boullan did not give up however. On his release from prison, he went on a pilgrimage to Assisi and, having returned to Paris, founded there the 'Annals of Holiness in the 19th Century' and once again set about the task of curing spells. On the death of Vintras (see **Vintras**), he claimed to be his successor as leader of the Carmelite Order of Elijah in Lyon.

Putting 1 into 0

Stanislas de Guaïta sent his secretary to enquire about Joseph Boullan. He heard tales of the 'ascension' Boullan practised, which was 'multiplied by 10'. This meant 'putting the 1 into the 0, the phallus in the cteis'. A tribunal rounding up Rosicrucian Cabalists condemned Boullan on 23 May 1887. Guaïta and the writer Huysmans claimed that Boullan had cast a spell on them and that he had tried to kill them by magic.

The accusations against Boullan

'Limitless promiscuity, all manner of lewd practices, incest, bestiality, incubi and onanism.' Stanislas de Guaïta

Three sorts of union

Boullan is perhaps best known for his 'law of sacred regeneration'. His biographer, Joanny Bricaud, wrote, 'Since the fall from grace resulted from an illicit act of love, the Redemption of Humanity can only be achieved through acts of love accomplished in a religious manner.' Guilty love must be combated through pure love, through a sexual approach, but in a heavenly manner, to the spirits in order to raise oneself: this is the 'union of wisdom'. Union in an infernal manner with inferior beings — even demons who might be improved — is, conversely, the 'union of charity'. For Boullan, bringing about harmony between the fluids of two equal beings striving after good was a 'duo of life'. He maintained that such a duo constituted this life on earth, in, an 'Edenic body', a 'glorious spiritual body'.

Joseph Boullan is a good example of someone who used scraps of occult thought without really knowing how to put them into practice. Details are few and far between, but Boullan appears to have taken his scatology from the *Liber Secretorum*, an apocryphal text attributed to Albert the Great. As for his sexual magic, it is far removed from Tantric yoga or other forms of sexual alchemy, especially since 'occult unions' can be 'unions from afar'.

Buonarroti, Philippe

1761–1837

A socialist conspirator

Buonarroti confused the struggle for freedom with the quest for the sacred. Could initiation be the same as human rights?

Buonarroti was an enthusiastic follower of Robespierre. A republican, he believed in the Supreme Being, but claimed to be anti-clerical. At the same time, he believed that liberty, the outcome of the French Revolution, was worth the sacrifice of his life. He was involved in numerous political societies of an esoteric nature, such as the Carbonari, the Philadelphians and the Grand Firmament. He took part, in one way or another, in all of the uprisings that took place in France between 1789 and 1837, and long after that he was symbolically present under the Commune in 1871 through the actions of his disciple, Blanqui.

The Conspiracy of Equals

Buonarroti allied himself with Gracchus Babeuf and Sylvain Maréchal to draw up the manifesto of the 'Movement of Equals', the first text to put communism on the agenda. He then went on to stir up the 'Conspiracy of Equals', for which he was arrested along with his accomplices; Babeuf died on the guillotine, while Buonarroti spent many years in prison. Far from breaking his spirit, though, this strengthened his revolutionary spirit. For him, revolution, rebellion and the affirmation of the rights of man corresponded to a quest for initiation. A secret society was necessarily political, because it participated in the unveiling of both spiritual and social freedom.

A source of influence
The influence of Buonarroti may well have been underestimated in the history of occultism, especially on the republican tendency of freemasonry. However, his influence persisted, in an underground but tangible manner, and the republicanism of the Grand Orient of France is one example of its lasting effect.

Two complementary dimensions

Buonarroti continued to refine his vision of a secret society. Without putting it into so many words, he considered that the initiatory society fitted into the socio-historic fabric obliquely and not directly. His theory distinguished between 'initiation' and 'exteriorization' (even if he sometimes confused the two in practice). Initiation, or rather the initiatory dimension, was therefore the source, while the lodge was an excellent place for training, which could only proceed through meditation. Exteriorization was the practice of applying, in this world, all that had been understood, learnt, tried out and verified within oneself. Real action is thus conceived as a continual coming and going between these two complementary dimensions. So, there is a time for philosophy and a time for action: the usual contradiction between them is removed. With Buonarroti, the secret society became a clandestine organization and, at the same time, a laboratory in which to experiment upon the future – or rather, where the future placed itself to develop.

Cagliostro

(alias of Giuseppe Balsamo)

1743–95

A man overtaken by his legend

Was he, as some believe, sent to pave the way for the French Revolution? Or was he simply a charlatan?

An extremely colourful historical character, Giuseppe Balsamo, better known as Alessandro, Count of Cagliostro, was immortalized in the writings of Alexandre Dumas. His life, the subject of much speculation, is shrouded in mystery. Was he a charlatan whose 'elixir of long life', reputed to cure all ills, was merely a placebo? Was he a spy? If so, in the service of whom? England? How did he become involved in the Affair of the Diamond Necklace which did so much damage to the reputation of Marie-Antoinette? Was he really so dangerous that he deserved to spend his last days imprisoned by the Inquisition? The Vatican certainly felt the need to justify its actions after his death by publishing an apocryphal 'Life of Joseph Balsamo'. Was he, on the other hand, just the symbol of a society crumbling into ruin and in need of scapegoats?

What is certain is that Cagliostro had had hermetic training, was an initiated freemason and also a clairvoyant. He founded masonic lodges, in particular the 'Lodge of Wisdom', and invented the ritual of Egyptian masonry, proclaiming himself the Grand Cophte and his wife, Lorenza Feliciani, the Grand Cophte of the women's lodges then very popular in high society. Overtaken by his own legend, he was dubbed a 'noble traveller' and seen as the emissary of a powerful secret society, probably freemasonry, which would change the world. To this day, he retains his fascination for, and hold on, the popular imagination.

'In herbis et in verbis'

Some of Cagliostro's prescriptions have been preserved. His biographer, Marc Haven, notes that his facial pomade, turpentine pills and Canada balsam pills were usually made up in a pharmacy. Clearly, then, Cagliostro was not a miracle-healer.

The physiognomist and mystic Lavater went to see him to find out his secret and was told that the whole of science was *in herbis et in verbis*. A woman who asked why well-known remedies worked better for him was told, 'It is the master touch, the secret I keep in my heart.'

Cagliostro had extraordinarily strong suggestive powers. He kept himself 'psychically fit', through very strict hygiene, rigorous ethics and the moral support of the lodges he had founded. Finally, the efficacy of his medication cannot simply be explained away by saying it is based on psychology. This begs the question of how, why and how far does the psychic work on the organic?

Self-sufficiency

'A mason who needs a doctor is not a true mason.'

The Carbonari

The freemasonry of the charcoal burners

A little-known initiatory society, the Carbonari played an influential part in the struggle for Italian independence.

'The Carbonari lived in the forest in long cabins (*barache*), where they drew up their own laws and constitutions. Their governing body was a kind of triumvirate, in office for three years, which oversaw three *vendite* or 'lodges' — the legislative, the administrative and the judicial. The last of these was called *l'alta vendita*. The lodges were themselves divided into a number of 'cabins', each one run by a 'good cousin'. One day, François I, king of France, became lost in the forest; he asked for shelter in a cabin and was kindly received. After he had been initiated, he made himself the protector of the good cousins' (H. Lepper).

Their influence in France

The Carbonari and the freemasons are parallel organizations. From legendary beginnings, they both passed through an operative phase to a speculative form. The rites of the Carbonari reached France around 1750, having been shaped, as Lepper points out above, in the forests in the Bourbonnais where the nobles proscribed by Charles VI and Charles VII had taken refuge and been initiated. The first lodge proper, called 'Workers of the Globe and Glory' was set up in Paris in a park in the Poissonnière district. We are told that the initiates were cheerful fellows given to the pleasures of the table, who went in for pranks and practical jokes, dressing up as bumpkins and wearing clogs.

A revolutionary organization

In 1766, the Carbonari merged with the freemasons. The organization re-emerged, however, around 1820, largely under the influence of Buonarroti. Ritual was reimported from Italy where the movement was still very much alive and had taken on a revolutionary tinge. However, apart from its influence on freemasonry in the 19th century and on socialists like Buchez and Leroux, and the appearance of the 'Universal Democratic Charbonnerie' of Buonarroti, the influence of the Carbonari on society was minimal.

The secrets

A few of the 'secrets' (passwords, signs and so on) of the Carbonari have been revealed. The rallying sign of a ladder was made by raising the hands to shoulder height and then letting them fall again, and 'good cousins' recognized one another by the slogan *Speranza, Fede, Carità* ('Hope, Faith, Love'). The password on entry to the lodge was 'Honour! Truth! Fatherland!'

Cardano, Girolamo

1501–76

A flamboyant genius

A visionary and an inveterate gambler, whose work is proof of his genius, Cardano's medical knowledge was founded on intuition.

Born the illegitimate son of a land-surveyor and procurator fiscal in Pavia, Cardano was a sickly child. He managed, nevertheless, to complete his schooling and went on to become a country doctor. He was married in 1532 and moved in the same year to Milan where, after many vicissitudes, he was allowed to teach medicine. His fame as a physician grew rapidly and a number of Europe's crowned heads sought his services. In 1551, he travelled to Scotland where he successfully treated the bishop of St Andrews for asthma. Visiting London, he cast the horoscope of Edward VI. He was, in addition, the outstanding mathematician of his time, setting out the solution of the cubic equation and giving his name to the cardan joint.

Cardano the Magnificent

Cardano was a flamboyant individual with a crippling fear of being poisoned; he was accompanied everywhere by two young servants who tasted everything he was about to eat or drink. His wardrobe consisted of four sumptuous garments from which he created 14 different outfits. He wore an emerald around his neck and put it in his mouth when given bad news (because he believed that sucking an emerald could dissipate sorrow). Subject to insomnia, he anointed his body in 17 places with a salve of poplar ointment, bear-grease or olive oil.

His last years were clouded by misfortune. Although he became famous, his son was condemned to death and executed for poisoning his wife. His younger brother terrorized him and his colleagues banded against him. In 1570 he was imprisoned by the Inquisition for heresy, recanted and went to Rome in the following year, where he was awarded a pension by Pope Pius V.

The art of hoping for nothing

Like all innovators, Girolamo Cardano was attacked from all sides. The French scholar Scaliger, for example, attempted to refute his *De Subtilitate* in a book longer than Cardano's own work. However, criticism seemed to act as a stimulant upon him. This was perhaps because, as he put it, he had learnt the 'art of hoping for nothing'. He maintained that his knowledge combined technique and inspiration, which he called

> '**Precious stones**, held under the tongue, can help in divination by increasing judgment and prudence.'

> 'The property of **red coral**, pure and brilliant as a carbuncle, is such that, when worn round the neck so as to touch the heart, if a man is ill or shortly about to fall ill, or if he has unknowingly drunk some poison, the coral becomes pale and loses its shine in a quite remarkable way. This has been observed several times.'

HIERONYMI
CARDANI MEDICI
MEDIOLANEN-
SIS
DE ANIMI IMMORTA-
LITATE LIBER,

Ad ſapientiſſimum uirum Iacobum Philippum Saccum, Galliæ Ciſalpinæ Præſidem optimum.

AEPE, ac diu dubitatũ eſt, An animus hic noſter immortalis, atq; incorruptibilis ſit, uelut diuinum aliquod numen: an potius, ut reliquorũ omniũ animãtium, morti obnoxius cũ ipſo corpore ſimul intereat. Atq; ſi ſuperſit, & illud etiã dubium eſt, an omnibus hominibus unus atq; idem exiſtat, uelut uno ſole cũcta

***Book on the Immortality of the Soul**, in Greek and Latin, 1545 (Arsenal Library, Paris)*

splendor; this *splendor* was often founded on an intuitive understanding of signs and portents.

Cardano believed that all things had a secret property or 'subtlety' specific to them which could be revealed by analogy. He therefore established correspondences between planets, colours and tastes: for example, black corresponded to bitterness and to Saturn, while blue had an affinity with salt and Mars, and so on. When he died, he left numerous works: 54 printed books and almost as many manuscripts on medicine, astrology, divination, moral philosophy, etc. All of these, furthermore, were in addition to some 130 other works he destroyed because he considered them failures. Cardano's autobiography was published, posthumously, in 1643 by Gabriel Naudé.

The vegetable kingdom

Plants, according to Cardano, can attract or repel one another. 'It is well known that plants can hate one another or love one another and that they have the means to indicate this to one another. The olive and the vine are said to hate the cabbage; the cucumber shuns the olive, as the vine shuns the elm. Similarly, myrtle planted by a pomegranate makes it more fertile and the myrtle itself smells more fragrant.

'The effect of the shadow of trees is remarkable. As I have said, deadly shade is that of the poisonous yew, walnut, old fig and rowan; healthy shade is that of the white-beam or service tree, and the beech.'

Cattan, Christopher

fl. c. 1550

Geomancy, or divination 'by the earth'

Cattan is known for his one book, Geomancy, a work of major importance.

The work of Christopher Cattan still has a following today. European interest in geomancy was first stimulated when Gerard of Cremona translated an Arabic work on the subject in 1160. This book on geomancy handed on Arab knowledge of Indian geomancy to Europe.

Drawing figures

Originally, geomancy was 'divination by the earth'. Figures were drawn on the ground and their meanings were then interpreted. Cattan modified the procedure slightly, as follows:

1. Sixteen lines of dots are drawn in one movement, without lifting the hand. Then these lines are grouped into four fours and four dot figures are chosen, starting from the right. These are the 'mothers'. All this time, the person drawing will be repeating mentally the question to which an answer is sought.
2. From the 'mothers', dots are chosen to form four more figures, the 'daughters'; from these 'mothers' and 'daughters', more are chosen to form four 'nieces'.
3. From the 'mothers' and 'daughters', two 'witnesses' are made and, from them, the 'judge'. It is the 'judge' which determines the ultimate significance, good or bad, of the whole drawing. There are now 15 figures drawn, which provide 16 different combinations of dots: 'The Track (or four dots one above another); the People (or four times two dots one above another); the Dragon's Head (or five dots in a Y-shape); the Dragon's Tail; the Boy; the Maiden; the Prison; the Conjunction; Minor Fortune; Major Fortune; Red; White; Sadness; Joy; Loss; and Gain.'

> Francis Warrain invented magic squares and **'geomantic necklaces'** of glass beads. He claimed that the figures of geomancy were based 'on the number 16, the only whole-number solution for the equation $x^y = y^{x4}$'.

Interpretation

The figures are ambivalent: 'loss' can be good as it sometimes means the loss of inhibitions or problems; 'conjunction' can be a love-affair or a business partnership. The figures are put in 'houses' to discern five 'aspects' (or the number of houses separating the figures): company, opposition and groups of three, four and six.

'Company' means associating one figure with the one immediately following it; 'opposition' compares a figure with the one in the seventh house; the 'group of four' is taken along with the fourth house and its 'company'; the 'group of three' takes two figures together, which are separated by three houses; and the 'group of six' takes three figures together, each separated by one house. The fundamental rule throughout is that only one question may be asked at a time.

Crowley, Aleister

1875–1947

An abortive quest for supernatural powers

From poetry to sexual magic, by way of drugs, Crowley spent his life in a fruitless search for supernatural powers.

Born into an upper middle-class puritan family, Crowley first became interested in the occult while an undergraduate at Cambridge. Always a controversial figure, the press first took him to task for his advocacy of eroticism in his *White Stains*. By way of reply, he gave a lecture in his mistress's home on 'sexual poverty in Britain'. He then joined the Order of the Golden Dawn, a secret society of which the poet W. B. Yeats and Bram Stoker, the author of *Dracula*, were also members. Crowley became the society's grand master and formed a homosexual partnership with Allan Bennett, known as Iohi Aour, another of its members. The two of them abandoned themselves to magic and Crowley declared his wish to become a 'saint of Satan' and to be known as the 'Great Beast' or 'the wickedest man alive'.

Mystical marriage

In *Magic in Theory and Practice*, Crowley set out his ideas on eroticism. The book was written so that 'all should realize their full potential'; the best prayer, according to Crowley, was 'ritual drama' and he preached 'Dionysiac ceremonies'. This was in fact a 'Gnostic mass'. After the introit Crowley, dressed as a priest, prayed to the 'four elements' and blessed 'cakes of light' for the communion of the faithful; the ceremony ended with a mystical marriage.

The Great Beast

In 1900, Crowley was expelled from the Order of the Golden Dawn for extreme practices. He founded his own order, the Silver Star, and set out to travel the world. Crowley settled for several years in Sicily with a group of disciples, but rumours of drugs, orgies and even sacrifices led to his expulsion from Italy. His travels also took him to Ceylon, where he met up again with Bennett, who had become a Buddhist monk, and to Madras where he was initiated into Tantrism. In Paris, he met Rodin, Rilke, Somerset Maugham and finally Rose Edith Kelley, his 'scarlet woman' whom he was to marry. It was in Cairo that a medium in a trance revealed the 'ultimate mysteries' of sexual magic to the young couple and urged them to set up the order of the Silver Star.

Rose died an alcoholic, leaving a daughter called Night my Athatour Hecate Sappho Jezabel Lilith, who was to die in tragic circumstances. Crowley, who lived for some time at Boleskine, on the shores of Loch Ness, continued to travel, surrounded by women. With Victor Neuburg, he journeyed into the Algerian desert to meet the spirit of evil. The two men were later found half-dead with exhaustion. Crowley finally came to believe he was a vampire, began to inject heroin, and adopted a wildly promiscuous lifestyle. When war broke out, he offered Churchill an infallible magic method to achieve victory. Churchill declined the offer!

Dee, John

1527–1606

The most famous summoner of spirits

John Dee started out a scholar and astrologer, but he fell under the influence of a crook.

As a young student, John Dee achieved celebrity and earned the reputation of a sorcerer with his invention of a mechanical beetle for a production of Aristophanes' *Peace*. At 23, he was lecturing on Pythagoras and Euclid in Paris. A year later, Henry VIII awarded this polymath a pension on account of his skill in astronomy. In 1553, when Mary Tudor came to the throne, she invited him to draw up her horoscope and received him at court. It was Dee who had the idea of founding a national library, gifted it 4000 of his own books and thus established the British Museum.

When Elizabeth I succeeded Mary in 1559, she chose January 14 as the date for her coronation because John Dee had pronounced it astrologically auspicious. A few years later, he published a treatise on Cabalistic alchemy, *The Hieroglyphic Monad* (1564), dedicated to Maximilian II, king of Bohemia and Hungary. While Dee's occult knowledge was clearly impressive, he was also interested in studies of a 'profane' or scientific nature, such as burning-mirrors, perspective, navigation, geography, mathematics and astronomy. Unfortunately, all too little is known about this aspect of his studies.

The angel at the window

In 1581, Dee met a reprobate by the name of Edward Kelley, who turned his life upside down. He fell completely under the influence of Kelley (which some have attributed to a latent homosexuality). On 21 November 1582, Dee claimed to have been visited by an angel in the form of a boy, who came to his study window and gave him a stone, which was like black crystal. This magic crystal is still to be seen in the British Museum. Whether this was a hallucination or one of Kelley's tricks, from that day forth they became a team: Kelley professed to receive visions from the heav-

A secret agent
There are many stories attached to the life of John Dee. He may have been a secret agent of Elizabeth I, but there is no definite proof of this.

A private diary
The Private Diary of Doctor John Dee was discovered in 1842. It contained some interesting tit-bits. Gustav Meyrink based his novel *The Angel at the Window* on it.

The medium
The John Dee — Edward Kelley team 'invented' the use of the medium. The messages dictated to them are explained in Dee's works, especially his *Liber Logaeth*, where he sets out the spells used to control the angels. Dee also produced *The 48 Angelic Keys, The Tablets of Enoch* and *The Table of Nalvage*, named after the angel which gave him the information. Spiritualists in the 19th century believed the medium could reveal the secrets of death; Dee and Kelley sought to decipher the mysteries of Creation by means of the 'original language' of Enoch.

Anonymous engraving from John Dee's autobiography (National Library, Paris)

enly stone and Dee wrote them down. On one occasion, the angel Uriel appeared and ordered Dee to give Kelley a pension of £50 a year.

Finally, the angels taught Dee the 'language of Enoch that Adam spoke before the Fall'. Kelley, in a trance, dictated to him *The Book of Enoch* which supposedly revealed the ultimate mysteries of Creation. On 21 September 1583, Dee received a warning that he was about to be murdered; the partners fled at once with their families to Poland, then to Prague. At Krakow, King Stephen was reportedly deeply alarmed by John Dee's powers. Dee's adventures are related in his autobiography, which was only published in 1859, *A True and Faithful Relation of What Passed for Many Years between Dr John Dee and Some Spirits.*

Wife-swapping

One day, the images of Kelley, Dee and their wives appeared spontaneously in the mirror. It was, to them, a clear sign and the two men solemnly exchanged wives on 3 May 1587. Their partnership eventually split up in 1589 and Kelley went to Prague, where King Rudolf II threw him into prison for life. Dee returned to England, but he was universally shunned. He died at the age of 81 in poverty, and is buried in Mortlake Church, London.

Della Porta, Gian Battista

1550–1615

A coherent vision of physiognomy

Della Porta became interested in and systematized physiognomy, because it was a branch of magic.

Gian Battista Della Porta was born in Naples. He was a scholar, playwright and occultist. He founded an 'Academy of Secrets', to which only those who had made an important discovery were admitted.

He was a man of many talents. His 'Natural Magic' published in 1589 is widely misunderstood, and the book he is best remembered for is his coherent treatise on physiognomy, *De Humana Physionomia.* Its aim is to provide a better knowledge of men through 'those signs fixed and permanent on the body or changed by accidents'. Intuitive knowledge, the 'immediate data of perception', is not enough: some tangible basis is needed, and every human being possesses signs which are common to all and others which are specific to him alone.

Correspondence of signs

Della Porta studied all parts of the body. He was careful not to extrapolate from one aspect alone, but looked always for agreement in several (eg eyes and feet) before drawing a conclusion. An innovative feature of his work was that he did not ignore sexual organs. 'The arts of the body have a mutual correspondence. For example, the size of a woman's mouth and the size and thickness of her lips will indicate the size of her private parts; the same holds for a man's nose and the membrum virile. 'If a man's penis hangs to the left, he will have sons, because it will cast his seed within the woman's body towards the right.'

De humana physionomia

Della Porta's work first examines the features of the human body and then attempts to define human types. Like his predecessors, he establishes an analogy between man and animal (NB an analogy, not an identity). The ideal woman for Della Porta is like a panther, both in body and in spirit. Her 'neck is long and slender, her chest formed of small ribs, her back long and her hips and thighs well covered with flesh. On her flanks and her belly she is rather flat, that is her body here does not stick out, nor is it hollow'. In the same way, the perfect man is like a lion. Envious people, according to Della Porta, have a loose lower lip, with a swelling around the canine teeth; they are made for biting. Misers 'have their neck bent forward and their shoulders drawn in over their chest; their body looks broken and their eyes are dim and watery'. Greedy people 'are longer between navel and chest than between chest and throat'. Lewd or unchaste people 'lean to the right and their feet and legs are not straight when they walk; they have long hair'. It is not by pure chance that one man's appearance might remind us of an owl and another's of a rat. Della Porta is the link between Aristotle and modern physiognomy. The most interesting of his followers was Marin Cureau de la Chambre who stated in his *Art de connaître les hommes* (1659) that temperament could be seen and read on the body.

Desbarolles, Adolphe

1801–86

Modern palmistry

Desbarolles brought palmistry up to date by attempting to rediscover its philosophical origin.

Desbarolles began his career by writing a book on the German character, which he attempted to explain through physiology. He also tried his hand at painting but, after various failures in the artistic field, he declared himself to be a palmist and a disciple of Eliphas Lévi.

He had wide success with the public; amongst those who consulted him he could count Alexandre Dumas, Proudhon and Corot. His books — *La Chiromancie nouvelle* (1859) and *Les mystères de la main* (1878) — ran through many editions. He was a pioneer of the practical use of chiromancy, applying it to vocational guidance so that children might avoid careers for which they had no aptitude.

A philosophical basis

Desbarolles tried to relate palmistry, which until his time had been purely empirical, to occult philosophy, and in particular that of Eliphas Lévi. He referred to 'astral light' or 'universal fluid', which was absorbed into the body, mainly through the thumb. He linked the phalanges hierarchically: the first to the world of God; the second to the world of thought; and the third to the material world. The joints stood for the transition between these various worlds. He also saw the four fingers (without the thumb) in terms of the four ages of our life, the four seasons and the twelve months.

Desbarolles' research gave rise in the 19th century to chirosophy, which was the study concerned with why we have lines on our hands. Papus and others attempted to answer this question and supposed that the hand was like the face of our astral body.

As we know, hermetism distinguishes the three bodies of the human being: the physical, the spiritual and the astral. The last of these is perceived through certain experiences and is, according to certain modern writers, a projection of the unconscious. Thus, the whole character of an individual, or rather of his unconscious, is inscribed upon his hand, as the hand is the unconscious revealing itself in concrete form. Papus wrote that 'the lines vary and modify themselves in proportion to the action of the will upon the unconscious,' that is, they are modified as the individual comes to an understanding of his unconscious.

Chiroscopy

The Congress of Experimental Physical Sciences held in Paris in 1913 decided to include chiromancy among the natural sciences, calling it 'chirology' and classing it as a branch of psychology. 'Medical chiroscopy' was invented to 'define the human co-ordinates' of the individual: constitution, temperament and type. The individual could be enabled thereby to realize the full potential of his personal evolution.

Donnolo, Sabbataï

fl. c.945

A master who left no trace

René Char said that the poet should leave traces, but no proof; Donnolo seems to have gone further, removing even these traces.

The matter of Donnolo's identity is not of such great importance. This master, about whom so little is known, saw himself as a modest link in a chain of initiates handing down knowledge which came from the mists of time. In about 930, more or less at the same time as another scholar, Saadia Gabon, he unearthed the *Sefer Yetsira* or 'Book of Creation', which promoted a move away from the ancient mysticism of the *Merkava*, or contemplation of the throne of God, and the 'invention' of the classical Cabala.

The Sefer Yetsira

The key idea of the Cabala appears probably most clearly in the *Sefer Yetsira*: speech is not simply communication, but also has an ontological and cosmological value. It reaches into the human being and the cosmos, and is at the root of that reality God revealed in his word. St John's Gospel, beginning with that lovely, enigmatic phrase, 'In the beginning was the Word', refers to the same idea. However, the *Sefer* is different from the Gospel, which is centred on God's incarnation, just as it is different from the Old Testament, which is centred on God's uniqueness. This is because it puts forward a cosmology, even if it refuses to give it a shape — rather like abstract art — and limits itself to letters and numbers.

In the Old Testament, in the Book of Genesis, God only had to say, 'Let there be Light' for light, and all creation, to come into existence. The act of Creation was speech and was quite independent of time. But how can the Word produce such effects? Religion provides no answer; for this we must turn to mythology. The *Sefer Yetsira* looks, at first sight, like a desperate attempt to reconcile the exuberance of mythology with the rigorousness of monotheism. Whatever the case may be, we find here the cosmology of the four elements of earth, air, fire and water, found also in esoterism and pre-Socratic philosophy, even if they are hiding behind apparently orthodox speculation.

The *Sefer Yetsira* was studied and commented on throughout the Middle Ages, particularly by philosophers and rabbis interested in Jewish esoteric thought. It was read throughout the world and in Germany was considered not only to be a major work

A great discovery
'Whether you accept it or reject it, the discovery of the Cabala is as important as the discovery of the New World.' P. Secret

Law and laws
'Moses wrote down the laws he had received, but not their explanation. He was content to entrust this to their memory ... This could be called the (spoken) Law, to distinguish it from written laws.' Leon Gorny

of theology, but also to be capable of working miracles and to contain the secret of the making of Golem, that creature of clay brought to life when the secret name of God, written on a piece of paper, was placed between his lips.

The 'true word'

'Every creature and every word, comes from a single name', says the *Sefer*. Cabalists believe that, by rediscovering the true word carved on Sinai when Moses received the tablets of the Law, it would be possible to reveal the language used to create the world. The scholar would then simply have to analyse this language and find out how its constituent parts combine. The author of the *Sefer* tells us that 231 doors open on to the mystery of the creation of the world; 231 is, it should be noted, the number of possible combinations of two letters from the 22 in the Hebrew alphabet.

The practical Cabala

'The effectiveness of the practical Cabala is not to be underestimated, even if it belongs to the realm of mythology, alchemy and magic. It has its own particular value, just like the speculative Cabala — or rather, the two are but branches of one and the same doctrine, and should not be separated. It is of no importance whether the Cabala corresponds to literal truth; it rests on historical fact.' H. Serouya

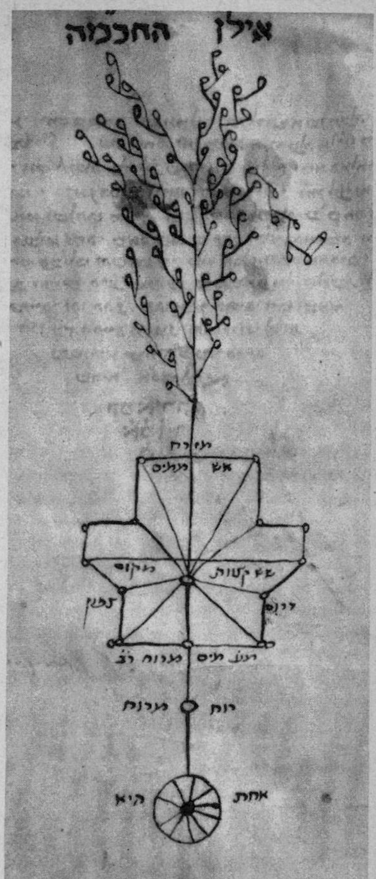

***Cabalistic plan** showing the order of Creation, from the* Book of Creation, *a Hebrew manuscript of the 13th century. (National Library, Paris)*

Etteila

(alias of Jean-François Aliette)

1738–91

The inventor of cartomancy

For Etteila, fortune-telling was a profitable business. He worked out rules for interpreting the cards.

Etteila was a teacher of mathematics, who developed a keen interest in the possibility of using cards as a means of fortune-telling. In 1770, he published *Etteila ou la Manière de se récréer avec un jeu de cartes* (Etteila or How to Amuse Oneself with a Pack of Cards), in which he proclaimed himself a 'master of cartomancy'. He set out the rules he had developed for the 32-card pack used in piquet. The meaning of the cards varied according to the name and number of the card, which trick and deal it came from, and so on. The meaning of any card could change, furthermore, according to whether the number on it was the right way up or not.

Memories of the 'Book of Thoth'

When Court de Gévelin, a Protestant minister from the Languedoc region, claimed in Book VIII of his *Monde primitif* (1782) that the tarot cards were derived from the Egyptian 'Book of Thoth', Etteila set about proving it. He published his *Manière de se récréer avec le jeu de cartes nommé tarots* (How to Amuse Oneself with a Pack of Tarot Cards) in 1783, revealing in it 'the key to the 78 hieroglyphs from the 'Book of Thoth', written in the year 1828 of Creation, or 171 years after the Flood'. He stated that the tarot cards are simply a summary of the chapters of this book made by 17 magi. He was made famous — and very rich — by this book.

Madame Lenormand was the only other fortune-teller to have as great a reputation as Etteila. She was the clairvoyant of Josephine de Beauharnais, Barras, Tallien, David and many other distinguished persons. Louis-Philippe's minister, Guizot, attended her funeral in 1843. Her major work was *Les Oracles sibyllins* (The Sibylline Books).

'The wheel of fortune'

Etteila appears to have been one of the first people to make his living from fortune-telling. He charged 30 francs per month for acting as a person's 'spiritual doctor' — a sort of official soothsayer — and also gave lessons. However, his place in the history of occultism is assured for having been the first to make rules for fortune-telling using tarot cards, and to make a success of it. In his 'wheel of fortune', he arranged the cards in a circle; and for his '15-card trick', he put them in three piles. His work inspired Oswald Wirth, secretary of Stanislas de Guaïta, also to write a book about the tarot.

Etteila had many followers, amongst them Jéjalel (whose real name was de Hugrand) who designed a 'planetary clock' to show correspondences between the planets and the tarot cards.

Evola, Giulio

1898–1974

From abstract artist to upholder of tradition

Evola turned his back on abstract art in a spectacular way.

The Italian Giulio Evola is seen nowadays as a traditionalist, but this was not always the case: his progress towards this position was achieved over a number of years. Evola first made his name within the field of modern art, where he took a particular interest in Marinetti and Futurism. He wrote *Arte astratta* (Abstract Art) but later, after experiencing a personal crisis, turned to the study of Nietzsche, from which sprang his *Teoria dell'individuo assoluto* (Theory of the Absolute Individual) in 1925.

'Spiritual mountaineering'

Evola began by stating that 'it is impossible to ask if woman is inferior or superior to man any more than it is possible to ask if water is superior to fire'. However, he finished rather lamely, countering feminist claims by merely stating that he respected the difference between the sexes. In this way, he anticipated the 'new right' which would later emphasize this difference — not inferiority — and stress the necessity of woman remaining in the place which was, historically, hers. In 1930, Evola took up spiritual mountaineering and became a follower of René Guénon. He published *La tradizione ermetica* (The Hermetic Tradition) in 1931, *Rivolta contro il mondo moderno* (Revolt against the Modern World) in 1934 and *Sintesi di dottrina della razza* (Synthesis of Racial Doctrine) in 1940. He claimed that far from being a racialist, he wanted merely to revive the Ghibelline tradition of support for the Empire against the Church, which Dante supported. However, Evola certainly influenced Italian Fascism and was, among Western interpreters of Tantrism, one of those who bent initiation towards masculine superiority in the interests of tradition (see 'Metaphysics of Sex', 'Riding the Tiger').

> 'The man who accepts extinction as extinction and, after having accepted extinction as extinction, thinks 'mine is extinction' and rejoices in extinction, that man, I say, does not know extinction.' Giulio Evola, *La Doctrine de l'éveil* (The Doctrine of Awakening).

Sexual magic

Evola's philosophy is based on sexuality, but unlike Freud, not on that of Eros. He believed that human beings are defined inwardly by their sex. However, 'masculinity and femininity are inner facts, and the inner sex does not necessarily correspond with the outer'. Abellio was intrigued by this idea and took it up in *La Structure absolue*, where he dealt with the 'transcendental effect of homosexuality.'

For Evola, occult sexual magic was akin to the musical pause: sexual practice in accordance with strict rules, handed down by masters and leading to true ecstasy.

Fabre d'Olivet, Antoine

1767–1825

A poet deranged by a lover's death

Poet, charlatan and plotter, Fabre d'Olivet was unlucky in love, then discovered occultism.

Fabre d'Olivet was born into a Protestant family in the Cévennes region of France. As an early follower of the philosopher, Delisle de Sasles, he began by writing poems and plays. At the French Revolution, he joined the Jacobin club, although he remained the friend of Thierry Ducloseau, a leading royalist conspirator. In 1797, he founded a political newspaper, *L'Invisible*, which survived 107 issues, thanks (claimed d'Olivet), to a magic ring which made him invisible and thus enabled him to observe the workings of the Legislature and the intrigues of the Palais-Royal without being seen!

Death deals him a terrible blow

Initially a supporter of the Republic against Napoleon, Fabre d'Olivet was condemned to deportation and was only pardoned at the last minute when a friend interceded on his behalf. He then turned to literature, writing in Provençal, one of many languages he knew, and attributing the work to a fictitious troubadour. In 1800, he fell passionately in love, but the young lady died, tragically, some two years later. Distraught, Fabre d'Olivet considered suicide until he experienced a visitation from his dead love. The incident overwhelmed him completely. 'The consequences of this event were immense for me — perhaps they will be so for all of mankind.' In the manuscript of his memoirs, he tells how this shock led him to his theory of occultism.

In 1805, he married the headmistress of a girls' school, who was to leave him in 1823, taking their three children with her. It seems that the ghost of his first love haunted the marriage. Meanwhile, he pursued his interest in occultism and, in 1811, he cured Rodolphe Grival, a lifelong deaf-mute, by hypnosis.

This was a productive time for him. He published: *Les Vers dorés de Pythagore* (The

Works

He published a love-story, *Azalaïs and the Gentle Ayma*, in 1799 and letters to his sister (*Lettres à Julie sur l'histoire*) in 1801. He described the latter as a 'cosmological, mythological, even historical novel' dealing mainly with Atlantis. *Le Savant de société*, a handbook of party games published under a pseudonym, also appeared in 1801.

Three worlds

'The universe we live in as men, belonging as it does to the kingdom of man, is divided into three worlds: the physical world we live in; the world of intellectual essences we strive towards; and the world of eternal principles, which is the goal of our existence.'

The kingdom of Man

'Beneath him is Destiny, needful of nature, above him Providence, free of nature. He, as the kingdom of man, remains the mediating Will, the efficient power between these two natures, to link them, unite their action and movement and allow them to communicate, for they would be incompatible without him.'

Golden Verses of Pythagoras) in 1813, the translation of a text he attributed to Lysis, written in non-rhyming alexandrines with a commentary; *La Langue hébraïque restituée* (The Hebrew Language Restored) (1815–1816), in which he developed his idea of an original language; *Notions sur le sens de l'ouïe* (On the Sense of Hearing) in 1819, in which he discussed his treatment of deafness; and, in 1824, his key work, *Histoire philosophique du genre humain* (Philosophical History of Mankind).

The universal man and Ram the druid

Fabre d'Olivet claimed to be interested in 'the abstract concept of the universal man', meaning 'that Being including in its universal essence all men who have lived, are living and will live'. That man is 'all men together, yet all men together are not him.' He divided the universe into three worlds: the world of physical realities where we are; that of essences; and that of eternal principles. They are all included in divinity and cannot exist without the mediation of the universal man between fatalism and freedom. For Fabre d'Olivet, the creative will is Aisha, the female dimension preceding Eve, who was herself merely an imperfect avatar or manifestation of this will. Mental energy, in this scheme of things, depends not on a magnetic fluid influenced by the stars, but by universal man himself, 'spurred on by his emotions'. Fabre d'Olivet then goes on to describe his history of the 'kingdom of Man'. The starting-point of its history was, he claimed, the 'theocratic empire founded by the druid Ram 6000 years before Christ. Ram travelled and was known as Rama in India, Osiris in Egypt and Apollo in Greece.'

Fabre d'Olivet eventually 'reconnected' with the spirit of his dead lover and, inspired by her, founded the 'Universal Theodoxical Cult' in 1824, with himself as 'Venerable Cultivator'. It was an order complete with its own rites, degrees and uniforms, which contacted the dead to invite them 'to partake of milk and honey with us as a sign of fraternal union and invisible harmony'. He died suddenly, probably of apoplexy, although one account of his death maintains that he committed suicide in full regalia, as a sort of cosmic sacrifice.

A thwarted passion

On 19 October 1824, Fabre d'Olivet revealed to his disciples, at one of their meetings, the difficulties he was having in his relationship with Julie Marcel, his deceased adviser ... 'A devilish spirit, whose name I cannot reveal, has become her enemy. There has been a terrible struggle ... My too faithful Julie was beaten and forced to withdraw and obey the laws of Destiny she had challenged in order to prove her love to me ... She has fallen from the world of Essences to the world of Reality; she has had to enter a body to be born again and take up once more the chains of mortal life.' The enemy turned out to be none other than Fabre d'Olivet's wife, exasperated by this mystical love affair! Fabre d'Olivet, convinced that Julie had been reincarnated in the body of a little girl of twelve, spent the rest of his life looking everywhere for her.

Flamel, Nicolas

1330–1418

Most famous of all the makers of gold

Nicolas Flamel and his wife are so famous that they each have a street named after them in Paris.

Nicolas Flamel was originally a public writer in Paris. He then acquired a bookshop and lived near the church of Saint-Jacques-la-Boucherie. In about 1360 he married Perrenelle and together they captured the public imagination.

History and legend

Nicolas Flamel has left an autobiography, *Le Livre des figures hiéroglyphiques*. We are told that, early on, he bought for two florins a book by Abraham the Jew containing pictures of some alchemical operations. Unable to decipher these, he went to Santiago de Compostella in the hope of meeting a Cabalist who might assist him. Happily, he met there a Jew, converted to Catholicism, who explained the secrets of the illustrations. Armed with this knowledge, Flamel returned to Paris where he worked with Pernelle on the transmutation of metals. He wrote, 'following my book word for word, I worked with a red stone ... Towards five o'clock in the evening, I truly transmuted it into as much pure gold, better certainly than common gold.'

However, Flamel was to keep his secret, for Charles V ordered the destruction of all alchemists' laboratories. So Nicolas Flamel turned instead to the endowment of numerous religious foundations and had a gate, covered with symbolic figures, constructed at Saint-Jacques-la-Boucherie. This obviously charismatic couple soon attained legendary status: as late as the 18th century, the traveller Paul Lucas claimed to have met a dervish who declared both were still alive! He was not alone; Alexis Monteil, author of the *Histoire des Français des divers Etats*, spoke of an 18th century intellectual who had often seen Flamel, still working in his underground laboratory.

> The **red colour** is 'like the lion, devouring all pure metallic Nature, by changing its true Substance into true and pure gold, finer than gold from the best mines.'

Man and myth

Nicolas Flamel is both an historical figure and the embodiment of a myth. Some six centuries later, the nature of this great alchemist is, intriguingly, itself the subject of continual transmutation: from man into myth, and vice versa.

In this illuminated figure, which Nicolas Flamel found in the book of Abraham the Jew, alchemy is likened to agriculture. (Arsenal Library, Paris)

Fludd, Robert

1574–1637

A mystic and yet a great experimenter

Fludd believed angels and demons were involved in health and sickness. He brought alchemy, astrology and the Cabala to his empirical observations.

Robert Fludd, or Robert de Fluctibus, was a member of the Royal College of London and left a remarkable work on medical theory, illustrated with engravings by Théodore de Brie. He believed that all diseases are rooted in original sin, and are caused by demons and combated by angels. For example, when the demon of fevers, Samael, comes, borne on the fetid east wind, he is opposed by St Michael and his peers, who build a 'mystical rampart of health'. Each of the demons occupies his own area of space and brings an illness — plague, pox, measles, and so on. Spells and prayers are as effective as medicine against them, and Fludd gives the appropriate formulae.

Fludd was, however, not only a mystic; he also carried out numerous experiments in his laboratory. It is even possible that he may have invented a steam engine before Denis Papin and, in 1815, Professor Kurt Sprengel expressed the opinion that Fludd had invented the barometer well before Torricelli. His work was, nonetheless, subject to a scathing attack by the philosopher, Gassendi; Fludd responded with his *Key to Fludd's Philosophy and Alchemy* (1633) in which he attacked his adversary's materialism in poetic terms, praising 'Nature, infinite and glorious'. In a posthumous work, *Philosophica Mosaica*, he established three principles of creation: darkness, which is the raw material or 'prime matter'; water, which is the 'second matter'; and light, which is life. The philosophical synthesis of idealism and materialism which he attempted was most unusual.

Apollo and Dionysus

Fludd believed in an 'archetypal Sun which gives all beings their beauty and their harmony. They celebrate the mystery of this divine Sun by reflecting it towards the visible created Sun, Apollo, who bears life, grace and health in his right hand and bow and arrows, as a sign of sternness, in his left. Apollo's alter ego is Dionysus, who tears all creatures to pieces. But they are in fact one and the same, known by day as Apollo and by night as Dionysus, Prince of Darkness. By night, Dionysus tears creatures into seven pieces; by day, Apollo restores them. However, they are really none other than the one God who makes all things.'

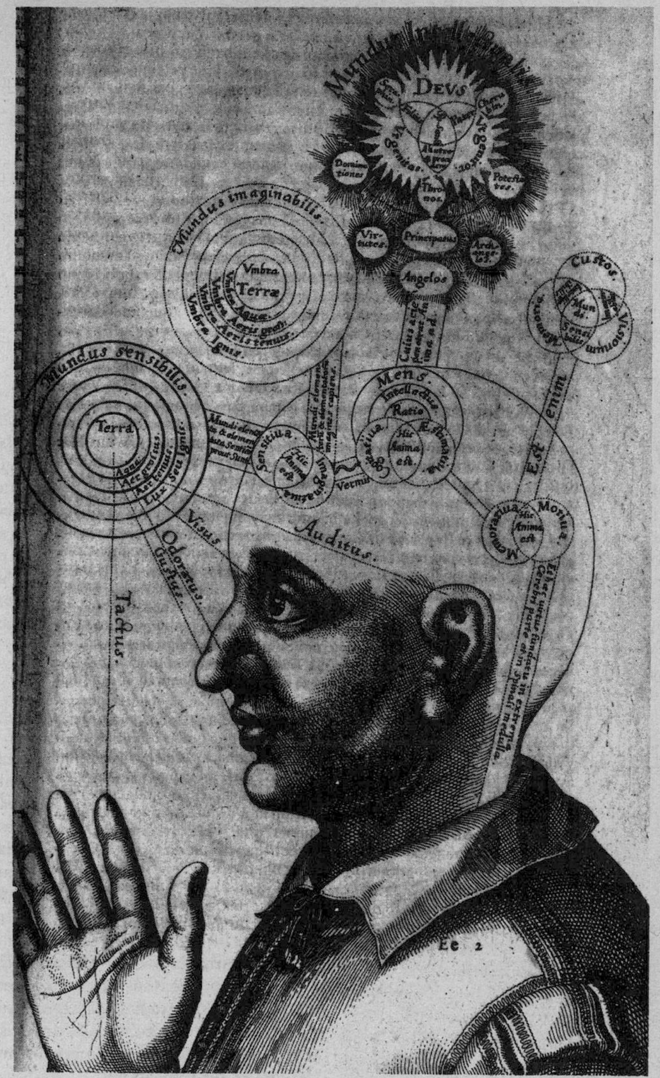

Robert Fludd's correspondences between the different worlds and man from Utriusque cosmi najhris salicet . . . , *1617–1619 (National Library, Paris)*

Fulcanelli

(alias of Jean-Julien Champagne)

1877–1932

The man who made the stones talk

An enigmatic character, Fulcanelli was one of the few alchemists of the 20th century.

The life and character of Fulcanelli remain shrouded in mystery despite the many books written about him. We know only what we can gleam from his books and the reports of his disciple, Eugène Canseliet. Fulcanelli reinvented phonetic Cabala, in such a way that, for example, 'argot' (the French word for 'popular slang'), could be reinterpreted as 'art goth' (or 'Gothic art'). He saw the alchemists' secrets in the very stones of the great cathedrals (and indeed the stages of the alchemists' work are depicted on the front of Notre Dame in Paris). 'As a sanctuary of tradition, science and art, the cathedral is not to be seen purely as a work devoted to the glory of Christ; it is a vast collection of ideas, of popular faith, perfect for revealing the thinking of our ancestors on any subject we choose.' Written in the 20th century, Fulcanelli's works reach back and link up with the thought of the old alchemist; they fascinated the surrealists including the poet André Breton.

Philosophers' houses

Fulcanelli listed 'philosophers' houses' in France and elsewhere. The carvings at the Manoir de Salamandre at Lisieux indicated, to him, that its owner was 'an adept of the philosopher's stone', and the same was true for the house of the 'wooden man' at Thiers. When he studied the sundial, dated 1633, at Holyrood Palace in Edinburgh, he wrote, 'We can reasonably regard this sundial as a monument to the 'philosopher's vitriol', which is the first stage in the quest for the philosopher's stone.' His approach was to blend art, history and alchemy.

Followers

Fulcanelli's main disciple, then, was Eugène Canseliet, whose main work *Le Symbolisme alchimique de la galette des rois* deals with the alchemical significance of the cake baked in France for Twelfth Night. The finder of the *galette* (or 'bean', hidden in the cake, and here standing for prime matter) is, according to custom, crowned (ie will become an adept of the royal art). Other 20th century writers influenced by Fulcanelli included René Alleau, author of the remarkable *Aspects traditionnels de l'alchimie*, and Armand Barbault, author of *L'Or du Millième matin*, who claimed to have discovered 'vegetable gold'.

Geber

(alias of Jabir ibn Hayyan)

c.721–c.815

Alchemy from first principles

Geber was an adept of non-experimental alchemy. For him, the order of the universe was expressed by numbers.

The son of a druggist, Geber (to use the Latinized form of his Arabic name) spent his youth in study of the Koran, mathematics and alchemy. Later he became the court alchemist of Harun al-Rashid and a friend of Ja'far al-Sadiq (700–65) the sixth Shi'ite imam.

Four elements and four natures

Geber took Aristotle's four elements (fire, water, earth and air) but dealt with them differently, by postulating four qualities or 'natures' of matter: heat, cold, dryness and moisture. The union of these natures with a substance produced the four elements in the following way:

fire = (heat + dryness + substance)
water = (cold + moisture + substance)
air = (heat + moisture + substance)
earth = (cold + dryness + substance)

The elixir

A beautiful slave-girl, one of the concubines of an important man, was attacked by a mysterious illness. Geber was called in and saved her. He related, 'I had an elixir with me and prepared a potion with two grains of it in three ounces of vinegar and honey. Half an hour later, the patient was in her usual good health and Yahya threw himself at my feet in gratitude. 'Do not do that, brother,' I said to him. He then questioned me about my elixir and I gave him what I had left of it, with instructions for its use.'

Thus, lead is cold and dry on the outside and warm and moist inside; this is the opposite of gold, which is warm and moist on the outside, and cold and dry inside.

A magic square

Geber believed that metals were formed in the bowels of the earth, under the influence of the planets, and were composed of sulphur and mercury. This theory was to become extremely influential in alchemical thought, and led to the phlogiston theory put forward by Georg Stahl in the 18th century.

Unlike Roger Bacon, though, Geber was convinced that empiricism could only lead to failure. In his 'Book of Balances', he explained that a balance is an equilibrium between natures. He sought to draw up for alchemy something like Mendeleyev's chemical periodic table. The world seemed to him to be dominated by the number 17; he believed that metals had 17 'powers' and he also pointed out that the numbers adding up to 17 (1, 3, 5 and 8) are found in the magic square:

4	9	2
3	5	7
8	1	6

The total sum of the square is 45; however, a gnomonic analysis of the square reveals the numbers 1, 3, 5, 8 in the lower square and the sum of the numbers of the gnomon (or numbers remaining when this square is removed) is 28 (4+9+2+7+6). The Sufis often referred to this magic square.

Geber was more than a philosopher, though. He left a considerable body of written work, translated by Gerard of Cremona, among others, in the 12th century.

Gichtel, Johann Georg

fl. c.1670

Can one marry a spirit?

Some things are classed as esoteric simply because we do not know what else to do with them.

Sexuality is sometimes involved in the quest for the occult (see **Tantrism**). Sometimes it is the denial, or suppression, of sexuality that is preached — often for the strangest reasons. One of the quirkiest of the non-problems which have exercised the human mind is whether or not it is possible to sleep with a succubus or an incubus, and whether children can be born of such a union.

A marriage with Sophia

It was probably a legacy of the most extreme intolerance of the Middle Ages that led the Abbé Montfaucon de Villars to suggest in his writings that his readers should renounce all knowledge of the flesh and save themselves for 'invisible mistresses'.

The same theory, in a slightly different guise, occurs in the works of Johann Georg Gichtel, a German publisher of esoteric texts. He claimed to be in love with Sophia (see **Sophia**) and forswore the company of all other women. Before we mock, we should recall Dante's Beatrice, Kierkegaard's Regine and Kafka's Milena. Gichtel was rewarded for his devotion: Sophia appeared to him on Christmas Day 1673 and, dazzling and heavenly, she 'consummated their marriage' in 'unimaginable delight'. Gichtel lived happily with her; she inspired him and encouraged him to publish the work of Böhme. He spoke to her as familiarly as to anyone else: 'Sophia had her own speech, which could not be heard in the air and was unlike any human speech, but he understood it as well as his native language.' Gichtel soon had followers and one of them, a scientist called Raadt, fell in love with Sophia, too. His wife even helped him to 'circumcise himself spiritually' so as to be worthy of Sophia. The group founded the 'Society of the Thirty', comprising those 'faithful in love'. Eventually the time came for Geichtel to choose a disciple; he selected a Frankfurt merchant, to whom he entrusted his Sophia, and who went on to have many spiritual children by her.

Irregular union

A doctor of law wrote in 1849, 'A child can sometimes be born from the union of a woman and an incubus, or devil. The real father is not the devil, though, but the man whose semen he stole.' There were strange ideas in this period; sexology had not been invented, and sex belonged in the domain of law rather than medicine, as the main concern was to 'normalize' it.

Guaïta, Stanislas de

1861–97

Was he really a black magician?

Was he a failed poet who blundered into magic, or did he really know something? The debate continues

A friend of Maurice Barrès, Guaïta was a poet whose major influence was Baudelaire. In 1886, he published *Au seuil du mystère* (On the Threshold of Mystery) which achieved considerable success and brought him many followers. A year later, he founded the Rosicrucian Cabalistic order along with Péladan, Papus and Julien Lejay, inventor of 'analogical sociology'. However, Guaïta turned aside from secular life in 1884 to 'explore the abyss of life'. He ended his days living as a recluse in a Parisian basement, venturing out only to buy rare books. Guaïta's secretary, Oswald Wirth, describing his library, said that only a select few were 'allowed into the Holy of Holies', his words reflecting the pompous, pedantic style adopted by certain intellectuals of the period, and still sometimes cultivated in esoteric circles today.

Maurice Barrès wrote of Guaïta:
'What a noble companion, dazzling in his loyalty and imaginative gifts.'

Oswald Wirth, Guaïta's secretary, left an interesting work on tarot cards, *le Tarot des imagiers du Moyen Âge*. He was also a distinguished freemason and spoke out against over-politicization (in the profane sense of the word) in the movement.

'Satan's Temple'

Guaïta had a reputation as a black magician. His main work, *Essais de science maudite*, was divided into four parts: *Au seuil du mystère* (On the Threshold of Mystery); *Le Temple de Satan* (Satan's Temple); *La Clef de la magie noire* (The Key to Black Magic); and *Le Problème du mal* (The Problem of Evil). In the second of these, he discusses the aims and practice of black magic in the service of Satan. The third describes Satanic forces and reads like a medieval book of spells. The last part is unfinished and might well have turned out to be the most interesting of all. In it, Guaïta shows himself to be Gnostic although, unlike Baudelaire, a Gnostic by his subject matter.

Birth of a current
'Alongside the classic figures of positivism, the Rosicrucians created the classic figures of the Cabala such as Eliphas Lévi, Wronski and Fabre d'Olivet, and also studied the works of true theosophists such as Jakob Böhme, Swedenborg, Martines de Pasqually and Saint-Martin, the only ones the Theosophical Society recognized as worthy of the name . . . Soon they attracted many followers already well-versed in the profane arts and sciences: engineers, doctors, teachers and writers . . . Thanks to this Rosicrucian order, a true intellectual aristocracy arose and quickly spread its influence.'

Guénon, René

1886–1951

The Marx of esoterism

René Guénon has done more than any other person to link culture with tradition in present times.

René Guénon began by studying for a degree in mathematics in Paris, but gave it up in 1906 to concentrate on spiritualism. He got to know Papus, then Synesius (or Fabre des Essarts), the self-styled 'patriarch of the Gnostic church', who helped him to start a magazine, *La Gnose* (Gnosis). In it Guénon set out the same ideas he developed in his books *L'Homme et son devenir selon le Vedanta* and *Le Symbolisme de la Croix* (Man and his Development in Hindu Philosophy and The Symbolism of the Cross). During this period he remained a freemason.

Guénon married in 1912 and, at about this time, began to be drawn to Sufism under the influence of the Swedish painter, Gustav Agueli, who had already converted to Islam. Islamic esoterism was the last link in Guénon's initiation. In 1917 he was a teacher of philosophy at Sétif in Algeria and his first books appeared in 1921, beginning with *Introduction générale aux doctrines hindoues* (A General Introduction to Hindu Doctrines), in which he explains the theory of cycles, according to which the present world is going through the Kali-Yuga and must be destroyed before it can be reborn. He followed this with *Le Théosophisme, histoire d'une pseudo-religion* (Theosophism, History of a Pseudo-Religion), *L'Erreur spirite* (The Spiritualist Error), *L'Ésotérisme de Dante* (Dante's Esoterism) and *Le Roi du monde* (The King of the World), which took up again the notion of the centre of the earth. In 1928, after the death of his wife, Guénon went to Cairo, where he converted to Islam in 1934, became a sheikh and married the daughter of a spiritual leader. He was by now confirmed in Sufism and continued his writing.

Offence
'Modern civilization, like all things, has its reason for being and, if it is really the end of a cycle, all we can say is that it must be, in its right time and its right place. But it must still be judged by the words of St Matthew, 'Come it must, but woe betide the man through whom the offence comes!'

A traditionalist
Guénon, as a traditionalist, was involved in extreme right-wing efforts to collect evidence. He wrote, 'History clearly shows that the failure to recognize a hierarchical order (based on the supremacy of the spiritual over the temporal) has the same consequences in all places at all times: social instability; confusion of duties; domination by the lower orders; and intellectual degeneration.'

Guénon's esoterism

His influence extends well beyond those interested in esoteric thought and has influenced modern French writers like Gide and Breton. His philosophy is in effect a summation of esoterism and it would not be inappropriate to call him the Karl Marx of occultism: Guénon identified the same aims in all kinds of esoterism and reduced them to a common tradition; there is the idea of an apocalypse in the Kali-Yuga and also in the class struggle; and the same sense of historical necessity dominates both philosophies. The difference is that Marx seeks justice and equality for all, whereas Guénon aims to restore 'elites'. A short resume cannot do justice to Guénon; it only serves to show that, like Marx, he should be read with care.

Gurdjieff, Georgi Ivanovich

1877–1949

A prophet or a crook?

His followers include the novelist Katherine Mansfield. There have been books and films about him — but what was his real contribution to knowledge?

Of Russian origin, Gurdjieff's biography contains many gaps which his followers have exploited to embroider a legend. A train-driver at the age of 20, Gurdjieff later travelled, to Cairo and Jerusalem, and also from town to town, searching out 'priests with secret knowledge'. He made his living by 'spinning yarns to tourists'. This, in fact, rather neatly sums up his life — a genuine thirst for knowledge, alloyed with charlatanism.

The removal of responsibility

Gurdjieff found a protector, which enabled him to take part in expeditions to discover 'fabulous cities' and to meet 'searchers after truth'. In 1900, during an expedition to India, he discovered a monastery, where the teaching of the 'Master of Justice' of the Essenes (the heretical Jewish sect of which Jesus may have been a member) had been preserved intact. In that monastery, he claimed to have learnt a neo-Pythagorean interpretation of the numbers of 'musical rhythm adapted to the functions of all parts of the body'. This was to be the essence of his teaching.

Up until 1913, Gurdjieff travelled in India, Tibet and Mongolia. He writes:

> I began to collect all the texts and oral information surviving in certain centres in Asia about that highly developed knowledge of ancient times known as 'Mekheness', a word which means the action of removing responsibility ... After two years of theoretical study, I began to work as a healer and applied the fruits of my studies to a great number of men.

From 1914, he began to give lectures, to practise his knowledge, and to amass a considerable fortune. The mathematician Ouspensky, whom he had met in Moscow several years earlier, become his follower and glorified him in his 'Fragments of Unknown Teaching'. In 1920, after the Russian Revolution, Gurdjieff fled to Tiflis, where the tsarists were holding out, re-establishing there his 'Institute for the Harmonic Development of Man', which was based on principles of asceticism and dance. In 1922, when he moved to Paris, he was the toast of the press. He bought a house in Fontainebleau-sur-Avon, setting up there a 'priory' where Katherine Mansfield went to die. He spent his last years staging ballets and enjoyed great social acclaim.

A sort of dervish

What exactly was Gurdjieff's teaching, then? According to Ouspensky, it involved 'rhythmic exercises to music, the dancing of the dervishes, mental training and breathing exercises ... However, he concentrated mainly on rhythm and on strange dances intended to prepare us to go on to dervish exercises.' He seems also to have relied on metapsychics to win inner freedom. Throughout, the master's strong character carried the enterprise along and he was even honest enough to write in his memoirs, *Meetings with Remarkable Men*, that he was not always to be held to the letter ...

Hermes Trismegistos

The mythical founder of occultism

Hermes is the central figure in occultism. He is also a mythical figure at the crossroads of many traditions.

Hermes has many forms. He is identified with the Egyptian god Thoth and also, by the ancient Greeks, with the messenger of Zeus. As Hermes Trismegistos, he is the patron of hermetism, to which he gave his name. It is Hermes who transmits light, paradoxically, by veiling it. However, this does not mean that he talks only in riddles; his world is simply the world of symbols. Hermetism, by definition, involves secrets, and secrets cannot be kept in the light or else they lose their secrecy. The invisible only becomes visible through concealment.

Solomon's seal, *two inverted triangles, refers to the teaching of Hermes by showing the world above and the world below.*

An elusive god

Quite literally mercurial, Hermes often eludes his observers. The epithet 'Trismegistos', which appears on the Rosetta Stone, comes from Greek and means 'thrice greatest'; it is therefore appropriate that Georges Dumézil should ascribe three functions to Hermes: to look after 'those who pray', 'those who go to war' and 'those who work'.

Numerous Gnostics have identified Hermes with Moses, Christ or St John. This is perhaps easier to understand if we remember that Hermes is the 'master of secrecy' and a mythological figure transmitting secret knowledge is at the heart of all religions.

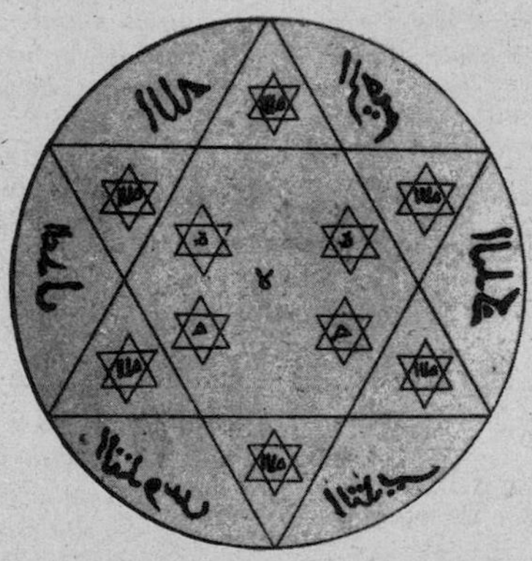

Hiram

The mythical figure of freemasonry

Hiram was killed to map out the way for his followers. This was no sacrifice: the hero 'died to his own death' to discover his 'true life'.

Who is Hiram? The Bible tells us that Solomon, having decided to build the Temple of Jerusalem, approached his ally, the king of Tyre. The latter sent cedars from Lebanon, along with other building materials and also an architect who had the same name as himself, Hiram. The architect, who may have possessed secret knowledge about building, and may have belonged to a secret society, organized the site, and arranged the builders according to their degree of skill. He designed and built the temple to Solomon's satisfaction.

Did Hiram really exist, though? There is no definite proof, but Judeo-Christian legend seized upon this figure, as it did with Solomon. The first operative masons, and later the speculative masons, perpetuated the legend by inventing the murder of Hiram by the three evil journeymen, embittered by not having been made masters.

The historical character of Hiram occurs in the Old Testament in 1st Kings and in Chronicles.

The legend of Hiram gave rise to a very ancient myth involving murder and the art of building. The legend, however, takes on a new meaning of liberation, thanks to the myth: man frees himself through work and art.

The three buried Hiram's body in a secret place and this episode has come to symbolize 'lost speech' for the masons.

Re-enacted at masonic initiation ceremonies, this legend has, at its heart, the theme of death and rebirth. The 'sacrifice' of Hiram has been likened to that of Christ; the glaring difference, however, is that Hiram does not die to take away man's sins but in order to 'open up the way' and encourage mankind to pursue the work he had begun in his own lifetime.

Original transcendence

So, if Hiram is Christ, he is the Christ of the Catharians, not that of the Church. It must be said that the legend of Hiram, within in a Christian setting, obviously takes on the aspect of a Christ-figure, but one influenced by Gnosticism. However, the legend has a decidedly esoteric side also: Hiram died because he refused to reveal the 'lost speech' contained within the secrets of building. This identification of Hiram with Christ far transcends the conventional Christian interpretation. The legend is a myth or, more precisely, a myth which gives human work its liberating dimension. By becoming Hiram, the initiate dies to his own 'death'; he is transformed by changing the world. Hiram is therefore a creator, in the lay sense of the word.

The Illuminati

A myth without foundation

The French Revolution was attributed to a plot by this society of Bavarian freethinkers. History has proved the accusation groundless.

In his *Soirées de Saint Pétersbourg* (St Petersburg Evenings), Joseph de Maistre, a Catholic traditionalist, spoke of those 'guilty men who dared to plan and even organize in Germany that dreadful, most criminal conspiracy to extinguish Christianity and royalty in Europe.' He was referring to the Bavarian Illuminati.

The Illuminati were a revolutionary initiatory group. Organized along the lines of freemasonry, they dreamed of the downfall of the monarchic and religious order and the creation of a pre-communist republic. The most noteworthy of their founders was Adam Weishaupt (1748–1830), a professor in the University of Ingolstadt. Widely persecuted, they were nonetheless an influence on the Carbonari, and Cagliostro and Mirabeau are said to have been members.

At the bottom of the plot

When the French Revolution broke out in 1789, many writers suggested it was the result of some secret plot. It was, therefore, but a short step to lay the blame for it at the door of the freemasons and the Illuminati. Numerous pamphlets, Abbé Lefranc's *Le Voile levé par les curieux ou le Secret de la Révolution révélé à l'aide de la franc-maçonnerie* (The Veil Lifted by the Curious, or The Secret of the Revolution Revealed by Way of Freemasonry) and the four volumes by Abbé Barruel, *Mémoires pour servir à l'histoire du jacobinisme* (Memoirs Towards a History of Jacobinism) only served to foster belief in this theory.

Abbé Barruel was then at least partly responsible for putting about the idea of a plot. All the usual pretexts for 'guilt' were found such as 'obscurity' (ie the masonic secret) and 'foreign influence' (the Illuminati were originally German). Nobody seems to have stopped to wonder how a small foreign plot could have been able to overthrow the king of France. As if a small foreign sect could have started a movement on the scale of the French Revolution, which was to shake the whole of Europe to its foundations! Clearly, history has given the lie to these claims.

The revolutionary dream

The freemasons had no direct influence on the French Revolution. Yet, because they symbolized the Enlightenment, they crystallized the dream from which modern democracy came. Historical analysis can no longer avoid the invisible dimension of the event and continue to be distorted by those such as Barruel and the modern extreme right.

Isaac the Blind

1165–1235

Can blindness lead to the light?

If we consider the case of this Cabalist, the answer is yes.

Isaac the Blind, the 'rich in light', was the central figure in southern French Cabalism; at the same period, a movement was paralleling it in northern France, led by Elhanan de Dampierre and Jacob de Corbeil. Isaac developed a highly structured system which was to form the basis of later forms of the Cabala.

En-soi, thought and word

According to his disciples, Isaac was the first to use the term 'Cabala' with respect to the esoteric tradition. His mysticism was contemplative and based on Neoplatonic Gnosis. Its three major concepts were: En Sof (or en-soi), thought and word. The En Sof is something beyond contemplation and quite inexpressible — a sort of God hidden from God Himself. The first emanation, or 'sefira', is nothingness in Jakob Böhme's sense of the word; 'It is the place of divine thought itself — which is nothingness in terms of human thought' (Roland Gotschel). Wisdom (or 'Hokhma') comes from nothingness and 'Mahshaba' is the symbol of the En Sof. In between Hokhma and Mahshaba is 'Haskel', ourselves.

The paths of wisdom
Isaac tells, among other things, of the 'marvellous paths of Hokhma'. He means 'intimate, subtle things which elude the meditation of all save those who draw the sap from them; this is *yeniga*, a different form of meditation from the way of knowledge'. Meditation continues progressively, 'from essences already formed to those not yet formed and, from an understanding of the thought surrounding them, it reaches the En Sof itself'.

Concerning speech, the third stage of manifestation, Isaac bases his reasoning here on a Hebrew word, *dabbar*, which means both 'word' and 'thing'. In this way, the sefirot are the words at the root of things, while Hokhma is the beginning of being, as well as the beginning of speech.

Meditation ultimately enables the Cabalist to attain the En Sof.

> Our master said, 'For mystics and those who meditate on God's name, it is essential to follow the words of Deuteronomy XIII, 4, which exhort us to hold fast to Him. It is a great principle of study and prayer to balance thought and faith as if thought clung to things above in order to unite the divine name with its letters and to embrace the ten sefirot within it, as flame licks around coals. All this must be expressed with the mouth, but connected in the heart to its true structure.'

The coincidence with Divinity — it is coincidence or adhesion, never fusion — is not acquired once and for all, but ceaselessly renewed in prayer, meditation and study. 'Study of the Law upholds the world,' says a Cabalistic proverb; coincidence with the En Sof is not a simple fact, but a cosmic event.

Jacques, Maître

The founding hero of the operative masons

The details of his fictitious life story are obviously symbolic. Born in Gaul, he worked on Solomon's temple and was murdered.

A symbolic character, Maître Jacques is one of the three patrons of the medieval operative masons' guild. He travelled to Jerusalem at the age of 36 and worked on Solomon's temple, where he was master of the stone-carvers, masons and joiners and was highly esteemed by both Solomon and Hiram. On Hiram's death, he left Judea along with another master, Father Soubise, but quarrelled with him later. He reached Marseilles with 13 journeymen and 40 disciples and continued his travels for a further three years. One day, he was attacked by the followers of Father Soubise who threw him into a marsh; he only survived by hiding among some rushes. After this close shave, he retired to Sainte-Baume, where Mary Magdalene is said to have lived as a hermit. However, there was to be no escape: Maître Jacques was betrayed by a man called Géron, who embraced him, upon which signal, his accomplices rushed forward to stab Maître Jacques. He died forgiving his enemies and was buried in a cave, which is visited by a guild pilgrimage every year on 22 July.

Two patrons
According to tradition, Maître Jacques, patron of the medieval operative masons' guild, was the colleague of Hiram, patron of freemasonry.

John (Saint)

The favourite disciple

According to tradition, Jesus gave St John the Evangelist a special, spoken, message.

There are two St Johns in the Christian tradition: St John the Baptist, with his feast-day on the summer solstice and St John the Evangelist with his on the winter solstice.

In the beginning was the Word and the Word was with God and the Word was God ... And the light shineth in the darkness, and the darkness comprehended it not.' (John I, 1–5)

The esoteric tradition maintains that this corresponds to the Roman double-headed god, Janus. The same esoteric tradition insists that there should always be a church dedicated to St John beside one dedicated to St Peter.

St John, author of the 'Gospel of Love', is the favourite gospel-writer of the Gnostics and the patron of many secret societies. He is traditionally supposed to have received special instruction (orally, and therefore secretly) from Christ himself. This knowledge was, according to esoterism, later transmitted to an invisible church and is therefore unknown to official Christianity, seen merely as a popular manifestation of the faith.

Jollivet-Castelot, François

b.1868

Alchemy as 'hyper chemistry'

Jollivet-Castelot was the 'renewer' of alchemy; a positivist in philosophy and a socialist in politics, he was the spiritual guide of Strindberg.

Born in Douai in northern France, and a chemist by profession, François Jollivet-Castelot was the confidant of Albert Poisson who wrote *Théorie et symboles de l'alchimie* (1891). We know about his life through his autobiography, *Le Destin ou les Fils d'Hermès* (Destiny or the Sons of Hermes), published in 1920, and through the work of his follower, Aimé Porte du Trait des Âges.

The doctrine of hylozoism

Jollivet-Castelot's first book, *L'Ame et la vie de la matière* (The Soul and Life of Matter, 1893), gave alchemy, which was at the time rather neglected, a new lease of life. The work's thesis was that the unity and dynamism of the universe correspond to an indivisible union of force and matter. Jollivet-Castelot then began to study astronomy in order to determine 'the influence of zodiacal light' on the cosmos. His aim was to found a new science lying half-way between chemistry and metaphysics, which he called 'hyperchemistry'. To his theory he gave the name 'hylozoism', a word he coined from the Greek words *hȳlē* and *zōē*, meaning 'matter' and 'life' to describe the indivisible nature of soul and matter.

In his philosophy, alchemy, which demonstrated the transmutation of spirit into matter and vice versa, provided irrefutable evidence; it exemplified the continuum he postulated. Jollivet-Castelot devoted himself to this research, founded a society and started a magazine. His book, *Comment on devient alchimiste* (How to Become an Alchemist, 1897), refers to the whole range of occult disciplines — astrology, Cabala, tarot — which he felt had to be combined. He also gave practical advice — on the purchase of an electric oven, Bunsen burner, blow-pipe, etc — as well as moral advice.

Jollivet-Castelot wanted to rescue alchemy from its dead past, and set it alongside the most up-to-date scientific discoveries. He was one of those who believed alchemy was the forerunner of modern chemistry; furthermore, he was convinced that the alchemy of his time foreshadowed future scientific developments. 'One day, the science of minerals will be seen to offer syntheses and series analogous to those of present-day organic chemistry. The formation, derivation and evolution of metals and metalloids will be studied, perhaps on the basis of ethereal whirlwinds and the polymeric condensation of hydrogen.'

From alchemy to socialism

Jollivet-Castelot was not interested only in alchemy. He was also active in the working-class movement and was a member of the Socialist Party; seeking to create a synthesis of his own idealism and the nascent Leninism, he founded the 'Non-Materialist Communist Union'. He explained this in *La Loi de l'histoire* (The Law of History, 1933): 'An alchemist must be a hylozoist; he must treat matter as living, respect it therefore and manipulate it in the awareness of its intellectual potential. He must see in it a part of Being, multiplied, fragmented, divided and suffering, but tending through endless evolution towards reconstitution in the Unity of substance.'

Julevno

(alias of Jules Eveno)

1845–1915

The renewal of astrology

Julevno is the best example of the astrologers who sought to incorporate the latest astronomical discoveries into their art.

As a teacher and later a librarian, Julevno lived an obscure life; he is known only in connection with late 19th century occultism. His main works, which were influential on contemporary astrology, were the *Traité d'astrologie pratique* (Treaty on Practical Astrology) and *Clef des directions* (Key to Directions).

The value of astrology

According to Voltaire, astrology is a 'universal extravagance infecting the human spirit' (*Dictionnaire philosophique*). This is surely shown by the fact that the signs of the zodiac and constellations no longer correspond as they did two millennia ago, although astrology ignores this and continues as though they do. It might be argued that the signs are only symbolic — but, if so, should some further explanation not be given? However, despite such criticism, astrology has not died out; indeed, it even revived in the latter part of the 19th century. Researchers like Julevno helped in this while others, like Ely Star, author of *Les Mystères de l'horoscope* (1880), and Selva, author of *Traité théorique et pratique d'astrologie généthliaque* (1900), tried to adapt astrology in the firm belief that true astrology had to link up with astronomy. In 1846, Le Verrier showed that Neptune orbits the zodiac in 160 years. The 'young astrologers' took account of this. Like Charles Hartfield, some believed Neptune had a malign influence and that, in conjunction with Saturn, it had led to the Crimean War. Others believed it had a beneficial influence. Julevno, an authority in this field, was on the side of the pessimists.

Fictitious planets?

Lilith, the 'black moon', may well be a fiction. It has, after all, only been seen by a few observers and that was in 1618 and 1700! Julevno himself announced the existence of two fictitious planets, Proserpine and Vulcan, which were, he said 'still to be discovered'. By reinforcing Venus, Proserpine represented sexual freedom; by reinforcing Mercury, Vulcan stood for social change. Perhaps these phenomena are best explained as astrological 'working fictions'.

Lilith

In his *Astrologie lunaire*, Alexandre Volguine, the founder of the *Cahiers astrologiques*, studied the influence of Lilith, the 'black moon', second satellite of the Earth. Certain astrologers put the occurrence of the First World War down to its influence.

Proserpine and Vulcan

In his *Des dialogues et du Verbe* (Of Dialogues and the Word, 1978), Jean Carteret established a cross with Proserpine and Vulcan. He wrote, 'I have worked out a cross with all the extrovert planets above the horizon and all the introvert planets below it, all the hard planets to the left and all the gentle ones to the right; thus it is a complete plan.'

Khalid

(alias of Khalid ibn Yazid)

c.660–c.704

The first Arab alchemist

Prince Khalid was probably the first Arab alchemist — he is certainly the first of whom we know for certain.

Prince Khalid was a historical character but it is uncertain whether he reigned. Legend tells that he refused to do so: political manoeuvring bored him and the crimes of power horrified him. He left the court to devote his life to study and Morienus, the pupil of the Alexandrian alchemist Stephanos, initiated him in the royal art.

Biography of an initiate

The initiation proceeded in the following way. Khalid found himself surrounded by charlatans masquerading as alchemists but, nonetheless, he persevered. Morienus, then living as a hermit in Jerusalem, came to see him and showed him how transmutation worked. Khalid was fired with enthusiasm, but furious with the charlatans, whom he had put to death. Morienus, shocked by this barbarism, fled; Khalid sought him everywhere and at last a servant, Ghalib, found him. Morienus agreed to reveal the secret of transmutation to Khalid on condition that he mended his vengeful ways.

The story is rather like that of Hiram; we recognize the same themes — execution, disappearance of the master, search and rediscovery. Khalid's very biography is like an initiation process; like Nicolas Flamel's life, it symbolizes the quest of alchemy. The legend of Khalid found its way to Europe in the *Composition of Alchemy* by Robert of Chester, who was persuaded to translate the Koran by Peter the Venerable in 1141 and had considerable influence on thinking in Christian Europe.

Khalid was also a prolific poet. Ibn al-Nadim mentions the poems by him found in 'The Book of Amulets', 'The Great Book of the Scroll', 'The Lesser Book of the Scroll' and 'The Book of the Testament on Art'. Hajji Khalfa (1599–1658), the biographer of Khalid, mentions the 'Book of Wisdom' as his major work and tells us that it contained 2315 verses.

Transmission

Alchemy was passed on to Islam via Alexandria. The academy at Jundi-Shapur in South-West Persia, which flourished in the time of Harun al-Rashid, was also a great influence in this respect. Christian intellectuals then began to study alchemy again through translations, notably by Robert of Chester, Adelard of Bath and, especially, Gerard of Cremona (1114–87). Besides translating the works of Ptolemy and Avicenna, it was he who probably adapted those of Geber in the 'Book of the 70'.

The first Arab alchemists paid **particular respect** to Hermes, Agathodemon, Plato, Zosimus, Democritus, Heraclitus, Ostanes, Stephanus, Apollonius, Alexander, Archelaus and Maria the Jew.

Lavater, Caspar

1741–1801

The face reveals the character

Lavater reinstated the old skill of physiognomy, a part of hermetism, and allowed modern science to benefit from it.

Lavater was born in Zurich and worked as a minister and hymn-writer before writing *De la physiognomonique* in 1772. He claimed that there was always a perfect correspondence between outward appearance and inward character; this was especially true of the lips. For example, firm lips, or soft, rapidly-moving lips betrayed a similar temperament. In the same way, 'a mouth twice the width of the eye is the mouth of a fool' and 'a deeply incised chin shows a firm, decisive man of sound judgment', and so on.

Followers

After Lavater, physiognomists tried to establish a scientific basis for their studies. In 1842, K.H. Baumgartner of the University of Freiburg showed how nervous diseases could be diagnosed by physiognomy. Biotypology was invented in 1925 by Nicolas Pende, but came dangerously close to racialism. 'Morphophysiology' was subsequently developed in 1948 to study the correlation between human form and physiological or psychological function, independently of racial classification.

Quotations

'[Physiognomy] judges the interior from the exterior.'

Ah! If a man knew and felt the dignity of his mouth, he would utter only godly words.'

The physiognomists

Hippocrates and Aristotle were physiognomists before their time. They distinguished four principles: apparent conformity (ie where appearance indicates temperament); analogy with animals (ie a man with a face like a fox will be sly); sexual differentiation (ie a man who looks feminine will lack virility); and climate. Albert the Great also developed these elements.

Gian Battista Della Porta, the Neapolitan physician, furthered the science by publishing his *De Humana Physionomia* in 1586. He was an astrologer, a magician (his 'Natural Magic' ran to 15 volumes) and a specialist in optics, foreseeing the telescope before Galileo. It was Della Porta who first included the genitalia in such studies. Long before Freud's friend Fliess, he noticed the correspondence between the nose and the penis.

After Della Porta, the most remarkable physiognomist was Marin Cureau de La Chambre, who published his *Art de connaître les hommes* in 1659. As a Cartesian, humanist and an advocate of sexual equality, he recognized that what was a fault in one man might be a virtue in another.

Levi, Eliphas

(alias of Alphonse Louis Constant)

1810–75

The last magician

Admired by André Breton and the surrealists for his openness to surrealism, his research into magic delighted them also.

Alphonse Louis Constant was born in Paris. After studying at the seminary at Saint-Nicolas-du-Chardonnet, he went on to the higher seminary of St Suplice at Issy where his interest in magic was first awakened by the Abbé. After becoming a deacon, he said that 'God had rewarded his sincere zeal by sending him what the uncharitable and sanctimonious called 'temptation' but he himself called 'initiation to life''. In fact, he had fallen passionately in love with Adèle Allenbach, a young girl who was in his class for catechism and whom he saw as the embodiment of the Virgin.

'**Occult philosophy** seems to have been the nurse or grandmother of all religions, the secret lever of all intellectual forces, the key to all divine obscurity and the absolute queen of society throughout the ages when it was the exclusive preserve of kings and priests.'

'There is **true and false science**, divine magic and devilish, or dark, magic; we are to reveal one and unmask the other. We must distinguish between the magician and the sorcerer, between the adept and the charlatan. The magician is the high priest of nature, the sorcerer is nature's profaner.'

A defrocked priest

Constant became a priest but resigned in 1836 as he was unable to renounce this passion. His mother committed suicide and he fell into deep moral and physical depression. It was then that he met Flora Tristan, a leading figure in the working-class and feminist movements. They enjoyed a stormy relationship, and it was she who introduced him to the literary circle, which included Balzac and Alphonse Esquiros, who had just published *Le Mage*, a book which greatly impressed Constant. After a while, he rediscovered his vocation and entered the Abbey of Solesmes in 1839, only to quarrel with the superior and leave after a year. It was in Solesmes that he discovered George Sand's *Spiridon* and he had the leisure to study the ancient Gnostics, the Fathers of the early Church, the books of Cassian and other ascetics, the writings of various mystics and, especially, the hitherto unknown yet remarkable books of Madame de Guyon. He also wrote *La Bible de la liberté* while at Solesmes.

Back in Paris in 1840, Constant lived in poverty, as a boarding student of the Oratorian fathers in Juilly. His *Bible de la liberté* went on sale but was confiscated immediately, for its sympathy with the theories of the Christian Socialist Lamennais. This did not, however, stop him going on to publish *Doctrines religieuses et sociales* and *Assomption de la femme*, both in 1841. He was, as a result, taken to court for 'attacking propriety and public and religious morality', sent to prison and ordered to pay a large fine far beyond his means. He spent eleven months in the prison at Sainte-Pélagie, where he discovered the works of Swedenborg in the library. On his release, he published *La Mère de Dieu*, in which divine love came rather too close to ordinary physical love for the church authorities. He also wrote songs which impressed the poet Béranger and, finally, abandoned the priesthood.

From mysticism to the barricades

Paul Chacornac tells us that, around 1845, Constant was ardently studying all the books and articles which aimed to transform society and abolish social inequality. He also 'kept company with republicans and spoke in political clubs'. It was about this time that he met Pierre Leroux and also fell in love with Noémie Cadiot, then 18 years old, who later became known as a sculptor under the name of Claude Vignon.

Constant was now working for the opposition press. A pamphlet, *La Voix de la famine*, earned him another year in prison and, in the 1848 revolution, as a fiery republican speaker, he came close to being shot. He seems to have 'calmed down' after this. His next great influence was Hoëné Wronski, who showed him that the Cabala is the 'algebra of the faith'. He then published *Dogme et rituel de haute magie* under the pseudonym Eliphas Lévi, the Hebrew translation of his two Christian names. According to his biographer, 'the invisible had just chosen him as one to fit into the great magic chain stretching from Hermes and Enoch to the present day'.

'There is a **tremendous secret** which has already turned the world upside down, as shown by the religious traditions of Egypt, which were symbolically resumed by Moses in the early chapters of Genesis.'

'There is a tremendous secret'

With his openness to 'another reality', as well as to social revolution, Eliphas Lévi obviously caught the imagination of the surrealists. Through his conflict with the Church, revolt and repentance, he resembles another friend of the poet André Breton, the defrocked priest Gegenbach. Briefly, Lévi personifies the surrealist quest by means of magic, by belief in talismans magic spells and so on. His was surrealism writ large, losing itself in myth, forgetting both literary and artistic creation.

Lévi believed in 'an occult science with true power, able to work miracles and compete with the miracles of authorized religion'. In a masterly synthesis, he set out all of hermetism (astrology, Cabala, and so on) and turned it into a weapon for freedom, capable of explaining both the meta-political world and the meta-poetical world. At the same time, rather naively, he was drawn towards operational magic as a source of practical exercises which could 'give power' to those who studied them. His ritual involved spells, exorcisms and clairvoyance, but — and herein lies his originality — it always relied on explicit symbols. In this way, the sign of the cross, or prayer, became means of rousing the psyche of the experimenter and acting, mysteriously, on matter.

'**Magic** is the traditional science of the secrets of nature, which comes to us from the magicians. Through it, the adept is invested with a sort of relative omnipotence and can act in a superhuman fashion.'

'**The soul** breathes in and out, just like the body. It breathes in happiness and breathes out the ideas resulting from its intimate feelings.'

Luria Ashkenazi, Isaac

1534–72

God suffers to create the world

Isaac Luria seems to be telling us that evil is the suffering God inflicts upon Himself so that freedom can be born.

Isaac Luria Ashkenazi (the 'German') was born in Jerusalem, initiated in Egypt, and died in Safed. The pupil of Moses Cordover and David ben Ziman, he founded a Cabalistic research circle and handed his teaching down orally.

The broken vases

In the beginning, according to Luria, there was the *Zimzum* (see **The Cabala**). Indeed how else can the world exist if the En Sof (or cosmic en-soi) fills all time and all space? It is only possible by the *Zimzum*, this self-concentration of the Divine Essence, whereby God drew into himself — towards and into his very centre — so that the world could realize its virtuality.

The *Zimzum* is a manifestation of God's rigour which, until then, was submerged in the ocean of His pity. By setting a limit to Himself, God thus allowed a return of divinity in the form of a ray of light. In the course of this process, the first three emanations, or sefirot, gather the light but it wells up so strongly in the six others that they shatter like vases. This breaking (the *Shebirat Kelim*) causes most of the light to return towards its source, while some sparks attached to the broken vases sink into the abyss.

The forces of Evil draw their strength from these *kelippot* ('husks'); this is an original catastrophe but the Evil from which it springs is itself part of God's plan, for it allows freedom of choice to exist in the world. The themes of Gnostic philosophy are all to be found here — the descent of the aeon into matter, the 'wounding' of God in the Creation, and so on.

Regeneration

The aeon (or the power emanating from God), in this way, descends and becomes matter, but rises again to join the Spirit. After the breaking of vases there is the *Tiqqun*, or 'restoration of the broken world'. There is the important nuance, however, that the impetus to rise again comes from below. God's name is thus sanctified, and man has won his creative freedom; Evil has become part of Creation.

The transmigration of souls
Luria developed the theory of the transmigration of souls (*Gilgul*) after the manner of Adam, who contained all souls. The positive side of the theory is that the soul is not exiled, or cast out, but is able to free and better itself through reincarnation within a living person.

Redemption
The *Tiqqun* has a parallel in human history. The 'task' of Israel in the world is to 'gather what has been scattered' and the Messiah will come to crown this process. The redemption of Israel is not an act of chauvinism: Luria believes that it coincides with the redemption of the world. The exile of Israel symbolizes the exile of all beings, and even of a part of God in the *Zimzum*.

'**Lurian philosophy** is the most extraordinary attempt to bridge the gap between the En Sof and a personal God.' Roland Goetschel, *La Kabbale*

Maïer, Michael

1569–1622

Mythology becomes alchemy

Is alchemy a form of mythology? Michael Maïer replies with a definite yes.

Michael Maïer was a doctor of both medicine and philosophy. Occultism, to him, seemed to provide the way to give coherence to his activities. He was invited to Prague by Rudolf II in 1608 but, on the death of his protector in 1612, came to England where he joined Robert Fludd.

An alchemistic reading of mythology

His first work, *The Secret of Secrets*, is of the greatest importance in the history of both alchemy and occultism. Later adapted by Dom Pernety (1716–96), the founder of the Illuminati in Avignon, and appearing under the title *Egyptian and Greek Fables Unveiled*, it interpreted mythology through the symbols of alchemy. This reading revealed the 'prime matter' (or the psychic dimension) for the alchemist to work on; to paraphrase Jung, it brought mythology to the human level and made it understandable.

Maïer's best-known work is *Atalanta Fugitiva* (1617) in which he describes the art of alchemy with 50 fine engravings, poems and commentaries. He believes that alchemy lies on the borderline between poetry and philosophy. Referring to the myth from which he derived the title of his work, he reminds us that in the race in the myth, Hippomenes beat Atalanta by throwing golden apples in front of her, which she stopped to pick up. This is an alchemistic allegory which, Maïer argued, must be seen as a reference to the 'coagulation of mercuric water ... The virgin is purely chemical; she is philosophical mercury, retained and fixed by the sulphur of gold.'

However, the allusion to the myth is only the prologue to the work. Alchemists often used this device, and, in no way, does it mean that they were confused. It is simply a means of setting forth the 'personal equation' of the author. Long before modern physics, the alchemists realised that the experimenter is an active part of his own experiment. He is aware that he is at work on his own subjectivity, or on his own being-in-the-world. It is the significance of his being-in-the-world that he seeks to grasp and that is, perhaps, the ultimate meaning of the alchemists' quest. In his prologue, therefore, the alchemist is simply stating the fundamental existential problem which inspires his endeavours.

The **'coagulation of mercuric water'** is the conjunction of knowledge of the subject matter and the methods of alchemy with one's own alchemistic quest.

A friend of the Rosicrucians

Michael Maïer spoke out on behalf of the Rosicrucians in 1617 in his *Silentium Post Clamorem* (The Silence after the Shouting). However, he does not seem to have been a member of the brotherhood.

Martines de Pasqually, Jacques

1724–74

A return to first principles

Martines de Pasqually founded the Elect of Cohen, which was affiliated to freemasonry. He called on men to rediscover the first principle which gave them life.

Martines de Pasqually played an essential role in mystical freemasonry. A Portuguese Jew who converted to Catholicism, we know that about 1750 he was travelling around France to publicize the 'Order of the Knight Masons, the Elect of Cohen' (*Cohen* is the Hebrew word for 'priest'). In 1767 he met Jean-Baptiste Willermoz and, in 1768, Louis Claude de Saint Martin, the 'unknown philosopher', became his secretary. When Pasqually left France in 1772, his system was flourishing (and is in fact carried on to this day in certain lodges). Martines de Pasqually died in Port-au-Prince, Haiti, where he had gone to claim an inheritance. He is said to have appeared to his wife (who was in Bordeaux) at the exact moment of his death, in order to bid her farewell.

The Thing

'At the first meetings, new disciples who have been invited to take part in the master's work will see the Thing accomplishing mysterious acts. They will leave the meeting fired with enthusiasm, yet terrified, like Saint-Martin, or drunk with pride and ambition, like the disciples of Paris. Apparitions have shown themselves and strange beings, different from earthly humans, have spoken.' Papus, *Martines de Pasqually*

How to become, once again, a 'creature of God'

The central idea here is that man, if he so wishes, can become God, or rather a 'creature of God' again, as he was before the Fall. Pasqually's cosmogony is built around the central figure of Christ, but against a background of esoterism and the Cabala. The aim of the initiate must be to return to the first principle, the creative principle which gave him birth. He does this by using magic to win over psychic powers (or 'spirits'). These operations are carried out in the presence of the 'angels'. Pasqually codified the procedures in which only the Elect of Cohen can succeed, after their training. This training comprises three stages: nourishment for the physical body; respiration for the astral body; and musical and psychic training for the spirit.

The three regular operations of the Elect of Cohen are: the 'daily invocation'; the 'three days' invocation' (monthly); and 'the work of the equinox' (twice yearly). In all these operations, the adept draws a circle, or several arcs of a circle, to protect himself, lights candles and repeats magic formulae. Those taking part must not wear anything metallic because steel drives away spiritual beings. The guiding principle is constancy: 'It is sometimes hard for those who desire something too fervently before the proper time; be constant and you will be rewarded.'

Mesmer, Franz Anton

1734–1815

Occultism anticipates psychoanalysis

Mesmer knew of conversion hysteria and the medical use of catharsis before Freud; he knew of the collective unconscious before Jung.

Mesmer was born near Lake Constance, at Iznang in Swabia. He first studied theology, then medicine, and presented his thesis, *De Inflexus Planetarium in Corpus Humanum* (The Influence of the Planets on the Human Body) in 1766. It postulated that man was subject to the regular effects of the 'tension' and 'relaxation' of the planets, which explained the female menstrual cycle and certain chronic illnesses.

Healing with magnetism

Shortly afterwards, Mesmer married a rich widow and they went to live in a luxurious house on the Danube where Mozart, Haydn, Gluck and others were invited to give concerts. Mesmer was, at this time, treating a young woman suffering from a 'convulsive illness' and, after applying magnets to her legs, he observed a marked improvement. He concluded — and this is his originality — that the magnet was only a catalyst, and that he himself, the doctor, was the agent of the cure. He deduced that the human body had properties similar to the poles of a magnet and that these can be changed, destroyed or reinforced.

The academics were sceptical but Mesmer undertook public healings. A young protégé of the Empress of Austria, a blind girl, recovered her sight thanks to him. (Psychoanalysts were later to attribute this to 'conversion hysteria'.) He went to Paris in 1778, where the scientific reception was just as cool, but the public reaction was wildly enthusiastic. Mesmer held group

Quotation

In a letter to a foreign colleague, Mesmer wrote, 'In the human body properties are manifested which are analogous to those of magnets; opposite poles can be seen, which can be communicated, changed, destroyed and reinforced. The phenomenon of inclination can even be observed.'

An artificial sixth sense

Mesmer's magnetic passes were intended to restore lost harmony. Perfect harmony in all our organs and their functions is health: illness is the loss of harmony. However, the passes first of all provoke a crisis, 'an attempt by nature to resist the illness'. For this reason, the crises must be induced: 'When nature is not strong enough to bring about the crisis, it can be helped by magnetism . . . The revolution which is thus produced is beneficial when the patient is filled with a feeling of well-being and relief, and especially if the crisis is followed by favourable evacuation.'

This is the principle of catharsis, rediscovered later by Freud and Bleule. Mesmer, though, was a doctor, not a faith-healer. He maintained that everybody possessed magnetism and only needed to learn how to express it — hence the use of magnets, basins, passes, etc. He called animal magnetism a sort of 'artificial sixth sense' in his hands.

Animal magnetism, *an important discovery of Mr Mesmer, a doctor from the Faculty of Vienna in Austria.' (Anonymous etching, National Library, Paris)*

healing sessions: patients learned how to become 'receptive' as they 'formed a chain', sitting in a circle around a basin full of magnetized water containing some iron filings, with knees, feet and thumbs touching. His scientific colleagues refused to attend such events.

Posthumous revenge

In 1785 Mesmer left France, denounced as an imposter by a learned commission. However he left behind him many followers, like the Marquis of Puységur, who discovered hypnosis and artificial sleepwalking, and Joseph Deleuze, who systematized the technique of magnetic passes in his *Histoire critique du magnétisme animal* (1813). Another disciple was Baron Jules du Potet, who carried out experiments in magnetism in front of doctors in Paris in 1820.

We should also mention Charles Lafontaine, the author of *L'Art de magnétiser* (1847), who seemed to believe he was the reincarnation of Simon the Magician, as he toured the highways and by-ways along with his medium, a prostitute. Henri Durville, author of *Traité du magnétisme* (1896), was also influenced by Mesmer and went on to found the School of Magnetism and Massage in Paris. It is also worth noting that Nicolas Bergasse integrated mesmerism into freemasonry during Mesmer's own lifetime; he set up the Lodge of Harmony and published *La Théorie du monde et des êtres organisés*, a book which resembles nothing so much as an opera score written in hieroglyphics!

Norton, Thomas

15th century

An unlucky alchemist

Once again, symbol is confused with reality.

Unfortunately, we know very little about Thomas Norton's life. What we do know, however, is that while still very young, he studied alchemy and corresponded with George Ripley, who initiated him in the royal art. At 28, Norton made the 'great red elixir', or philosopher's stone, subsequently stolen by a servant.

Getting over this misfortune, Norton once again set to work and produced an 'elixir of life'; again it was stolen, this time by the wife of the mason/architect, William Canynges, who went on to use it in the construction of the church of St-Mary-Redcliffe. The episode is significant insofar as it illustrates the relationship between alchemy and church-building (see **Fulcanelli**).

Putting it in writing

In 1477, Norton wrote his major work, which Ashmole published as part of his *Theatrum Chimicum*. He explained in the *Canon* that, although it was generally held that alchemy could only be taught orally (ie by initiation), he was, nonetheless, trying to pass it on by means of the written word. Alchemy enabled adepts to make gold and to raise themselves spiritually at one and the same time, provided the alchemist understood the meaning of the operations he carried out.

Norton writes that the alchemist cannot grow metals like vegetables (although some claimed this was possible); he can, however, transmute existing metals. He then goes on to describe the seven figures erected by Raymond Lulle in a town in Catalonia: Three of them, ladies dressed in luxurious garments, are made of good silver; the four others, which look like knights, are made of gold. The letters decorating the hems of their clothing make up the following sentences:

1. Once a horse shoe, said one lady, I am now made of as fine silver as you could wish.
2. Once iron in a mine, said another, I am now perfect, fine gold.
3. Formerly an old red copper saucepan, I am now silver, said the third lady.
4. Once copper formed in loathsome places, I am now, by the grace of God, made perfect gold, said the fourth.
5. The fifth said, Once perfect, fine silver, I am now perfect, excellent gold, the finest of all.
6. For two hundred years I was a lead pipe; now I appear to all as a silver of good alloy, said the sixth.
7. The seventh said, I am lead turned to gold by the art. But in truth my companions are nearer to it than I.

Symbolic bad luck

Norton compared himself to his predecessor in alchemy, Thomas Daulton, a man of great virtue and wisdom who also discovered the philosopher's stone and suffered a similar misfortune. Daulton was living quietly in an abbey when the court of Edward IV, including John Delves, came to see him. Delves told the King that Daulton had made 1000 pounds of gold in half a day. The alchemist was arrested but declared he had thrown the elixir he had used to the bottom of a lake and the King had him released. However, Daulton was later kidnapped and thrown into a dungeon by another courtier, Thomas Herbert; Daulton's secret was to die with him on the scaffold.

Nostradamus

(alias of Michel de Nostre-Dame)

1503–66

The *Centuries*

Nostradamus' work acts like a myth; those who believe, plunge into it and reveal themselves in it.

Nostradamus was born in St Rémy in Provence. He practised as a doctor before studying astrology and publishing his *Centuries*, a book of rhymed prophecies, in 1555. It was a great success; Henri II, Catherine de' Medici and François II consulted him, and he was appointed personal physician and adviser to Charles IX.

Nostradamus' work is in the form of a thousand questions and is supposed to foretell events up to the year 3797. The predictions are coded, in an early sort of backslang (eg 'Rapis' = Paris), or puns (eg Dort-léans = d'Orléans) etc. Nostradamus claimed that the *Centuries* came to him by divine, supernatural inspiration at night; he excused the verse by explaining that it was composed by natural instinct and with poetic fervour, rather than according to poetic rules.

St Malachi and others

Nostradamus had many precursors. In 1175, Geoffrey of Monmouth published the prophecies of Merlin, dating from around 465. These announced the coming of a great king who would reign over all the world, and mark the birth of the myth of the 'King of the World'.

Commenting on the Apocalypse in the 13th century, Joachim de Flore predicted the coming of the reign of the Spirit. A century later, a monk named Brother Liberatus discovered historical prophecies in his work, which he revealed in *Vaticinia Joachimi* (1303). However, the most famous of all predictions are those of St Malachi (1097–1148), who drew up a list of 111 popes, beginning with Celestine II, elected in 1143, and going right up to the Last Judgment. René Thibeau, the theologian, calculated, on this basis, that the world would end in 2012.

The use of prophecy

The *Centuries* have been the subject of many commentaries and have been exploited by numerous individuals as a means of justifying their (sometimes dubious) ends. In this way, the priest Torné-Chavigny, in *L'Histoire prédite et jugée par Nostradamus* (1860–62) used the *Centuries* for political purposes. This happened again when the French socialist government came to power in 1981, and Nostradamus was used to start rumours of impending catastrophe.

An example of interpretation

In 1938, Dr Fontbrune suggested that this quatrain of Nostradamus had foretold Hitler:

> Nine years that thin man will hold in peace
> Then he will fall into thirst so bloody
> For their peoples he will die without faith or law
> Killed by one much more mild and good-natured.

According to Dr Fontbrune, the third line obviously refers to Hitler. For confirmation, he directs us to the first line: Hitler must be the 'thin man' because he was a vegetarian!

Papus

(alias of Gérard Encausse)

1865–1916

The author of 260 popular works

Papus is said to have been able to perform faith-healing and to have restored occult medicine. He was a great popularizer and tireless organizer.

Gérard Encausse was born in Spain but his parents moved to Paris when he was a few years old. He began by studying medicine and became a hospital intern, but abandoned medicine to study occultism. He read the *Médecine nouvelle* of Louis Lucas, which described a 'life principle' governed by the *enormon*, a condensation of movement, which was defined as an 'organic spectre', analogous to the luminous spectre and stretching from its centre to its periphery. Encausse was so deeply affected by this that he decided to take up occult studies. He was initiated into martinism by Henri Delaage and chose the pseudonym 'Papus', the name of the genius of medicine in the *Nuctemeron* of Apollonius of Tyana.

A man of action

As Papus, he joined Stanislas de Guaïta and Péladan to found the Cabalistic Rosicrucian order. In 1889, he founded the Independent Group for Esoteric Studies with 350 members and, at the same time, set up the martinist lodges in Paris. The lodges launched a journal, *L'Initiation*, a monthly magazine, *L'Union occulte* and also a weekly called *Le Voile d'Isis*. The time seems to have been ripe for such preoccupations.

Papus submitted his thesis in 1894 and began to develop his philosophy of the anatomy (a concept which also attracted Goethe), and which was based on histological analogies between organs (eg the lungs and the kidneys). Three years later, he opened a school of hermetic sciences along with Jollivet-Castelot and Sédir. Tsar Nicholas II had heard of Papus and summoned him in 1905 for a spiritualist séance, at which he produced the spirit of Alexander III.

Papus was a doctor in the ambulance corps during the First World War when he died of tuberculosis. He left no less than 260 works and he is still remembered in esoteric circles. He wrote widely, on the Cabala, tarot cards, medicine, palmistry, and so on, and is also remembered as a tireless organizer, faith-healer and reformer of occult medicine.

Anatole France wrote, 'I wish they would create a chair in magic for Mr Papus.'

The spirit of the cells

'He [Papus] taught that the esoteric view of the human body is that it is made up of thousands of living cells, each with its individual conscience and spirit ... The task of the spirit of the medicine or the magnetic fluid is to 'talk' to these tiny beings, rouse their energy and show them where and how they can find their own cure.' Dr Philippe Encausse, *Papus, sa vie, son oeuvre*

Paracelsus

(alias of Theophrastus Bombastus von Hohenheim)

1493–1541

'The Christ of Medicine'

Paracelsus was alchemist, magician and philosopher, and is widely believed to have invented homeopathy. He styled himself 'The Christ of Medicine'.

Paracelsus was born in Einsieden in Switzerland. He studied alchemy and chemistry at Basle University and then made a study of metals, minerals and mining diseases in the Tirol. He then set out on his travels through Europe and the Middle East, where he increased his already considerable knowledge, particularly in medicine. In 1526, he returned to Basel as town physician and his friend Erasmus secured him a lectureship at the University; here he used German, not Latin, in his lectures, and was driven out in 1528. He eventually moved to Salzburg, where he died in 1541.

Body and spirit
'If the spirit suffers, the body suffers also.'
Paracelsus, *Traité des trois essences premières*

A global view

The medicine of Paracelsus was based on esoteric ideas; the fundamental principle was his law of similarity — like acted on like, and it acted in infinitesimal doses, not on the physical body but on the subtle body, ie 'the intersection of the organism and the universe'. Stripped of its metaphysical trappings, this philosophy of medicine is still of interest with respect to the formation of scientific thought.

But has Paracelsus anything practical to teach us? Unquestionably, yes. Despite his obsession with alchemy, it was Paracelsus who invented ether as an anaesthetic and laudanum as a tranquillizer, and who first described silicosis and traced goitre to minerals found in drinking water. He encouraged research, observation and experimentation, and revolutionized the medical methods of his day. He also improved both pharmacy and therapeutics and established the role of chemistry in medicine. In his claim that 'every part of the body contains the effective cause of its cure' he can even be said to have been the father of modern psychosomatics.

Union with the macrocosm
'That which comes from the heart of the macrocosm comforts the heart of man — gold, emerald, coral; that which comes from the liver of the macrocosm comforts the liver of man.'

Péladan, Joséphin

(properly Joseph)

1858–1918

The quest for an esoteric Christianity

Péladan tried to rediscover St John's esoteric teaching of Christianity.

Joséphin Péladan believed that the Catholic Church, even if it was unaware of the fact, was the repository of secret knowledge. According to Péladan — and this is a belief running throughout hermetism — popular religion is only the exoteric manifestation of an esoteric, initiatory philosophy. The school he belonged to made special reference to St John's Gospel, and allied magic with its spiritual quest.

It was Péladan's father who taught him the rudiments of hermetism; he continued his studies with Guaïta, Papus and the Rosicrucians. When the group and its journal, *L'Initiation*, were banned by the Catholic Church, Péladan immediately broke with it and founded the 'Catholic Rosicrucians', protesting his orthodoxy, but nevertheless reducing the importance of the Old Testament and refusing to believe in Hell.

A Catholic 'magician'

Péladan left a considerable body of work, notably *Comment on devient mage* (How to Become a Magician), *L'Occultisme catholique* (Catholic Occultism) and works on Rembrandt and Courbet. He was a figure of considerable influence around the turn of the century and inspired violent opposition as well as enthusiasm.

The 'Amphitheatre of the Dead Sciences', which appeared in *L'Occultisme catholique*, set out his position as a catholic 'magician':

1. Occultism is the plainest form mystery can adopt. The occult is abstract, without shape, independent of race, time, place and even of the personality of the person formulating it.
2. Religion is the most highly-prized state mystery can achieve. Religion is mystery in concrete form, adapted to one particular cycle, race, climate and personalized by its founder.
3. Symbolism is language manifesting the Word. From one civilization to another, the Word is identical but the symbols are not.
4. To understand Tradition, it must be translated into its present mode.
5. Before the time of Christianity, occult thought was kept locked away in the temple; priest and magician were one and the same person.
6. Since that time, priest and magician mistrust one another and each one guards jealously his half of the truth which was torn in two when their roles were separated . . .
10. The occult is the science of relationships par excellence and, in moral terms, the science of responsibilities. Magic is the practical form of the occult . . .
15. Analogy proceeds from known to unknown, from body to soul, from phenomenon to numen, from man to the world and from the world to God, from visible to invisible and from finite to infinite.

Intellectual charity

'Our order is a brotherhood of intellectual charity . . . which visits the sick who lack will-power and cures them of the giddiness of passivity, comforts the prisoners of material need and redeems the captives of prejudice.'

Peucer, Kaspar

fl. c. 1550

The reviewer of divination

Kaspar Peucer was no occultist but he is important in the history of divination because of the information contained in his books.

Throughout history, the Church has had to fight against soothsayers, astrologers and magicians. Divination was always particularly popular, both with the aristocracy and the ordinary people. At the time of the Reformation, a reassessment of the various methods of divination was called for, and it was to Kaspar Peucer, a doctor and a mathematician, that this task fell.

Divination and superstition

Peucer started off with two assumptions: firstly, the grain must be separated from the chaff (ie 'good' or 'useful' divination must be differentiated from the 'harmful' kind); and secondly, Christianity is compatible with 'good' divination. The book in which he sets out the distinctions between 'natural predictions' and 'superstitions', *Commentarius de Praecipiis Generibus Divinatonum* (1553), is encyclopaedic in its scope.

Peucer begins by casting doubt on many popular practices such as: the use of knucklebones or beans; pyromancy (in which some offering was thrown into a fire and predictions were based on the shape of the flames); and capnomancy, which 'considered the smoke of sacrifices, its twisting and turning, the way it sometimes rose straight up, or slanted, or folded back on itself, and whether the smoke had the correct smell or not, according to the flesh that was being burnt'. These methods, said Peucer, come from neither God nor nature. He praised instead the merits of astrology and acknowledged predictions based on experience, such as the means by which ploughmen foretell the weather.

It was Peucer's aim to bring some order to the mishmash of beliefs in fortune-telling. Physiognomy finds greatest favour with him, and he also approves of chiromancy, which he sees as a derivative of medical diagnostics. He had faith in divination based on meteorology and that based on the study of malformations or abnormal growths (teratology), believing that these were God's way of sending warnings to man. Peucer was even convinced that a man could turn into a werewolf, and a witch into a butterfly.

Peucer's work, ultimately, is not the work of an occultist, but rather a mine of information about the type of superstitions occultism is always encountering and with which it is sometimes confused.

Natural phenomena

Perhaps rain, snow and thunder foretell nothing special, but unusual events have a meaning, if only we can decipher them. Floods foretell war and revolution. Comets always tell of catastrophe: 'All men are agreed, of a certainty, that comets not only cause death and ruin by filling the air with their pestiferous exhalations . . . but also, after they have been seen, war, sedition, all manner of violence, cruelty, murder and confusion ensue.' If two suns are seen at the same time, this announces an alliance between two kings.

Pico della Mirandola, Giovanni

1463–94

The inventor of the Christian Cabala

A man of prodigious knowledge, Pico della Mirandola was accused of heresy. He influenced Renaissance thought nonetheless.

Giovanni Pico della Mirandola was a child prodigy and was already studying canon law in the University of Bologna at 14. At 23, he tried to run off with the wife of a cousin of Lorenzo de Medici. In the ensuing fight, in which about 20 men were killed, he was wounded and fled to Perugia. There he met a converted Jew, Raimondo Moncada, who taught him Hebrew and introduced him to the Cabala. In 1486 he published his *Conclusiones Philosophicae, Cabalisticae et Theologicae* in which he declared that the Cabala was the best way of understanding the mysteries of the Christian religion as well as of bridging the gap between the latter and the Greek philosophy of Plato and Pythagoras. His work is an a posteriori refutation of the accusations of heresy levelled against him, for which he had been condemned.

Pico della Mirandola associated with rabbis and took Savonarola's side against his critics. In *De Hominis Dignitate*, he inaugurated a Christian Cabala, distinguishing true magic from black magic, arguing that the true magician is the one who works in God's cause.

> '**Magic** is the highest and holiest form of philosphy.'

> '**Angels** only understand Hebrew.'

> **Positive mythology**
> Mythology must be approached positively and not in the minimizing way of the profane world. The world or the universe acts on a mythological stage, with Christ or any other figure assuming a cosmic and historic meaning which impregnates the psyche. In other words, the coming of Christ can leave nobody indifferent—not even those who deny him. The event is therefore, *nolens volens*, at work in the Jewish unconscious to reveal the foundation of Christianity.

The Incarnation: where two traditions meet

Pico della Mirandola argues that the Cabala throws light on many of the mysteries of Christianity including the teachings of the Incarnation, the Trinity, original sin and so on. Of course, the Cabala is the Jewish heresy, par excellence. The official Jewish faith, and the Talmud in particular, reject it utterly. Rabbis have never looked kindly upon Cabalists, viewing them in the same way as their Christian and Muslim counterparts did the alchemists.

The Cabala is a quest for the 'secret' of Judaism (ie its 'roots'). Its speculation, on occasions, can be wildly fanciful, but it always has meaning when related to the Jewish cultural and spiritual unconscious. Moreover, the Cabala is interested in the incarnation of the Word and poses questions, especially by way of the sefirotic tree, about how it can exist in the world. This links up quite naturally with the Christian Gnostic tradition, which also asks questions about the Incarnation. For Pico della Mirandola, both the Cabala and Christianity sang of God-become-man. From a hermetic point of view, this is seen slightly differently: the religious dimension of the figure of Christ is played down somewhat, and the mythological aspect is stressed.

Postel, Guillaume

1510–81

Ecumenism before its time

Guillaume Postel worked for universal agreement by stressing the point shared in common by the three religions of the Book, their esoterism.

Guillaume Postel was born at Dolerie near Avranches. He was a village school-master before going to the Collège Sainte-Barbe in Paris as a servant. He learnt Greek, Hebrew and Arabic in his free time, was noticed, and sent on a diplomatic mission to Suleyman the Magnificent in 1537. While there, he was given a book on the Cabala by the sultan's Jewish doctor. He had found his way.

Back in Paris, a year later, he published the first European translation from Arabic as well as a book claiming the derivation of all languages from Hebrew. He was appointed Professor of Mathematics and Oriental Languages at the Collège Royal in 1539, which brought him to public attention. François I considered him one of the greatest scholars of the time.

Joanna, the Redeemer

A few years later, we find a changed man; perhaps success had gone to his head. Postel had come to believe that he had been called to bring about universal peace by uniting the three religions of the Book (See his *De Orbis Terrae Concordia*, 1544). 'The first man born after the Flood was Gomer, son of Japheth, son of Noah, and he was founder of the Gaulish and Celtic people and their law' wrote Postel in his *Les Raisons de la monarchie*. He even travelled to Rome to try to win over Ignatius Loyola to his strange ideas, but was put in prison instead.

On his release, Postel translated a book of the Cabala, *Bahir*, then published in quick succession *La Dernière Naissance du médiateur* (dictated, he said, by the Holy Ghost) and, under a pseudonym, *La Clé des choses cachées depuis la création du monde*. In the latter he told of the four ages of humanity: the age of nature; the age of law; the age of grace; and, finally, the age of concord, when original sin would be expunged. To earn a living (he had resigned from the Collège Royal), he worked as an almoner at the San Giovanni hospital in Venice. Here he was the confessor of Joanna, an illiterate cook of about 50. He saw in her the 'sacred Mother of the world' and believed that she would save the *anima* (or dark part of the human soul) and arouse the *animus* (or its bright part). The *anima* had been compromised by Eve's sin and, like her, could not be redeemed by Christ; it could only be redeemed by Joanna, the female Messiah. (It should be noted here that the *Zohar* (or 'Book of Creation') speaks of two Messiahs.) The Inquisition subsequently declared Postel mad.

'The world was made for man'

When Joanna died in 1551, Postel was prostrate with grief. This was then followed by an ecstatic phase, in which he wrote 'The Venetian Virgin' in Joanna's memory, and by a period of *Gilgul*, the Cabalist term for the reincarnation of the soul of a dead person within a living person (see the Yiddish film *The Dibbuk*). Back in Paris in 1553, he published *La Doctrine du siècle doré* (The Golden Age). Postel dated this 'golden age', in which the world was made for man and not vice versa, from 1551, the year of Joanna's death, whereas Isaac Luria put its start later, in 1568.

Postel took up teaching again, in the College of the Lombards. An imposing figure, with a grey beard down to his waist, his lectures were so popular that many of his students were forced to stand in the courtyard if they wished to listen to him. However, the publication of his *Merveilleuses Victoires des femmes du Nouveau Monde* in 1553, in which he spoke of his *gilgul*, caused a scandal. He withdrew to a monastery in 1564, after retracting out of sheer weariness, and spent the last 17 years of his life in meditation.

Followers of Postel

Postel, like other great names, had his followers. There were, for example, Guy Le Fèvre De La Borderie, who published *La Galliade* in 1578, and Jacques Gaffarel (1601–81), the author of *Curiosités inouïes*. This book, which told of talismans and other charms, was outlawed by the Sorbonne in 1629. The Church also reacted, especially in the person of Marin Mersenne, a correspondent of Descartes.

Mersenne developed his criticisms in 1623, in *Questions sur la Genèse*; Gaffarel, a doctor of theology, answered in his *Abdita Divinae Cabalae Mysteria*, dedicated to Cardinal Richelieu. Gaffarel insisted that the Cabala was a mystical explanation of the Scriptures. The explanation was given to man before Christ's coming, and in Hebrew, because that was the language Adam spoke. In *Curiosités inouïes*, he explained the code of nature. This led him closer and closer towards magic and he began to believe in 'natural talismans', such as stones, animals and plants. The most interesting were those found in stones called *gamahés* (a word derived from *camaïeu* or 'cameo', he believed); this is also the name given to figured agate in France. When asked why other theologians had not managed to decode these signs, he pointed out that they did not know Hebrew.

Ptolemy

(alias of Claudius Ptolemaeus)

c.90–168

The founder of astrology

Ptolemy laid the foundations of astrology. His system remains valid today, despite its flagrant astronomical errors.

Very little is known about Ptolemy's life. It appears, however, that he was born in Greece, and we know that his main work was carried out in Alexandria in Egypt. This celebrated astronomer, geographer and mathematician held supreme sway over the minds of men of science right down to the 16th and 17th centuries.

Works

Ptolemy's main works are: the *Almagest*, his 'great compendium of astronomy'; the *Tetrabiblos Syntaxis*, which is combined with the *Karpos* or *Centiloquium*, and deals with astrology; and the *Geographia*, a form of almanac. He wrote, in addition, works on map-making, the musical scale and chronology.

The *Tetrabiblos* is perhaps the work of greatest interest to those exploring the occult. In this work, Ptolemy explains how to deduce the pattern of a person's life — his illnesses, successes and 'destiny' — from observations of the stars and planets. First of all, it is necessary to work out the planetary 'aspects' (ie their relative positions) within the subject's horoscope. There are six aspects: conjunction (when two planets are in the same area of the sky); sextile (when they are 60° apart); quartile (90°); trine (120°); opposition (180°); and antiscian (at equal distances from the equator on opposite sides). Aspects can be favourable or unfavourable; the conjunction can be either, depending on the case, but sextile and trine are always favourable.

The horoscope may be established, for example, by observing the configuration of the heavens at the moment of the subject's birth ('casting nativities'); another method is cathartic astrology, which can be very precise, although the period covered by the prediction is severely restricted. In the case of the former, a zodiacal circle is drawn where the positions of the planets make angles, the aspects conforming with the angles of the regular polygons which can be drawn within them. Calculations are then based upon both the date and time of birth, and the latitude of the place of birth; often tables are used as an aid.

The divination is then carried out by determining 'directions' and 'transits' in the horoscope. Directions represent the symbolic unfolding of the birth chart, and can indicate significant phases in the individual's life; transits occur when certain planets pass through significant parts of the horoscope.

Validity

As the first astrologers only worked with 22 fixed stars and seven planets, one might wonder how their calculations could be valid. Furthermore, Ptolemy's cosmology was based on the prevailing opinion that the Earth stood still and the Sun went around it. Most authors, including Papus, dismiss this objection by explaining that the system is symbolic. It remains, nonetheless, an irksome problem.

Pythagoras

c.592–c.510 BC

The mystique of numbers becomes great art

In his own lifetime, Pythagoras was considered a demi god. He was a mathematician and metaphysician of genius and one of the great figures of hermetism.

Pythagoras was born in Samos between 592 and 575 BC, in the same century therefore as Buddha, Zoroaster and Lao Tzu. By the fourth century BC, he was already classed as a demi god. His biographer, Iamblichus, called him the 'harmonic deity' half-way between gods and men. He was then named the 'northern Apollo with the golden thigh'.

Although his life is shrouded in myth and legend, it is almost certain that he took part in the 48th Olympiad as a young man, winning the olive branch for heavyweight boxing. He then set off on a long journey of apprenticeship, to Egypt (where he was initiated into the mysteries of geometry and formulated his famous theorem), Phoenicia and Chaldaea. He was passionately interested in all he learnt and was almost 50 when he returned to open a school of philosophy in Samos. He attracted numerous pupils, but his teaching displeased the tyrant Polycrates and he was forced to go into exile in Crotona, a Greek colony in Southern Italy.

The contemplation of numbers

At Crotona, he established an organization which emphasized moral asceticism and purification, the doctrine of the transmigration of souls and the kinship of all living things. It also prescribed certain rites and abstinences (the most famous of which was not to eat beans). Pythagoreanism was then first and foremost a way of life, rather than a philosophy. Heraclitus records that Pythagoras counted supreme happiness as the 'contemplation of the perfection of numbers': number as rhythm and perfection, a kind of mathematical approach to Gnosticism.

The organization was composed of three degrees of initiates: the 'wise' (or mathematicians): the 'politicians' (or the agents in the profane world); and the 'nomothetes' who came between the other two grades. The first stage of initiation took three years; five further years of study, together with proof of ability, were needed to reach the status of master. In the end, the society developed into a political force and, by the time of Pythagoras' death, one to be reckoned with.

In the middle of the fifth century BC, the movement was the victim of violent persecution and all those Pythagoreans who survived sought refuge abroad. However, in the first century BC it rose once again from the ashes.

Pythagoreanism had an important influence on Plato who owed it his 'harmonic philosophy' and reflections on

Aetius wrote that Pythagoras was the first to give the name 'cosmos' to the universe which surrounds us, because of the order that can be seen in it.

numbers. A century after Plato's death, Neo platonism and Neo pythagoreanism, mixed with Syrian and Egyptian thought, made Alexandria into the cultural capital of the world and a centre of Gnosticism. The influence of Pythagoras was felt throughout society, even among builders, for it was he who was reputed to have calculated the golden mean.

Cosmos, number and harmony

Pythagorean metaphysics is structured around the ideas of cosmos, number and harmony. Pythagoras seems to have been the first thinker to apply the idea of 'cosmos', ie order, to the universe. This order is expressed in the harmony in the world, in men and in the relationship between the two. However, the order remains hidden from those who wallow in the mud and clay from which the Creator made them. Souls, according to Pythagoreanism, undergo palingenesis, or successive reincarnation, until they are sufficiently pure to be admitted to heaven 'beyond the Milky Way'. A true understanding of the doctrine of universal harmony and of the analogy between microcosm and macrocosm was central to the philosophy and was the ultimate goal of the initiate's quest.

Porphyry wrote that much of what Pythagoras taught in mathematics had been learnt from the Egyptians, the Chaldaeans and the Phoenicians. Indeed, if the Egyptians had been fascinated by geometry since earliest times, the Phoenicians had specialized in numbers and arithmetic, and the Chaldaeans in astronomy. As for religious rites and other rules for living, this was apparently teaching Pythagoras had received from magi. However, whereas the Pythagoreans' views on religion are well-documented, their rules for living are far more obscure. Eudoxus of Cnidos, though, in the eighth volume of his *Revolution of the Earth*, tells us that they took their concern for purity and abstinence so far in matters of shedding blood and meeting others who shed blood, that they ate no animal flesh and even avoided the company of cooks and hunters.

Particular importance seems to have been attached to friendship, which lay somewhere between comradeship and love and was considered to have real initiatory value. Life within the Pythagorean brotherhood revolved around meals taken together, animal sacrifices, ritual ceremonies and physical and spiritual exercises. After reaching the first degree, the postulant was initiated in the 'Law of Number', the Pythagorean philosophy in which 'all is arranged by Number'.

The secrets of Nature

Initiation into mathematical secrets only came after a long preparatory period. Some idea of the cast of mind of those in the order can be gained from these verses:

> Work to put into practice these precepts and meditate upon them. Love them and you will find in them the way of divine virtue; this I swear by him who gave us the holy Quadrant, source of eternal Nature. But do not accomplish this work without asking the gods to help you finish it. When the precepts are familiar to you, you will know the constitution of the Immortal Gods and that of men. You will know how things separate and how they reassemble. You will understand that Nature is always like itself, so that you will not hope for that which cannot be won and nothing will remain hidden to you ... So take courage, for you know that man is of the divine essence; you know that holy Nature can reveal all things to him. And if Nature reveals her secrets to you, you will achieve all I have prescribed.

The philosophy of numbers, which deals with 'pure number', is the secret teaching of Pythagoreanism. A commentary on Plato's *Charmides* says:

> Logistics (counting) is the theory of things which can be counted and not of true number. It does not take number in the true sense of the term, but takes 1 as unity, supposing that all counting is number. Thus, it takes 3 in place of the triad or trinity, and 10 in place of

the decade, and applies arithmetical theorems.

Nicomachus of Gerasa said in his *Introductio Arithmetica*, 'All that is in Nature seems to have been determined, in part as in whole, in accordance with Number, by the wisdom of Him who created all things; the model was established, like a preliminary sketch, by the domination of Number which pre-existed in the spirit of God, creator of the world.' Theon of Smyrna explained further that 'the Pythagoreans treat all numbers as principles, so that 3, for example, is the triad and the principle of three for all things, and so on.'

The manifestation of divinity

The Greeks did not use figures to represent numbers; instead they made use of letters of the alphabet or other signs. The Pythagoreans of Sicily employed groups of dots and may well have invented figures. There is little doubt that the decimal system and the use of Arabic numerals has helped us to forget the distinction between the philosophy of numbers and mere arithmetic. Philosophically, however, the figure 2, the number two, the couple or dyad, and Duality are all quite different things, as Ghyka reminds us. Number speculation was, therefore, really a manifestation of divinity which man can still explore if he so wishes. In so doing, man is not seeking to lose himself in divinity, but to identify his own personality. This mystical approach to mathematics leads to a cosmogony of a musical type, as we shall see.

The story of Creation is, accordingly, expressed in the most concise way possible (after all, what is more concise than mathematics?), pairing Love with Discord, Eros with Thanatos, and so on. The underlying philosophy is that of same and other, as Plato put it: a harmony of opposites. Moderatus of Cadiz, writing about the time of Nero, said, 'The Pythagoreans, when they speak of 'one', mean identity, unity, equality, harmony and sympathy in the world; when they speak of 'two', they mean 'other', discrimination and inequality.' This is a fundamental point as art, society, and all of life result from a dialectic between same and other and the constant exchange between sympathetic and destructive forces.

The universe sings

Pythagoras and his followers reflected on the idea of proportion. Nicomachus explains that a ratio is the relation between two terms, whereas proportion is the correlation between at least two ratios. So, at least three terms are needed to establish a proportion. This led to the idea of 'continuous proportion', the 'golden section' and the golden mean. These speculations were started by the Pythagoreans, taken up again by Vitruvius, Fra Luca Pacioli di Borgo in his *Divina Proporzione* (1509) and Leonardo da Vinci. The Pythagoreans also developed the idea of the 'middle' or 'mean', the theory which explains the harmony of musical chords. Pythagoras realized that all musical intervals depended on fixed arithmetical ratios of lengths of strings at the same tension. In this way, the ratio 2:1 gave the octave, 3:2 the fifth, and so on. To give a value to the interval between two terms is indeed the same as defining the mean which yields proportion. These ideas apply equally to mathematics, music and architecture. In Plato's *Republic*, we read that the typical problem of harmony is getting the intervals to agree, something equally true of poetry and speech.

Quintessence, the 'fifth essence'

Hesiod had a great fear of the number 5 and believed the fifth day of each month was always unlucky. Pythagoras stripped away such superstition and gave 5 its place in the symbolic order: it does, after all, represent the hypotenuse of the right-angled triangle with other sides of 3 and 4. The five-pointed star or pentagram, much used in occultism, also came to occupy an important place in Pythagoreanism, as it symbolized the harmony of the five senses and hence health. In alchemy, quintessence, or the 'fifth essence', is the fifth entity resulting from the four elements mixed in various proportions.

The initiatory secret of the Pythagoreans is that the whole universe sings. They speak of the 'music of the spheres', an idea they passed on to early astronomy. Man sings too; he is a note in the huge cosmic symphony. However, he is unaware of this, because, as a spark of light fallen into matter, he is, in current terms, alienated. To achieve completeness, we must discover this musical vibration we bear within ourselves, like a wound; this is where initiation comes in. But can such a secret be told? Can the music of the universe really be revealed? It was Pythagoras who discovered the *tetractys*, the triangular figure composed of 10 dots, which was held to be so important that it figured in the Pythagorean oath. The *tetractys* is a beautifully simple symbol, formed of four rows of respectively four, three, two and one dots, where the single dot is the apex of the figure. It was identified with harmony itself by the Pythagoreans. The song of god and the song of the world are love songs, only heard by man if he finds the spark of divinity within himself; the love of God is perfect, unalloyed — the cosmic number.

From Iamblichus:

'The doctrine of Pythagoras has been preserved with amazing exactness, for no one was able to gain access, for many generations, to his archives until Philolaus, the first person to edit his works. According to tradition, Dion of Syracuse bought them, at Plato's request, for a hundred minas from Philolaus, who had fallen into utter poverty. Indeed, the latter also belonged to the brotherhood of the Pythagoreans, which is how he came to have the books in his possession.'

Randolph, Paschal

1815–75

Initiation celebrates sexuality

For Randolph, eroticism led to the invisible; orgasm harmonized a couple and was a form of magic.

The American Paschal Randolph was the son of a black saloon dancer and a doctor from Virginia. His life was the sea, first as a cabin-boy on a sailing ship, then as the master of his own vessel. He travelled widely and also published some novels, including *Master Passion* and *Astoris*. In 1840, he was received into the 'Hermetic Brotherhood of Luxor' which opposed the wave of spiritualism then washing over the USA. In the Civil War he sided with the North, his resolute stand even drawing the attention of Abraham Lincoln. In 1868, after several trips to France, he founded in Boston his own secret society, the 'Eulis Brotherhood', which soon attracted a considerable following.

Maria de Naglowska was one of Randolph's most prominent disciples. Her *Sacred Ritual of Magic Love* set out a sort of westernized Tantrism and mentioned two secret ceremonies, the 'golden mass' and the 'sacred hanging'. *The Light of Sex* (1933) claimed that evil could be neutralized by opposing it with sexual acts carried out under the direction of sacred prostitutes.

A defence of bisexuality

Randolph set out his views in his book, *Magia Sexualis*. His central idea was that sexuality is the driving force behind creation: 'Man is the positive pole of its manifestation; woman is the negative. The phallus is positive, but man's brain is negative; similarly, the yoni (or female genitalia) is negative, but woman's brain is positive.' In this way, Randolph touched on bisexuality: man is both masculine and feminine at the same time.

The orgasm was, for him, something sacred and also magical. 'When the sexual act is perfect, the union of man and woman is achieved at every level of their beings and their strength increases tenfold; all their wishes are granted.' It is, however, important to note that this is a spiritual quest, not simply sexual intercourse. 'For this magical act, never take a prostitute, nor an inexperienced virgin, nor an adulteress: carry out the sacred act only with your chosen companion. Aim for the union of souls beyond carnal union.'

'Do not couple more than once or twice a week. Before, during and after the **act of love**, have within you quite clearly the image of what you desire.'

Reuchlin, Johann

1455–1522

A lesson in tolerance

The Christian Cabala, especially Reuchlin's version, takes up the idea that all religions, in their own way, express the same divine, cosmic truth.

Johann Reuchlin was born at Pforzheim in Germany. He became a doctor of philosophy in Basle in 1477, before receiving a degree in law at Poitiers in 1481. He next travelled to Rome as an embassy attaché, and finally settled in Stuttgart. In 1492 he learnt Hebrew from a Jewish doctor and was then able to study the Cabala directly. Two years later, in *De Verbo Mirifico*, which attracted the attention of the educated classes throughout Europe, he wrote that God 'revealed His secrets to man in Hebrew'. Reuchlin claimed to have established the 'correct spelling of Jesus' name', and thence the 'ultimate meaning' of His coming.

'The Bible of the Christian Cabala'

On 15 August 1509, the Emperor Maximilian I had all books in Hebrew burnt. The authorities asked Reuchlin if he considered it just to take all books from the Jews, leaving them only the Bible. He answered in the negative and was therefore commanded to appear immediately before the Grand Inquisitor in Mainz where, however, the representatives of 53 towns in Swabia spoke up in his favour. By way of thanks, the rabbis of Pforzheim gave him the documents he later used to write *De Arte Cabalistica*.

This book, the 'Bible of the Christian Cabala', was published in 1516 and dedicated to Pope Leo X, who was interested in Pythagoreanism. It is written in the form of a dialogue between a Pythagorean and a Muslim, to whom a Jew is explaining the Cabala. The Jew teaches the two that 'the Cabala must never be sought through the crude contact of the senses, nor by logic; its domain lies elsewhere, in a third sphere, so to speak.'

The Pythagorean and the Muslim discover that the Cabala is the carrier of the oldest tradition of all, as it is 'a symbolic theology, in which letters and names are not only the signs for things, but also their very essence.' *De Arte Cabalistica* refers to the *Zohar* and the *Sefer Raziel* (or 'Book of Magic'). It speaks of the 50 doors of the intelligence, of which even Solomon and Moses could only open 49.

Reuchlin had many followers, including Francesco Georgi (*De Harmonia Mundi*, 1525) and Paulus Ricius (*De Caelesti Agricultura*, 1541). In modern times, Franz Kafka was an avid reader of *De Arte Cabalistica*.

Cabalistic degrees

A distinction is drawn between *cabalici* (true initiates), *cabalaei* (their pupils) and *cabalistae* (imitators).

Rosenkreuz, Christian

The mythical hero of Rosicrucianism

A fine literary invention springing from a troubled age, the figure of Christian Rosenkreuz has fired the imagination of men of all ages.

All we know about Christian Rosenkreuz is gleaned from the *Fama Fraternitatis*, the central text of the Rosicrucians. He was born into the penniless lesser nobility in Germany and, during his convent education, became fascinated by the Holy Land where he travelled at the age of 16. On the journey, he heard tell of the wise men of Arabia, gave up his pilgrimage and went instead to Damcar (in modern Yemen). The wise men made him welcome and taught him Arabic, mathematics and physics, and he translated into Latin the famous *Liber M*, which was said to contain all the secrets of the universe.

He then spent several years in various Arab countries before returning to Europe where he tried, in vain, to communicate his knowledge. In Germany, he built a huge house and devoted himself to personal study. After some five years, he sent for five brothers he had known in his school-days and together they founded the Brotherhood. They formulated a secret language, performed miracles, healed the sick and recruited new members. They also swore to keep their organization secret for a hundred years.

Rosenkreuz's burial-place was discovered 120 years after his death, by a brother in the course of a transmutation. His body was perfectly preserved, and in his hand he held a little book tooled in gold. This book showed that Rosenkreuz knew of all events past, present and future. The brothers closed their master's tomb and went out into the world to continue his work.

The **elect** is 'the man who, in the quest for knowledge, is ceaselessly renewed in the image of his Creator'.

Apart from Rosenkreuz's biography, the *Fama* reveals a philosophy which criticizes certain authorities such as the Pope, Aristotle and Galen, but praises Paracelsus and the Cabala. It tells of the exact correspondence between microcosm and macrocosm (man and universe) which was grasped by means of a branch of mathematics known only to Rosenkreuz, who then used it for the good of mankind.

'The Chemical Wedding'

Another founding text, *The Chemical Wedding*, is an extraordinary 'spiritual novel'. After a visitation by an angel and a premonition in a dream, Christian sets off on the quest for initiation. Sometimes he uses a compass, with which he finds his way towards his spiritual dawn; sometimes Hermes Psychopompus, the leader of souls, guides him in person. At sunset, Christian reaches a royal castle on a mountain peak. There, he must undergo a series of tests. He passes the first, the weighing of souls, and offers the young girl in charge of the ceremony some roses he takes from his hat.

Celestial portents

The *Fama Fraternitatis* refers to the *Trigoneum Igneum*, the triangle formed in the heavens in 1603 by Aries, Leo and Sagittarius, which was believed to mark the start of a favourable period. One year later, the astronomer Kepler observed a new star within the triangle and deduced that an apocalyptic period was about to begin. This led the Rosicrucians to expect a period of political and historical upheaval.

Christian then experiences an apocalypse and is reborn, purified. On the fifth day, Christian pays a remarkable visit to Venus, as she sleeps, naked. An inscription explains that she will awaken 'when the tree melts'. Christian is engrossed by the scene and Cupid wounds him with an arrow. For Jung, this represents the 'descent into Hell' (in both psychological and alchemical terms), the discovery of the secret that will transform sexuality into love.

However, a book like this cannot really be summarized, abounding as it does with the most amazing episodes — from beheadings to thrilling sea voyages — and dazzling poetic images. The author (or authors) displays consummate skill, planning endless surprises for the reader as he leads his hero on towards his destiny.

Some (see **Andreae**) see this as pure fiction, but the Rosicrucian message had considerable influence at the time. Adam Haselmayer, secretary to the Archduke Maximilian, in his 'Reply to the Rosicrucian Brothers', called attention to the prevailing social injustice, war and barbarism of the times, and urged the brothers to 'make their presence visible' so that the 'Great Judgment' could take place. The myth, however, has come down to us today.

Celebrity
Descartes tried to make contact with the Rosicrucians, and Leibniz and Goethe were also fascinated by the order.

The successors of Rosenkreuz
Apart from the original Rosicrucian Order, the following are worth noting:
—the Golden Rosicrucians of 1630, which had many followers, such as the *Rose-Croix d'Ancien Système* of 1777;
—the *Rosicrucians of Florence*;
—the *Societas Rosicruciana in Anglia*, 1867, of which Eliphas Lévi was a member;
—the *Ordre kabbalistique de la Rose-Croix*, founded by Stanislas de Guaïta;
—the *AMORC (Anticus Mysticus Ordo Rosae Crucis)*, founded in the USA in 1909 by H. Spencer Lewis, which spread throughout the world. In his *History of the Order Rosae Crucis* (1915–1916), Lewis attributes the original founding of the Order to the Pharoah Tuthmosis III (1500–1447 BC);
—the *Rosicrucian Fellowship*, founded by the Dane, Max Heindel (1865–1919); and
—the *Lectorium Rosicrucianum*, with its base in the Netherlands, which is Gnostic in outlook.

Saint-Germain, Claude Louis, Count of

1743–84

The man who found the elixir of life

Saint-Germain is a legendary figure; there are even those who believe he is still alive.

Saint-Germain was an adventurer of unknown origin. He arrived in Paris in 1758, where he immediately charmed Madame de Pompadour; amongst other things, he told her that he was immortal and that he had known François I.

He turned up again in Leipzig in 1775, where he went by the name of the Count of Weldonne. Emperor Joseph II was one of those who believed in him, and Saint-Germain showed him his 'elixir of life' (a mixture of scented herbs) and 'industrial processes' for washing paper, improving silk and so on. He then moved to Altona, where the Landgrave of Hesse put a laboratory at his disposal for his experiments. His 'pupil', Etteila, claimed for a year after his final disappearance that he was still alive, aged 325, and that they had lunched together. Saint-Germain is credited with having written *La Très Sainte Trinosophie* which Cagliostro had in his possession.

Saint-Martin, Louis Claude de

1743–1803

A master of the occult and of love

The 'unknown philosopher' was a follower of Martines de Pasqually. He sought to restore the magic of initiation ceremonies and followed Jakob Böhme in his quest for Sophia.

Louis Claude de Saint-Martin, the 'unknown philosopher', was deeply affected by the early loss of his mother. His father wished him to become a magistrate but he abandoned his legal studies for a military career. He bought a commission, as was the custom in those days, and joined a regiment stationed at Bordeaux. There, a colleague introduced him to the 'Elect of Cohen' and he became secretary to the founder, Martines de Pasqually.

He was initiated in 1765 and, shortly afterwards, met Jean-Baptiste Willermoz, the 'mason of Christ'. He then embarked upon a spiritual quest and, discovering the works of Jakob Böhme, set about translating them into French.

'Entering God's heart'

Saint-Martin was deeply influenced by Martines de Pasqually and his *Traité de la réintégration*. He, too, believed that the 'man of desire' (ie you, me, anybody) must get back to his creative principle. He believed that magic was necessary to achieve this but, where Pasqually contrived to use spirits in this work. Saint-Martin intended to use the power of Christ. He declared that the approach to the creative principle was internal: the seeker had to draw strength from within himself through a labour of knowledge and love, and 'through blood'. (This labour 'through blood' is linked to 'inferior forces' and concerns the imagination, gestures and words, ie the magical side of ritual ceremonies.)

So, if it is internal, how can the method of the Unknown Philosopher become operative? The answer comes from Jakob Böhme. The idea of Sophia, or divine wisdom, the feminine principle of the 'Great Architect of the Universe', and equivalent of the Soul of the World, becomes the object of the initiate's quest. Saint-Martin wrote:

> The only initiation that I preach and seek with all my soul is that which takes us into the heart of God and brings the heart of God into us for that indissoluble marriage which makes us friend, brother and spouse of our Divine Restorer. There is no other means to this holy initiation but to dive deeper and deeper into the depths of our being and not to let go until we can draw out the living and life-giving root.

In summary, we can describe Saint-Martin's method thus: Sophia (or wisdom) blossoms when the individual truly discovers his own 'sensitivity', which is normally buried beneath his inner darkness. Note that this 'sensitivity' is supposed to open out to both cosmic and divine influences at the same time. Saint-Martin intended to achieve this by combining the spiritual and the magical, the latter providing the 'matter' by means of which the former can discover itself (he spoke of 'opening the spiritual centre').

Saint-Martin never married and had no mistresses, remarking 'I feel in the depths of my being a voice telling me I come from a land where there are no women.' However,

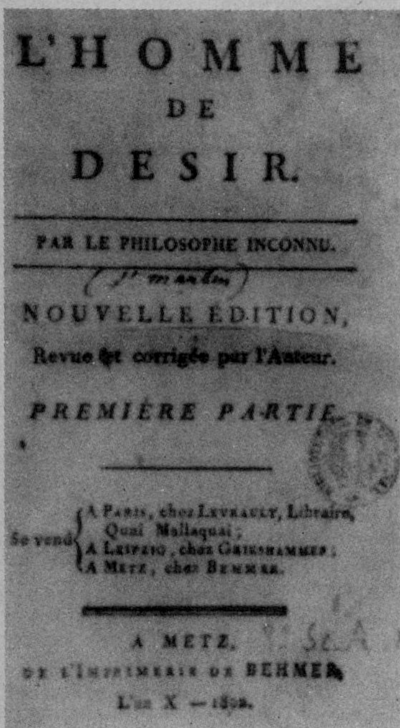

L'HOMME

DE

DESIR.

PAR LE PHILOSOPHE INCONNU.

NOUVELLE ÉDITION,

Revue et corrigée par l'Auteur.

PREMIÈRE PARTIE.

Se vend { A Paris, chez Levrault, Libraire, Quai Mallaquai; A Leipzig, chez Griesshammer; A Metz, chez Behmer.

A METZ,

DE L'IMPRIMERIE DE BEHMER.

L'an X — 1802.

End paper of L'Homme de désir, the best-known work of Louis Claude de Saint-Martin (National Library, Paris)

from about 1778, he enjoyed a platonic relationship with Charlotte de Boecklin, a lady of 48, separated from her husband, who helped him to translate Böhme's works.

A gifted writer

Saint-Martin left many books, including *L'Homme de désir* (The Man of Desire), *Le Ministère de l'homme-esprit* (The Ministry of Man-Spirit) and *Le Tableau naturel des rapports qui existent entre Dieu, l'homme et l'univers* (The Natural Description of the Relations Existing Between God, Man and the Universe). These go to make up a 'divinist' system — the term the author preferred to 'spiritual'. His works have a certain charm which earned him the title of the 'French Novalis'. Sainte-Beuve praised his talent and considered some of the Unknown Philosopher's writings among the finest works in the French language. Chateaubriand, in his *Mémoires d'outre-tombe*, recalls a meeting with Saint-Germain with amusement but no little admiration.

Anguish

'The heart of man is chosen to be the repository of God's anguish.'

'The words of anguish are always new; therein lies the principle of language.'

Saint-Yves d'Alveidre

1842–1909

Master of esoterism and 'synarchy'

Saint-Yves d'Alveidre understood that symbolism must not be confused with sociology.

Saint-Yves spent his early years in a children's institution — virtually a prison — where he had been placed by his father. On leaving it, he studied medicine and, in 1877, he married the Countess of Keller, who had been Balzac's second wife, and brought him a considerable fortune. She also obtained for him the title of Marquis d'Alveidre.

The 'archaeometer'

Saint-Yves was a prolific writer, of everything from bad verse to the works which earned his reputation in hermetic circles — *Mission actuelle des ouvriers* (The Present Mission of the Working Class), *Mission des juifs* (The Mission of the Jews), *La France vraie* (The True France), *L'Archéomètre* and *Mission de l'Inde* (The Mission of India). In these he developed his idea of 'synarchy', or joint sovereignty, a tripartite government whose 'three essential functions' (education, justice and economy) were represented by three chambers of which one (the 'metaphysical') bound the whole structure together.

Saint-Yves also 'invented' the archaeometer (see **Wronski**'s 'progonometer'). V.-E. Michelet wrote, 'What is this archaeometer or 'measure of Archaeus' (or universal cosmic force) to which the hermetists refer in coded terms? It is a process, a 'key', which opens up, almost automatically, the arcane secrets of the Word to science and the arts. It is an instrument which measures first principles.' So what is this fabulous instrument, this divine computer? 'Cardboard circles covered with the secrets of the Zodiac' which provide answers to the questions that are put to them!

The great circle
'Millions of divijas (those born twice) and yogis (those united in God) form a great circle, or rather a semi-circle. Above them, moving towards the Centre, we see five thousand pundits (or pandavan), some of whom are engaged in education proper, while others are a sort of internal police service ... There are 5000 of them, a number corresponding to the roots of the Vedic language ... The highest circle, nearest to the mysterious centre, is made up of twelve members who are initiated to the highest degree.'

The centre of the world

Saint-Yves was also a believer in the 'centre of the world' (see **Agartha**), in this case an underground city in the centre of Asia. This may be nothing more than a harmless vision, but Saint-Yves' work is quite unlike that of Wronski or Fourier. And, whereas such works have been considered prophetic (*Mission des juifs, Mission des ouvriers*, etc), his metaphysics leaves no room for freedom; the functions he describes are predetermined by tradition and similar to those of a caste system.

Sédir, Paul

1871–1926

'The rabbis showed me unknown manuscripts'

Sédir broke with esoteric circles, claiming he had received revelations from initiates.

Sédir was the pseudonym (an anagram of the French word *désir* ('desire')) of Yvon Le Loup, a bank clerk. He published numerous pamphlets and also articles in Papus' journal, *L'Initiation*, and then, quite suddenly, broke with esoteric circles. In an autobiographical work, he explained that 'some rabbis have shown me hitherto unknown manuscripts; alchemists have admitted me to their laboratories; Sufis, Buddhists and Taoists have long kept vigils with me in the places where their gods are to be found. But one evening, after a certain meeting, all that these remarkable men had taught me was as the mist rising at dusk from the overheated earth.'

We know nothing of the men Sédir had met. However, from that moment on, he dedicated his life to Christ. He established a movement known as the *Amitiés Spirituelles* (Spiritual Friendships) whose main activities were charity and the spreading of the master's thought. The latter took the form of lectures devoted mainly to the 'message of Christ' for which Sédir tried to produce the 'original authentication'. Interestingly, Sédir remained at the same time an occultist who had frequent recourse to magic and magnetism.

'**Mirrors** are of three sorts: discs and other instruments black in colour — saturnian mirrors; vases and crystals filled with water — lunar mirrors; and (parts of) metallic spheres — solar mirrors.' Sédir, *Les Miroirs magiques*

Divination by mirrors

In divination by mirrors, Sédir took up the old technique of Cagliostro and others. Psychologists have always been interested in this practice. In 19th century London, it was studied, especially by Myers, by way of the 'sensory automatism and hallucinations provoked by it'. The use of mirrors, or a crystal ball, can indeed produce 'visions' which are usually the product of the subject's unconscious, fancifully exaggerated. That, at least, is the theory of Pierre Janet who recognized the reality of visions, but added, 'You knew very well what you would see appearing — memories of certain occasions, knowledge and deeply embedded thoughts and attitudes and so on.'

Simeon bar Yokhai

2nd century AD

The master of the Cabala

Whether he existed or not, Rabbi Simeon bar Yokhai is the central character of the Zohar, the 'master of the secret'.

The *Zohar*, the key book of the Cabala, was published (or 'revealed') in 1290 by Rabbi Moses ben Shemtov of Leon (1250–1305) who lived most of his life in Avila in Spain. It is possible that he even wrote the book, although he claimed merely to be recording an ancient tradition.

According to this tradition, Rabbi Simeon bar Yokhai — much praised in the Talmud — was condemned to death by the Romans. He hid in a cave to evade capture and the *Zohar* records his conversations there with his son, Rabbi Eleazar, and followers. Whether authentic, an inspired forgery, or even a compilation, the *Zohar* (or 'Book of Splendours') is the 'crown of the mystical tree of Judaism'. Here, more clearly than anywhere else, we see the mystic undergo transmutation in the course of the initiatory quest and we discover technical means of achieving this transition.

The roundness of the Earth

'In the book of Rabbi Hammenuna it is explained that all the inhabited Earth turns as in a circle. Some parts are at the top, others at the bottom ... That is why, when one region is lit by daylight, the other is in darkness. One has day and the other has night ... This mystery was entrusted to the Masters of Wisdom, not to geographers, for it is one of the deep mysteries of the Law.'

The exegesis of the *Zohar*

Rabbi Simeon tells us: 'When the Mystery of Mysteries wished to manifest itself, it created firstly a point which became God's thought.' Genesis only came later: the word *Zohar* means that spark which the Mystery created in the void, and which is the origin of the universe.' So the *Zohar* begins with a theory of the origin of the universe. In the section entitled 'The Book of Secrets', it explores the ways leading to the ineffable, and 'The Head of the Academy' provides information about death. But what of love above? 'By day, men and women are separated, but at night husband unites with wife for the midnight hour is the hour of union above, just as it is below. Just as on earth one body cleaves to another, so in Paradise the soul of the husband embraces the soul of the wife and their two lights melt into one.' The section called 'The Old Man' explains the philosophy of the transmigration of souls, while 'The Small and Saintly Assembly' tells of the death of Rabbi Simeon, who died with the word 'life' on his lips.

Other sections are more 'scientific' in nature. 'The Secret of Secrets', for example, deals with physiognomy: 'The physiognomy of a man is the book in which are written his acts and the state of his soul.' Finally, let us not forget that the Cabalists knew that the earth is round and that it revolves around the sun.

Simon the Magician

1st century AD

Christ's most dangerous rival

He was perhaps the most important representative of Gnosticism, a legendary figure. Could he have taken Christ's place?

The Father of All Heretics, as he was called, was a contemporary of Christ. He was born in Samaria and became a philosopher-cum-preacher-cum-magician after travelling to Alexandria. He attained legendary status within his own life time: 'he made statues walk, could roll in fire without burning himself, and could even fly,' according to one of his childhood friends. Clement I, secretary to St Peter, called him 'Simon the Precursor'; he saw him as God's left hand and the syzygy, or counterpart, of St Paul.

'The Root of All'

Simon summed up his philosophy in a work entitled *The Root of All* which allies him closely with the thinking of some of the pre-Socratic philosophers. Fire is the 'root of all' — referring, evidently, to a hidden fire, the axis of the world from which the soul was born. This fire gave rise to six principles, expressed in pairs, of which the cosmos is woven: Spirit/Thought, Breath/Name and Reason/Meditation. On earth, these principles come together harmoniously in *hestos*, 'that which stands upright'. Simon himself is an incarnation of *hestos*.

His system is essentially a form of Gnostic philosophy. Wisdom falls to earth and yearns to rise again to heaven. Simon sets out in search of Wisdom and finds it in a brothel in Tyre. Can any more terrible 'prison of flesh' be imagined for such purity? Here Simon encounters a prostitute who is a reincarnation of Helen, the cause of the Trojan War. Together Simon and Helen symbolize the incarnation of God. Simon is a forerunner of the Catharians: he preaches that the Old Testament God is an imperfect demiurge. In a polemic against St Paul, he declares that 'Adam was created blind' and argues that original sin is, therefore, attributable not to a stain Adam might have avoided, but to the existence of some hitherto unexplained aspect of the unconscious.

A rival to Christ?

As a rival to Christ, Simon the Magician is a historical character without equal. Hippolytus and many others report that he was identified by his followers with God come down to earth. The Church eventually overcame his ascendancy, though, and we read its answering counter-myth in Acts. He was eventually converted and went to Rome where he practised levitation. This was, however, to be his undoing: while Simon was in the course of self-levitation, St Peter concentrated his being upon him and Simon fell headlong, breaking his skull.

'Thus, according to the Gnostics, God took the **shape of a man**, although He was not a man. Remarkably, He appeared to suffer in Judea without suffering really. To the Jews He appeared as the Son, to the Samaritans as the Father and to other nations as the Holy Spirit.'
Hippolytus of Rome, *Philosophumena* (Refutation of All Heresies)

Steiner, Rudolf

1861–1925

A strict scientist and spiritualist philosopher

Steiner is one of the modern masters whose work has had — and continues to have — the greatest influence.

Rudolf Steiner was a brilliant student. He discovered Goethe when he was 18, wrote two books about him and then became the archivist of the great philosopher's scientific manuscripts. In 1897, he published *Goethe and his Conception of the Cosmos*, became secretary of the German branch of the Theosophical Society and began to give lectures.

Anthroposophy

Steiner founded the philosophy of anthroposophy, which postulated the existence of a spiritual world, fully accessible only through man's innate spiritual perception which has become dulled by the materialism of the world. He set up the Anthroposophical Society in 1912 and the following year began to build his first 'Goetheanum', a 'school of spiritual science' at Dornach near Basle. Students flocked there from all over Europe to study and act out mysteries. The centre was destroyed in 1922 in a fire, probably started by members of the National Socialist Party, but was immediately rebuilt and became the centre of the society, which proceeded to spread throughout the world.

An ideal of humanity
'My meeting with Rudolf Steiner took place in Strasbourg . . . We saw that we were both intent on the same mission: the awakening of a true culture, inspired and dominated by an ideal of humanity.' Albert Schweitzer

Research in all directions

Dr Albert Schweitzer, one of the most remarkable figures of the 20th century, frequently spoke of Steiner's influence. 'I rejoice,' said Dr Schweitzer 'at the effect of his great personality and deep humanity in the world. Everyone ought to follow his path.' Like his master Goethe, Steiner was a strict scientist and a spiritualist philosopher, an initiate and a man of action. His teaching is still very much alive, in a variety of spheres throughout the world.

Steiner wrote on subjects as diverse as death, the history of the cosmos, philosophy, medicine and morality. To this day, there is a study centre in Dornach, where research into cancer is carried out: the aim is to discover a cure combining modern discoveries and ancient empirical techniques. Steiner's 'biodynamic' method of farming and gardening is still applied and his teaching methods continue to be used for mentally handicapped, maladjusted and other children. There are Steiner schools practising his educational approach in Paris, Edinburgh and other cities. The teaching concentrates on the inner development of the child, in an attempt to achieve his or her 'psychic awakening', and takes particular account of the dream dimension all children inhabit.

Swedenborg, Emanuel

1688–1772

The prophet of the New Jerusalem

Swedenborg influenced some freemasons' lodges as well as many authors. He tried to get back to the original simplicity of the Gospels.

Swedenborg came from a wealthy family of Swedish scholars. He was a child prodigy and performed brilliantly in his studies. He received his doctorate in philosophy in 1709, travelled widely and, by 1716, was distinguished in many fields, including mathematics, crystallography and geodesy. His remarkable achievements brought him ennoblement and honours from most of the learned societies of Europe.

'Social blood which will be love'

Swedenborg fell gravely ill in 1743 and, on his recovery, discovered that he had become a visionary. Until his death he claimed to receive messages from the angels regarding both trivial and profound matters. This marked a new direction in his work. For him, man is placed at the junction of heaven and earth. Every cell in the human body obeys its own inner necessity, and life as a couple is the crowning of the human being. God is all goodness. 'The Lord casts none into Hell, but the spirit of the sinner goes there by itself, for he makes unswervingly towards those like himself.' But more importantly, Swedenborg believed that in 1757 mankind entered the age of the New Jerusalem, the age of universal religion, close to the coming Golden Age. 'Worship will be reduced to a minimum and Scripture will be seen in a new light, with the Trinity abolished.'

With less poetic and religious fervour, Swedenborg anticipates Fourier. 'Within the human body, the heart carries life-giving blood to every organ. Very soon, society will have the social blood which is the love of man for man. Charity is acting with faith and justice in all circumstances. We are part of one another; the crime of one is the crime of all; the virtue of one is the virtue of all.' He was denounced by the Lutheran church, but had numerous disciples after his death and influenced many writers, including Balzac.

The angels

'We must understand that angels cannot be seen with the eyes of the body, but only with the eyes of the spirit which is within man. Like sees like, because their origin is the same.'
Swedenborg, *Of Heaven and its Marvels and of Hell According to What Has Been Heard and Seen*

How to have visions

Swedenborg was subject to catalepic fits and every day practised 'representative visions' with his eyes open. He trained himself to stop breathing, in order to let the spirit develop its 'inner breathing' which manifests itself clearly after death.

The Templars

An occult order of chivalry

Originally perfectly orthodox, the Order of the Templars seems to have become influenced by Gnosticism and occultism.

The Order of the Militia of the Knights of the Temple was founded in 1118 by Geoffrey of St Omer, Hugh of Payns and seven companions. Members were either knights or sergeants, soldier-monks with the duty of protecting pilgrims to the holy places of Jerusalem, Bethlehem, and so on. The rule of the order was sanctioned by the council of Troyes, thanks to the support of the all-powerful abbot, Bernard of Clairvaux (later to become St Bernard). The Templars made three vows, of poverty, chastity and obedience.

A historic role

The order went from strength to strength and soon became one of the wealthiest and most influential groupings in European politics. However, the enormous economic and political power of the Templars was eventually to bring about their downfall. The king and the pope could not tolerate an organization so powerful they could not control it. In Paris the Templars had even drained the marshy ground of the area called the *marais* and ruled over it with their own craftsmen, peasants, masons, guilds, etc. Rumours began to circulate about them. They were accused, amongst other charges, of institutionalized homosexuality. However, the most serious accusations were that they worshipped an idol, Baphomet, a devilish androgynous figure, seen as the denial of Christ, and that they spat upon the cross. They were also supposed to be in league with the Muslim Shi'ite order of Assassins, who had developed the philosophy of the 'will for power' before its time and used drugs and crime to achieve their ends.

The order was, therefore, too dangerous for the authorities and its members were arrested by decree of Pope Clement V. The Templars died along with Jacques de Molay, their 22nd grand master, who was burnt at the stake by order of King Philip IV of France in 1314.

Masonic followers
'Thus, freemasonry did not claim to be the legitimate heir of the Temple, but nor did it deny the existence of established traditional links between the Temple and Lodges.' Jean Tourniac, 'The Principles and Spiritual Problems of the Revised Scottish Rite'

A masonic degree

The masonic degree of Templar was established in 1760. Various organizations of an initiate nature have claimed to be survivals of the original order: the Order of Christ, in Portugal in 1317; the Order of the Temple, in France in 1808; and the Order of the Eastern Temple, in Germany in 1905. Even today, such orders exist, claiming descent from the 12th century knights of the Temple.

Trithemius, John

(alias of Johann von Heidenberg)

1462–1516

Monk and magician

From worship of the Virgin to magic is a strange move. But his initiation is uncertain, as he is surrounded in mystery.

Trithemius had an unhappy childhood, ill-treated by his stepfather. He entered the University of Trier thanks to his maternal uncle and, at the age of 18, he founded the 'Sodalitas Celtica' (Celtic Brotherhood) along with some students. One day when travelling to visit his mother in the depths of winter, he was caught in a snowstorm and forced to stop at the Benedictine monastery of Sponheim. He decided there and then to become a monk, which he did on his 20th birthday, and a year later was running the monastery himself.

His arrival turned the monastery upside-down. The building was in a sorry state of repair and Trithemius restored it. He obliged the monks to work regular hours and also set up a library of some 2000 volumes which quickly became famous. He wrote books on the Virgin, the Benedictine Order and ascetics, as well as homilies. Visitors flocked to Sponheim, amongst them Johann Reuchlin.

However, Trithemius's conversion did not diminish his passion for the occult sciences. He wrote to his friend Arnold Bostins in 1498 and told him he was working on a book called *Stenographia*. He confided, 'This book, in which I teach many little-known secrets and mysteries, will seem to all, especially the ignorant, full of superhuman, amazing, incredible things. Nobody has ever spoken or written of them before me.' Unfortunately, the letter was intercepted and rumour spread that Trithemius was writing a book on magic. The emperor, Maximilian I, summoned him in 1505 to interrogate him on questions of faith and Trithemius is said to have caused the spirit of the Emperor's deceased wife, Mary of Burgundy, to appear in a darkened room.

'This good and holy science of magic'

It was only after his death that any real idea of Trithemius's activities was formed. He certainly studied the Cabala, 'this good and holy science of magic'. He also knew of Faust, and perhaps even met him. Amongst Trithemius's works was *Antipalus Maleficiorum Comprehensus*, a book classifying witches according to their specialities; in it he listed 44 methods of divination and provided an interesting biliography. Another work, *De Septem Secundeis*, develops certain gnostic concepts. He writes of seven angels governing the seven planets from Creation to the end of the world, each one holding power for 354 years and 4 months. History is made up of three cycles of these seven reigns, so that time will end in 2235, when Algol, known as Medusa's Head, will reach a certain point in the constellation Gemini. Trithemius is considered by some to have foretold Luther's schism two years before it occurred and, using his methods, his English translator, William Lilly, pre-

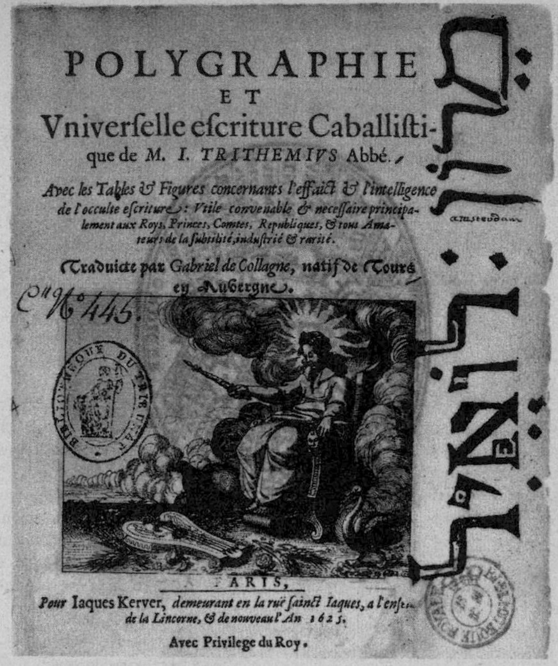

POLYGRAPHIE
ET
Vniverſelle eſcriture Caballiſti-
que de M. I. TRITHEMIVS Abbé.

Avec les Tables & Figures concernants l'effaict & l'intelligence de l'occulte eſcriture: Vtile convenable & neceſſaire principalement aux Roys, Princes, Comtes, Republiques, & tous Amateurs de la ſubtilité, induſtrie & rarité.

Traduicte par *Gabriel de Collagne,* natif de Tours en Auvergne.

PARIS,
Pour Iaques Kerver, *demeurant en la ruë ſainct Iaques, a l'enſei... de la Lincorne, & de nouveau l'An 1625.*
Avec Privilege du Roy.

John Trithemius's treatise on 'polygraphy' and 'universal Cabalistic writing' (National Library, Paris)

dicted in 1647 the Great Fire of London (1666).

However, the *Stenographia* is his most representative work although it was not published until 1676. It contains codes (or 'conjurations') and the various scripts he employs are prayers which, he claims, cause the angels to act on our behalf. It is uncertain whether these are a clever trick, a genuine enigma, or an occult technique.

Valentin, Basil

b.1394

Alchemy takes an interest in antimony

Basil Valentin was several characters rolled into one. His life and work are veiled in mystery.

Although a doctor and superior of the Benedictines in Erfurt, Basil Valentin was first and foremost an alchemist. His works were unknown until, a century after his death, a pillar of the church in Erfurt was split open by lightning to reveal where he had hidden them.

A myth

The character of Basil is in fact a myth. There never was a monastery in Erfurt and the works attributed to him are full of anachronisms and could never have been written in the 15th century. Moreover, his name is a pun, consisting of the Greek word for 'king' and a Latin word meaning 'in good health' — and, as we know, alchemy is known as the 'royal art' and the philosopher's stone can reveal the 'elixir of life'.

The most notable of the works bearing his name (all edited long after his death) are *The Great Stone of the Ancients* (1599), *Of Natural and Supernatural Things* (1603) and *The Microcosm* (1608). *The Chariot* was however the most successful, appearing as it did at the height of the quarrel between those for and against the use of antimony. Those in favour of its use called upon Basil's authority as he had 'proved' its ability to 'purge' gold and men. He gave directions for obtaining oil from antimony (used in the treatment of ulcers) and for preparing tincture of antimony. Malicious rumours at the height of the quarrel maintained that Basil had poisoned the monks he was supposed to be looking after by trying to use antimony as a tonic.

The *Last Testament* of Basil Valentin, clearly apocryphal and published only in 1626, is very interesting. It deals with the 'feeding' of metals, their 'heavenly and hellish qualities' and even their 'excrement'. It takes the anthropomorphic vision underlying the principles of alchemy to its limit and was analyzed by Gaston Bachelard in the 20th century.

'Alchemy was the art of **using the most appealing lies** to attain truth.' Alexandrian, *Histoire de la philosophie occulte*

The Amphitheatre of Eternal Wisdom of the doctor and alchemist Heinrich Kühnrath (1560–1609), completed by Erasmus Wolfurt in 1609, establishes a correspondence between Christ and the philosopher's stone. According to Jung, it marks an essential turning-point in the European psyche. In brief, it was a successful attempt to integrate Gnosticism with official religion.

Alchemical engravings

A good part of the alchemical corpus consists of texts accompanied by engravings. Basil Valentin's *Twelve Keys of Occult Philosophy*, presented as twelve engravings, with anonymous glosses added later, is a case in point. Clovis Hesteau de Nulsement wrote a philosophical poem about it. Many other such works could be named, including *Mutus Liber, The Amphitheatre of Eternal Wisdom, Splendor Solis, De Re Metallica and Della transmutazione metallica.*

Villeneuve, Arnaud de

1240–1313

Occultist, doctor and humanist

Arnaud de Villeneuve was an alchemist of some repute but his work is riddled with unbridled speculation.

Arnaud de Villeneuve is thought to have been the first humanist doctor. He was born in Provence, took his Master of Arts degree in Paris and travelled in Spain and Italy. Gaining a considerable reputation as an alchemist, he carried out his first transmutation in Rome in 1286. He was subsequently appointed professor of medicine at Montpellier, where his lectures drew large crowds. In 1299, however, he was arrested on account of a book in which he predicted the coming of the Antichrist in 1355 and the end of the world in 1464. He was eventually released and fled to Italy. He was denounced by the theologians of Paris but the pope, Clement V, pardoned him and summoned him to Avignon. Arnaud de Villeneuve died on his journey there.

'Spiritus animalis'

Arnaud de Villeneuve based his work on the old theory of the four humours, but he took account of a fifth principle, the *spiritus animalis*, a sort of mediator between body and soul. It had its seat in the heart and produced vital phenomena as well as mental images. It flowed through the human being just as the sun's rays permeate space, but could be affected by external agents or passions. Each man is born with his own temperament, but Villeneuve believed every temperament needed the correct hygiene and diet to realize its full potential. He believed in the benefits of hydrotherapy, which he described in his book *De Regimine Sanitatis*.

Arnaud de Villeneuve combined astrology and philosophy with his medicine, believing it necessary to interpret the patient's dreams and to cast his horoscope as part of the diagnosis and treatment (see his *Tractatus Visionum*). His work seems in many ways to anticipate psychosomatic medicine. He further believed that the contra-indications of drugs were governed by the moon's phases: for seven days of the month, blood is dominant among the humours, for seven others, it is bile, and so on. Recent observations have indeed established a connection between the moon's phases and psychological disturbances.

Treatments

Arnaud de Villeneuve was not only a theoretician. He administered certain treatments using his knowledge of the absorption of the skin, discovered how to massage the bladder and used narcotics against pain. He also perfected the distillation of wine and used aromatic wines as tonics. Sixty-five such treatises are gathered together in his *Opera Omnia* of 1504.

According to Galen (b.131), the human body is made up of four humours: blood; bile; black bile; and phlegm. These correspond respectively to heat, cold, dryness and moisture.

Vintras, Eugène

1807–75

A crook on the fringes of occultism

The affair of Eugène Vintras was a mixture of charlatanism, politics and religion; that was the essence of his sect.

Eugène Vintras was born illegitimate and grew up in poverty. He had various jobs, but on 6 August 1839 his life changed completely. An old man 'whose face shone so brightly you could not look at him' visited him. This was St Joseph, come to announce the 'reign of Love' in order to prevent the impending 'end of the world'.

Vintras immediately founded the Institute of Pity, taking the name Sthratanael. His Institute was funded by a countess who with him formed the union of 'Adam and Eve of the regenerate world'. As Vintras was already married, the countess had to sleep in a single bed beside the double bed of Vintras and his wife. He claimed to have visions directed by the Virgin Mary and wore a cross on which the figure of Christ had addressed him, saying 'I want this cross to be known as the cross of grace, because this is an age of crime and corruption, having drawn down on all the earth the terrible effects of my Father's justice.'

Vintras and his followers

Followers flocked to him and Vintras offered them communion by giving them holy wafers dipped in blood. However, in April 1842 Vintras was arrested and sent to prison for five years: he had been collecting money from people to whom he claimed to reveal the name of their guardian angel.

While he was in prison, the Abbé Maréchal, known as Ruthmael, took over the community. He began with the extraordinary revelation that the sexual organs of his followers were blessed by the Holy Ghost. He therefore encouraged them to use them, and to masturbate together. He told them, 'Those who feel love for one another should share it often. Every time they do, they are sure to create a spirit in heaven.' On his release from prison, Vintras rejoined his mystic wife. Maréchal, who had meanwhile been sentenced, in absentia, by the courts for his excesses, went into hiding in a brothel.

From 1852 to 1862, Vintras lived in London. While there he published *L'Évangile éternel* (The Eternal Gospel) and attracted fresh recruits. On his return to France, he formed centres (which he called 'carmels') all over France, especially around Lyons. This was where Vintras founded his 'college of prophets'. He died, firmly convinced that he was a reincarnation of the prophet Elijah and that his order would survive the end of the world.

Guru, charlatan and visionary, he is still considered a saint in certain fundamentalist circles, although in fact he had little to do with occultism.

'I want the man bearing the cross to be **its only victim**.'

Against Vintras
Eliphas Lévi was aware of the dangerousness of Vintras and his order and violently denounced this 'absurd, anarchic sect'.

Willermoz, Jean-Baptiste

1730–1824

The organizer of Christian rites in freemasonry

Jean-Baptiste Willermoz was a mystic 'in touch with spirits' who gave him their orders. He played an important part in the history of freemasonry.

Jean-Baptiste Willermoz was a rich silk manufacturer from Lyons. He became a mason in 1753 and soon became a leading figure in the movement. He organized lodges and worked on the corrected Scottish Rite, which was Christian with aristocratic leanings and was distinct from the Ancient Accepted Rite that was more general at the time. At the convention of 1778, the rituals which he had written himself were accepted. He knew all the masonic dignitaries of Europe, including the Prince of Hesse-Kassel, and was a member of Martines de Pasqually's 'Elect of Cohen'.

A forerunner of spiritualism

From 1785 to 1799 Willermoz devoted himself to spiritualism with the help of a medium, Madame de Vallière. The accounts of their seances are held in the library in Lyons. Willermoz told the Prince of Hesse-Kassel that the spirits (or 'Unknown Superiors') had revealed to him the secret of long life. The prince invited him to Hamburg in 1790 to tell him of his 'luminous oracles'. Gerard van Ringsberg recorded their meeting: 'The simplest exercises consisted in staring at an object until it appeared to shine or was surrounded in luminous clouds. Another exercise was to stare at a dark spot in the sky at night to see a star appear in it.' The prince also had a portrait of Christ which, miraculously, illuminated as he looked on. He began to seek advice from it and one day the portrait proceeded to dictate 'secret' commentaries concerning the Apocalypse.

Willermoz's 'communications with the spirits' anticipated the wave of spiritualism about to wash over Europe and America.

Freud would doubtless call these messages 'products of the unconscious mind'. Nevertheless, it is interesting to see how such 'products' draw their material and their vocabulary from occultism.

In conclusion, Willermoz was, on the one hand, a mystic with an interest in prophecy and, on the other, a gifted organizer and powerful reactionary force in freemasonry.

Wronski, (José Marie) Hoëné

1776–1853

From advanced mathematics to esoterism

A seeker of the absolute, Wronski finally abandoned mathematics for metaphysics. This led him to hermetism.

Hoëné Wronski was the son of the architect to the last king of Poland. As a young army officer, he plotted for the independence of his country and performed heroic acts during the siege of Warsaw by the Prussians. He later set off to travel Europe, arriving in 1800 in Marseille, where he was granted French nationality.

At first he worked with the astronomer Lalande, who put the Marseilles observatory at his disposal. However, Wronski then became quite obsessed with his 'search for the absolute' (Balzac even based his character Balthasar Cloës on him). This ended in failure, though, and Wronski fell into poverty. It was also at this time that he lost both his wife and daughter.

A 'visionary of reason'

In 1810, Wronski published *La Loi suprême des mathématiques* (The Supreme Law of Mathematics), which drew praise from the Academy of Sciences and, in the following year, *Problème universel des mathématiques* (The Universal Problem of Mathematics). More books followed, including *Philosophie de l'infini* (The Philosophy of the Infinite) and *Réforme du calcul des probabilités* (A Reform of the Calculation of Probabilities), in which he reintroduced to mathematics the notion of infinity which had been rejected in Lagrange's theory of functions. Édouard Krakowski wrote, 'Wronski is gaining a certain notoriety — there is no denying it. The scale of his subjects, the bizarre titles and the peculiar fondness he has for dealing with increasingly metaphysical ideas in mathematical language, drive away his readers. Where they expect a mathematician, they find a visionary.'

Soon Wronski began to believe that he really was a prophet. His mathematical research led him to develop an 'infallible martingale' (a sort of double or quits bet), based on the 'teleological law of chance', with which he claimed to be able to make exact predictions. He then wrote a series of messages to the great men of his time and travelled all over Europe to effect his 'holy alliance of men' which would 'reconcile God's law and man's law'. His benefactors included an unsavoury character called Arson, whom he eventually sued, and later the engineer Durutte, whose money enabled him to print *Messianisme ou la Réforme absolue du savoir humain* (The Messiah or the Absolute Reform of Human Knowledge) in 1847.

Science and chimera

Wronski is typical of a certain kind of talented person with an interest in the occult sciences who suddenly becomes obsessed by some wild fancy. For example, he dreamt of inventing a device to 'calculate' past, present and future events. This is how

LE SPHINX,

OU

LA NOMOTHÉTIQUE SÉHÉLIENNE.

N°. I.

PAR HOËNÉ WRONSKI.

אם תבקשנה תמצאנה
(SALOMON)

A PARIS,

DE L'IMPRIMERIE DE DOUBLET,

RUE GIT-LE-CŒUR, N°. 7.

Décembre 1818.

In his review Le Sphinx, *Wronski established by scientific means the existence of the Absolute and came to 'schelian religion'. 'Schel' is the Hebrew word for 'proof', the opposite of 'revelation'. (National Library, Paris)*

Eliphas Lévi described the 'progonometer', as the device was known: 'All the sciences are the degrees of a circle turning on the same axis. The future is in the past, but it is not entirely contained in the present. Knowledge associated with the sciences makes up the spokes of the progonometer.' This same idea was taken up by Saint-Yves d'Alveidre, but with Wronski it became a utopian philosophy which began to resemble the 19th century Messianism of Pierre Leroux and Charles Fourier.

Finally, Wronski was also a tireless inventor. Amongst his most notable creations were an automobile chariot (which anticipated the tank), a 'pneumatic wheel' for use on railways, a small boiler and a calculating machine. Clearly a man ahead of his time, none of Wronski's contemporaries was able to see the potential of his inventions.

Zachaire, Denis

16th century

The Don Quixote of alchemy

Zachaire is to alchemy what Don Quixote is to chivalry.

The life of Zachaire seems to have been dreamt up by Marchodeo del Delle, court poet of Rudolf II of Austria. Whether or not he existed, the story goes that he was a gentleman from Guyenne, sent by his parents at the age of 20 to the College of Arts in Bordeaux and then to study law in Toulouse.

Tilting at windmills

In Bordeaux, Zachaire became passionately interested in alchemy:

> As soon as I was established in Toulouse, my master encouraged me to set up little furnaces, then larger ones, so that before long I had a whole room full of them. Some of them were for distilling, some for sublimating and some for burning and yet others were for dissolving and for melting. In this way I spent, in a single year, two hundred crowns of the money set aside to keep us in our studies for two years. As well as setting up furnaces, I bought coal, all sorts of drugs and various glass vessels at six crowns each, not to mention two ounces of gold for use in experiments and two or three marks of silver of which precious little was recovered. It was so tainted and blackened by being mixed as the experiments and recipes directed that it was almost useless. Thus, by the end of the year, my two hundred crowns had gone up in smoke and my master had also died of a fever.

This ruined Zachaire financially and he returned to Toulouse, only to be driven out again by an epidemic of plague. At Cahors, he was shown how to obtain the philosopher's stone. He returned once again to Toulouse, but finally sold his property there and made his way to Paris where he hoped to meet adepts of the art.

In Paris, the adepts used to meet near Notre-Dame to exchange ideas. One of this group, soon to reveal himself as a mere charlatan, promised to show Zachaire how to produce gold from cinnabar. Utterly disheartened by this experience, he returned to his studies. 'I began to read Raymond Lulle again with great diligence, especially his testament and codicil. I spent about another year reading and thinking of nothing day and night except my resolution.' Zachaire met his death in Cologne, murdered by a servant in an inn where he was spending the night.

Zanne

(alias of Auguste Van Dekerkove)

1838–1923

A crude blend of beliefs

It is uncertain whether Zanne had any real esoteric knowledge, whether he was inspired or merely a hoaxer. A Jack-of-all-trades, he left a profusion of works.

Auguste Van Dekerkove led a varied and eventful life; he was a journalist, labourer, draughtsman and magnetizer, to name only some of his occupations. It was in 1894 that his mysterious 'spiritual masters' conferred upon him the 'sacred name' of Zanne. Unfortunately, he does not tell us anywhere in his writings who these spiritual masters were. It is likely that he was at some point in contact with a group of Tibetan lamas, although this solution to the riddle of his name must remain mere speculation.

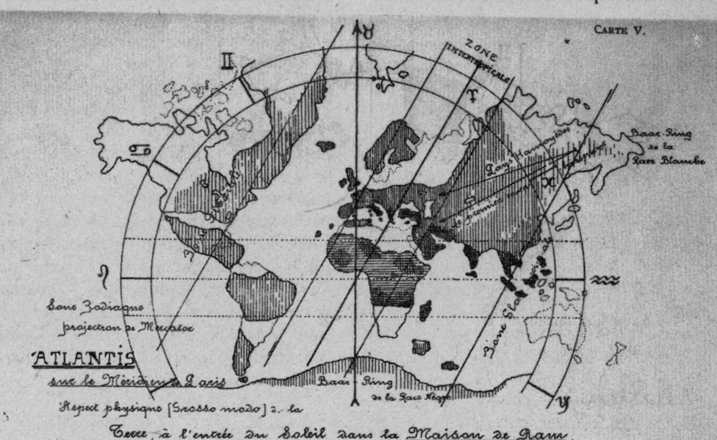

Zanne used complex overlays to create his occult history of the world. Map V of the appendix to his book Western Occultism and Eastern Esoterism *(National Library, Paris)*

A circular method

The texts of Zanne are profusely illustrated; he himself said, 'Every drawing is created by design.' His *Grande Cosmogonie* contains more than 2000 pages, in which he sets out his philosophy according to his 'circular method', full of twists and repetitions. His great interest was the primordial language of all mankind. He developed his theory in *Principes et Eléments de la langue sacrée* (Principles and Elements of the Holy Language), which was based on a comparison of the Hebrew and Roman alphabets. This primordial language was, for him, a true 'lost speech' which, although it had never been spoken, was the secret source of the speech of the inhabitants of Atlantis, the Hebrews and the Iberians, among others. Zanne also subscribed to the theory that sexuality was the way to initiation.

Zanne's work is largely unknown and he certainly merits greater attention, although Abellio perhaps went rather far in declaring him a major writer. His writings are patchy and inconsistent, though they also contain some occasional, remarkable insights. They are, further, pervaded by an often abstruse intuitive philosophy which conspires with the tautology of his 'circular method' to produce a rather turgid effect.

Examples of Occult Thought in Literature

Hermetism and art have a lot in common; Rimbaud, for example, spoke of the 'alchemy of the Word'. The resemblance is particularly striking when we consider the creative process; just like the occultist, the artist works on his 'raw material' or 'prime matter' (be it musical, literary or pictorial) and is constantly required to reassess his creation aesthetically, emotionally and ideologically.

Like the occultist, the artist works upon himself using an operative fiction: for the novelist, it is his characters; for the astrologer, it is his astrological theme. In the course of their creativity can they then teach us something about the universe and ourselves? In the case of the artist, the answer is obviously yes, but in the case of the occultist, the response is less clearcut.

Hermetism reveals the artist's raw material in its unfinished state; it is roughly crystallized. In its rough state it allows the artist's desire, not to be, but to 'be desired', as Flamel expressed it.

To establish a link between art and hermetism, as we are doing here, requires that the artist necessarily uses a hermetic process, and indeed a poem like Nerval's *El Desdichado* illustrates how this can happen. Some artists, of course, are clearly steeped in occult philosophy — Shakespeare is a good example. Others, like the French poet André Breton, use it simply as an intermediate stage.

Occultism, or at least the leaning towards it — the creative urge — occurs spontaneously in the artist's psyche as soon as he sets out to express himself in word, colour or form. Gnostic philosophy appeared in the very same way as soon as mankind began to look beyond his primordial, torpid state. It is, however, the artist who has the means to escape from the inner darkness the occult reveals to him. It is the artist who can 'transmute' himself through his works. In this way art develops by transcending its occult content.

Balzac, Honoré de

1799–1850

The rival of the demiurge

A body of work as monumental as Balzac's inevitably made him into a godlike figure. Perhaps that is why he was so interested in esoteric thought.

Balzac's philosophical outlook owes a great deal to occultism. He wrote, 'Politically, I belong to the Catholic religion; I am on the side of Bossuet and Bonald. Before God, I am on the side of St John; I belong to the mystical Church which alone has kept the true doctrine' (*Letters to a Foreign Lady*, 12 July 1842). Nevertheless, he was influenced by the Unknown Philosopher, Louis Claude de Saint Martin, who wrote in *L'Homme de désir* (The Man of Desire), 'The light rang out, the melody produced light and the colours moved because they were alive.' Balzac himself wrote in *Seraphita*, 'Light produced melody, melody produced light, colours were light and melody and Movement was a Number with the gift of speech.' This striking resemblance is only one of many. Balzac was also influenced by Swedenborg. He wrote, 'Swedenborg's philosophy is only a Christian repetition of ancient ideas; it becomes my religion when I add the unfathomable nature of God.'

Number and Movement

'1. All that is here below exists purely through Movement and Number.
2. Movement is like Number in action.
3. Movement is the product of a force engendered by the Word and a resistance called Matter ... Newton's gravity is not a law, but one effect of the general law of universal Movement.
6. Number, which produces such variety, also creates Harmony, which in its highest acceptation is the relationship between the parts and Unity.
14. Three is the formula for the worlds which have been created. It is the spiritual side of creation just as it is the material sign of the circumference. Indeed, God only worked in circular lines. The straight line is the attribute of infinity, as man who has his feeling for the infinite, uses it in his works. Two is the number for creation. Three is the number for existence, which includes both creation and created. Add the Quaternary and you have seven, the number for Heaven. God is above that – he is Unity.' Balzac, *Seraphita*

Visionary realism

'In the hundred years since his death, the general view of Balzac's work has changed radically. Judged at first to be excessively romantic, it was later classified as 'realist'. Gradually it has been released from this rigid view as critics realized that if Balzac was faithful to any reality, it was the reality of his visions.'
R. Amadou and R. Kanters, *Anthologie littéraire de l'occultisme*

Baudelaire, Charles

1821–67

Beauty and terror lead to Gnosticism

A vein of Gnosticism runs through Baudelaire's work, although this in no way mars the beauty of his poetry.

The literary critics Robert Amadou and Robert Kanters tell us that it was Gérard de Nerval and Balzac who guided Baudelaire towards his study of hermetism. In *Les Paradis artificiels*, Baudelaire certainly evokes both Fourier and Swedenborg, and also Lavater. However, it was his discovery of the writings of Edgar Allan Poe (1809–1849) which was to prove decisive, for here the quest for the mysterious was combined with the most exacting literary standards.

'Poetry has only itself'

Rimbaud paid Baudelaire the compliment of hailing him as 'the first seer, the king of poets and a true god'. But what was it that Baudelaire 'saw'? Some critics, to whom initiation appeared a rather passive affair, focused on his *Correspondances*, with their apparent references to hermetism. Rimbaud felt that they completely overlooked the aspect of the 'angel of morbidity' he so admired in lines like '*O Satan, prends pitié de ma longue misère*' ('Oh Satan, take pity on my lifelong misery').

René Char considered Baudelaire the most human of all poets. Baudelaire confronted death and its terrors, the ultimate human mystery, and tried to recover from it the beauty it stole from life. His song was not the music of the spheres, but human music tearing itself free from the distress Pascal described so vividly. Baudelaire was no hermetist, but a poet: 'Poetry has no Truth as an object, it has only itself'. However, sometimes his lines do sound like Gnostic texts. He is filled with the most utter despair at times and seems, like the Catharians, not to be of this world.

Baudelaire's metaphysical philosophy remains obscure as he elegantly contrived to leave us only his poetry. However, if the claims of Paul Arnold are to be believed, he referred secretly and constantly to *Poïmandrès*, the Gnostic text where we read of the soul's fall into matter — into the 'prison of flesh' — and its struggle to return to the light. This text tells how anguish is transmuted into love and, certainly, if Baudelaire was influenced by it, we would thus learn a lot about his personal philosophy.

> 'The **insatiable thirst** revealed in life for all that is beyond, is the most vivid proof of immortality.'

Blake, William

1757–1827

Poet, prophet and revolutionary

'I must Create a System, or be enslav'd by another Man's; I will not Reason and Compare: my business is to Create.'

Poet, mystic, artist and engraver, William Blake defies all formal definition or classification.

Works

In addition to Blake's quite remarkable imaginative intensity as an artist, he also brought this same beauty, imagination and visionary power to his literary works.

His *Songs of Innocence* (1789) and *Songs of Experience* (1794) include some of the purest lyrics in the English language and express his ardent belief in the freedom of the imagination. His mystical and prophetical works include the *Book of Thel* (1789), *The Marriage of Heaven and Hell* (1791) and *The Song of Los* (1795). All his works reflect his vivid and unshakeable faith in the invisible, and his conviction that he was in receipt of perpetual spiritual guidance and support.

A poet and visionary, he has all the attributes of the bard. His work reveals a cosmogony, relates the history of our world and tells of 'natural religion', that system of ethics which takes account of all aspects of our nature, including our yearning to revolutionize our planet and unite with God in love. Art occupies a central place in Blake's philosophy as a necessary refuge, for it is in this way that his vision is sustained and preserved.

Premises

'Man does not have a body distinct from his Soul, for what is called his Body is a fragment of the Soul, discovered by the senses, the great evasion of the Soul in our time.'

'Energy is the only life and proceeds from the Body; Reason is the boundary, the outer circumference, of Energy.'

'Energy is Eternal Pleasure.'

The existential myth

The critics fell upon Blake's work and tried to analyze its strangeness. The influence of the Cabala can certainly be seen, as well as that of Swedenborg, Böhme and alchemy itself. But this simply serves to heighten the mystery. For what, after all, is alchemy, or the Cabala? No one knows exactly what Hegel or Balzac or Baudelaire sought in those old books, or what sort of confirmation they provided to them in their intuitive quests.

William Blake listens to 'something' speaking within him and then transcribes it in the 'words of the tribe'; this 'something' is nature, the world, in fact anything you like, for Blake believed, in accordance with the principle of alchemy, that a work of art was not only the manifestation of liberty but also the means by which nature is perfected.

This creed is perhaps what gives such exquisite intensity to his writings, now wild and prophetic, now gentle and candid. In his works, redolent with fable, Blake invites us to contemplate the question underlying all hermetism: does the language of art not contain more truth than that of experimental science? This may be the question that drove Blake on; it may be his 'existential myth'. To find out why Blake believed that he had succeeded in his personal quest, we can do no better than to study his works.

Cyrano de Bergerac, Savinien de

1619–55

A master of esoterism in burlesque clothing

Rostand made this spiritual dreamer into the model of disinterested love.

Best known as a character in Edmond Rostand's famous play, Cyrano was a real person who lived in the time of Louis XIII and Mazarin. A playwright, from whom Molière borrowed, perhaps his most important works are the *États et Empires de la Lune* and *États et Empires du Soleil* which reveal a hermetic philosopher hiding his reflections in burlesque works of fiction.

Amadou and Kanters write, 'Cyrano's works anticipate travel by balloon and gramophone records, as well as discussing serious points of alchemy; this is what makes reading them, even today, an extraordinary spiritual journey.'

Discourse on Truth

'I arrived at a bog where I found a little man, quite naked, sitting resting on a stone. He talked to me for three good hours in a language I know I had never heard, which was not like any other in this world, but which I understood more quickly and easily than the language my nurse had used. He explained, when I enquired about such a wondrous thing, that in science there is a Truth, and outside this Truth all things are far from easy; the further speech moved away from this Truth, the further it fell below understanding. "Similarly," he continued, "in Music this Truth is never met, but the soul is immediately uplifted and borne blindly towards it. We do not see it, but we sense Nature sees it. And, without understanding how we are absorbed in it, it does not fail to delight us, even if we do not know where it is." I said to him that the first man in our world had undoubtedly used this language because the name he had put to each thing declared its essence. He interrupted me and went on, "When I speak, your soul encounters, in every one of my words, this Truth it is groping after, and although by reason it cannot grasp it, it has in itself a Nature which cannot fail to understand it." I exclaimed: "Alas, no doubt this powerful tongue was once used by our first forefather to talk to the animals and be understood by them! And therefore, because this language is lost, they no longer come to us as they once did for they no longer understand us."'

Fourier, Charles François Marie

1772–1837

Utopian socialism and esoterism

'Of cabbages and kings': Fourier's philosophy was all-embracing.

Occult mythology did not ignore the rising working-class, and the historians of the 19th century were the first to see that the archaic guild movement was responsible for helping working-class culture to move into the modern world. It should come as no surprise to find freemasons running the finances of the Paris Commune or directing the first Workers' International. Just as in art, the dream of liberty expresses itself in the quest for a 'lost speech', even if that is not stated explicitly in the ideology.

The age of gold is yet to come

The reformer Saint-Simon (1760–1825) was perhaps the first to inform the modern revolutionaries that the age of gold spoken of in mythology was before us, not behind us, as was traditionally believed. The same idea occurs in Rimbaud's verse and among the surrealists. However, the best representative of this zealous search for a new world is Charles Fourier. Scorned as a utopian by Marx and idolized by the poet André Breton, his philosophy was rediscovered in the 1970s.

The flowering of humanity

Marx did not agree with Fourier, because he centred his system, not on the real economic problems of exchange, production or consumption, but on his Theory of Attraction. This was the force which, when rediscovered, would lead humanity on to realize its full potential and achieve harmony with the universe. Although he was concerned above all with social problems, Fourier's solution was not sociological, but philosophical, although he did not forget the actor who reveals these problems and from whom they draw their meaning. The regeneration of nature, for Fourier, depends on the liberation of man: macrocosm and microcosm coincide in a kind of analogy, hence the importance to his system of the underlying cosmogony. This cosmogony takes up archaic themes and brings them up to date; for example, it makes reference to the 'copulation of the stars' which symbolizes the marriage of the gods, a common motif in mythology and alchemy.

The passion for analogy

Fourier believed that the alienation of both society and cosmos was caused by the failure to give free rein to our passions. The effect of moralism had been disastrous: it had created artificial duties and thrown society and the entire universe into disorder. Fourier chose this extract from Schelling for the epigraph to *De l'analogie*: 'It is impossible to read destiny in part only; the universe is built on the model of the human soul.' He notes, in *Théorie des quatre mouvements* (Theory of the Four Movements), that the passions so decried by philosophers are 'the most noble thing after God, since He desired that all the universe should be arranged according to the effects that they produce in terms of the social Movement.' These four movements ring throughout the

Women and freedom

'Social progress and change depends on the progress of women towards freedom, and social decay goes hand in hand with their loss of freedom.'

cosmos, with animal, organic and material movements all linked to the predominant social one. Fourier tried to elucidate his theory with an astronomical analogy: 'Groups of stars in the Milky Way represent 'ambition', while groups of planets round their suns represent 'love', and groups of satellites round planets represent 'paternity'.' He continues: 'The properties of friendship are based on those of the circle; the properties of love are based on those of the ellipse.'

Carried away by his passion for analogy, he wrote:

> These analogies need to be reinforced with plenty of detail, first of all with respect to the leaves of vegetables. The tense twisted leaf of the beetroot represents the violent nature of the work of slaves or the working-class; the grotesque leaf of rape is the image of the head of the village family helping himself to all profits in the name of morality. The cabbage is the image of mysterious love, its secret intrigues masked; its billowing, wavy-edged leaves represent the cunning efforts of lovers who must keep their passion hidden.

Fourier even goes so far as to state that every man develops around a 'tree of passions' (like the Cabalistic tree of the sefirot) which yields 12 passions and 810 different types of character.

If 'association', the central motif of his system, is desired and is to be achieved, we must give free rein to our passions, and not suppress them.

> 'A child seems to be full of all vices — greedy, argumentative, fanciful, cheeky, rebellious, inquisitive, uncontrollable — but he is the most perfect of all; he will be keenest in the work of the Combined Order. From the age of ten, he will be promoted to be among the leading children in the parish and will have the honour of presiding over them, and leading them on parade and in work.'

'**Social education** aims to develop fully all material and intellectual faculties and to apply them, even the pleasures, in productive industry.'

Goethe, Johann Wolfgang von

1749–1832

His genius was largely founded on hermetism

Goethe does not seem to have treated esoterism incidentally; it was certainly one of his sources of inspiration.

During his legal studies, Goethe was assailed by an apparently incurable illness of a psychosomatic nature. 'I was a shipwrecked sailor,' he wrote, 'more ill in my soul than in my body'. His parents entrusted him to the care of Dr Johann Friedrich Metz, described by Christian Lepinte as an 'enigmatic character, a real doctor in the Rosicrucian tradition, for whom the treatment of the body must lead

'Faust and Mephisto' by Eugène Delacroix (1798–1863). Lithograph selected from a series of 17 for Goethe's Faust *in 1823. (National Library, Paris)*

to the healing of the soul.' He cured Goethe and introduced him to the devout, occultist circle of Suzanne von Klettenberg. Goethe began to read Paracelsus, Basil Valentin, Jakob Böhme, Giordano Bruno and others, and *Aurea Catena*, a work on alchemy, became his standard reference. Some critics claim that the character Makarie in *Wilhelm Meister* is based on Dr Metz and the Society of the Tower recalls the Klettenberg circle.

In 1780, Goethe became a freemason. This did not, however, prevent him from writing that 'freemasonry is a State within the State, and it is never advisable to introduce it where it does not already exist'. As a freemason inspired by occultism, who maintained close relations with esoteric groups in spite of his high position, Goethe produced works impregnated with symbolism and alchemy. Hermetism was his constant, deep preoccupation, as is proved in particular by his work on colours.

Humanism, hermetism and wisdom

Lepinte tells us that:

> Goethe's thinking is dominated by the idea of a society of elects or initiates perpetuating a sacred myth ... The poem *Geheimnisse* (Secrets) haunts his spirit. The monastic order, whose mysteries are revealed in the fragments of the poem, shares in the order of the Templars, in Rosicrucianism, freemasonry and the mystic quest for the Holy Grail.

Goethe was extremely wary of impostors, and his *Grand Cophte* satirized Cagliostro whom he accused of 'casting pearls before swine'.

The character of Makarie, referred to above, tells us much about Goethe's ideal. Makarie is detached from the corporeal but is nonetheless linked to it by the 'umbilical cord of human brotherhood'. For Goethe, truth must lie in humanism. The winning of wisdom is no small matter, as he shows in *Faust*, in which Goethe takes us to the very heart of Gnostic legend. At the end of the book entitled *Dichtung und Wahrheit* (Poetry and Truth), he states that if Neoplatonism is the basis of his philosophy, hermetism, mysticism and the Cabala are also important elements in it. He is not only a powerful hermetist, he is also — and this is far from incompatible — a humanist and a scientist. He is the very image of the Wise Man. Rudolf Steiner considered that Goethe had, after long maturation, 'attained the supreme mysteries'.

> Goethe's *Faust* contains the main elements of Gnosticism: the principles of good and evil (God and Satan); the Gnostic himself (Faust); Sophia (Gretchen-Helen) and so on.

Jean de Meung

c.1240–c.1305

A literary alchemist

Jean de Meung discovered hermetism through the Catharians and the troubadours. He was probably an alchemist, so the Roman de la Rose is a work in code.

The *Roman de la Rose* (Romance of the Rose) is in two parts; the second part, written by Jean de Meung around 1277, is incontestably hermetist.

'Gay sçavoir'

Jean de Meung was denounced by the chancellor Gerson (see his *Vision* published in 1240) for being a Catharian and a troubadour. However, as far as Jean de Meung was concerned, there could be but one object of research, the *gay sçavoir* (or 'joy of knowledge') of the troubadours, which was symbolized by the Fountain of Youth. He wrote:

> The fountain I tell you of is a health-giving fountain, wondrously beautiful . . . We never saw such a fountain, for it springs from itself, as others which are not fed by their own veins, do not. It is sufficient unto itself; it needs no marble and no leafy shade, for the water which never fails comes from a source so high that no tree can reach it . . . To drink of this fountain, think to honour Nature.

There is a science which teaches how to drink from this fountain — alchemy, the true art. In the *Roman de la Rose*, Jean de Meung provides a comprehensive review of occult theory; the work is in effect a complete miniature encyclopedia on the subject. Eliphas Lévi wrote, 'The roses of Flamel, de Meung and Dante flowered on the same tree,' in his *Histoire de la magie*. This may be true of Flamel and de Meung, but is less obviously true of Dante, whose quest was spiritual rather than esoteric.

The loving relationship

Careful reading of the *Roman de la Rose* will reveal the theme of the alchemy of love, for that is what it is all about despite the dry, prosaic, didactic tone of some pages. The alchemist himself is the subject of his work, but this implies neither egocentricity nor sentimentality. The alchemist is a man in love and it is as such that he discovers nature (or the cosmos). So the subject of alchemy is a relationship. The human being is defined in terms of a triple relationship: with himself, with his loving partner and with the universe.

The Fountain of the Beautiful Narcissus *The lover drinks the 'living water', ie he discovers the first principle. Miniature from the* Roman de la Rose *by Jean de Meung, 14th-century manuscript. (National Library, Paris)*

Jung, Carl Gustav

1875–1961

Psychoanalysis, alchemy and initiation

According to Jung, the process of psychoanalysis is related to that of initiation, and transfer is comparable to transmutation in alchemy.

Carl Gustav Jung was the writer who opened up psychoanalysis to the influence of hermetism. The proof of this lies in his theory of symbols which owes far more to esoteric thinking than to, say, the linguistics of Saussure. His personal manner of deciphering the unconscious also recalls a rather clumsy quest for the invisible. Finally, and inescapably, his works contain numerous references to alchemy, which he used as a model for the completed 'individuation process' and from which he borrowed the operative concepts of his psychology (see especially *Psychology and Alchemy*, 1944). However, *My Life* is the book in which his most significant ideas on the subject appear.

An apologia for secrecy

> At the primitive stage, the need to surround ourselves in mystery is of vital importance, and the shared secret is the bond which holds the group together. At the social level, secrecy is a necessary compensation for the lack of cohesion in the individual's personality which, after constant relapses into the unconscious original identity shared with others, is always breaking up and scattering again . . .
>
> A secret society is an intermediate stage along the path to individuation: the individual entrusts the collective organization with the task of differentiating him with respect to others, ie he has yet to understand that strictly speaking it is up to the individual to stand on his own feet and be different from others.
>
> . . . It would be quite wrong to consider the intermediate stage as an obstacle to individuation. On the contrary, it will continue for a long time to be the only way the individual can exist independently, as he is increasingly threatened with anonymity.
>
> . . . Just as the initiate, thanks to the secrecy of the society, can prevent himself from passing into an undifferentiated collective, in the same way an isolated individual, in order to pursue his solitary way, needs some secret which, for whatever reason, he cannot and must not reveal. It is only a secret we cannot betray, a secret that fills us with fear or that cannot be put clearly into words, that can stop us from slipping back into the collective. *My Life.*

A comprehensive approach

Jung took an interest not only in alchemy and Gnosticism, but also in astrology, divination, spiritualism and parapsychology.

For Jung, the unconscious draws its definitive structure from a Gnostic and alchemistic language and grammar. The idea is fascinating, even if Jung's conclusions are sometimes debatable.

Maeterlinck, Maurice

1862–1949

Poetry impregnated with hermetism

Hermetism lies at the heart of Maeterlinck's works; Debussy's musical interpretation perhaps illuminates something of their mystery.

The works of Maeterlinck, including *Pelléas et Mélisande* and *Grand Secret*, are studded with reflections on occultism, by which he sought to explore the ancient mysteries of existence. Maeterlinck's approach lies midway between so-called 'traditionalism' and spiritualism.

> Thus we see that occultism ... was always a protest by human reason, true to its prehistoric traditions, against the arbitrary declarations and supposed revelations of public, official religions. Against their dubious dogma and anthropomorphic and illogical manifestations, too trivial to be taken seriously, it avowed a total and invincible ignorance on all essential points. From this avowal, which seems at first glance to destroy everything, but which in reality leads almost inevitably to a spiritual conception of the universe, it drew its metaphysics and its morality; these are purer, higher, more disinterested and, above all, more rational than those to which religions gave rise as they stifled occultism. *Grand Secret*

'I see a rose in the darkness.'

'Pelléas et Mélisande'

In his play *Pelléas et Mélisande*, Maeterlinck sought to restore to the theatre the dream dimension; this is what caught Debussy's interest and inspired him to compose an operatic setting of the work. The study of man is, for Maeterlinck, not merely an exploration of sociology, psychology or the unconscious; it is also a duality, a dynamic equation, uniting and contrasting reality and dream, here and elsewhere.

Maeterlinck, in company with the symbolists, wanted to stress the mystery which surrounds and forms humanity. However, whereas Mallarmé, for example, concerned himself with language alone (the *mots de la tribu*, or 'words of the tribe'), Maeterlinck concentrated on the mythological aspect. Thus *Pelléas et Mélisande* contains elements found in the legend of Melusine, amongst other figures taken from folklore. Maeterlinck's genius springs from an intensity of feeling which imbues his work and fills it with images of remarkable beauty and richness.

Mallarmé, Stéphane

1842–98

Mallarmé and the philosopher's stone

One of the founding fathers of modernism, he seems to have drawn extensively on hermetism. How else can his poetic quest be understood?

Literature owes far more to esoteric thought than we often like to think. Let us take, for example, Virgil (70–19 BC), whose *Eclogues*, according to Paul Maury, revealed a numerical construction which was derived from the golden mean. It has also been claimed (by Jerome Carcopino) that the fourth of these poems was directly inspired by Pythagoreanism. As for Apuleius (125–170), his *Golden Ass* ends with an initiation into the mysteries of Isis. We could also cite Shakespeare, Dante, Milton, Rabelais and Poe among the many writers who have taken an interest in hermetism.

A 'commentary of pure signs'

Stéphane Mallarmé was another writer much influenced by hermetism. As a freemason, he frequented the Independent Art bookshop where, according to V. E. Michelet, the author of *L'Ésotérisme dans l'art* (with which Mallarmé was familiar), the 'spirits of symbolism joined those of esoterism'. This was where he met Villiers de L'Isle-Adam, the author of *Isis* and *Axel*, as well as Debussy and others. Mallarmé was fascinated by the Cabala and alchemy, and wrote that occultism is the 'commentary of pure signs obeyed by all literature in the immediate outpouring of the spirit'. It is an interesting definition: hermetism provides the explanation — the only possible explanation — of the signs or forms which make up any work of art, literary, artistic or musical.

The absolute structure

In essence, Mallarmé attempted to grasp the very root of the act of writing. He tried to relocate himself with respect to the invisible, of which writing is but a trace. He set off in search of a 'speech' (a lost speech?) whose elusive iridescence he longed to capture. His talk of 'the throw of the dice which will never abolish chance' and his obsessive fear of the book as a rigid, definitive structure are evidence of this.

Some writers have likened Mallarmé's verse to certain theories of esoterism, especially Helena Blavatsky's 'secret doctrine' and Rudolf Steiner's 'theosophy'. It could also be argued that Mallarmé's first vision recalls the 'broken vases' (*Zimzum*) of the Cabala which the poet must confront, aided only by his verse. Interesting though these comparisons may be, they completely overlook Mallarmé's utter originality, which gave new life to the tradition to which he belonged. While the surrealists were haunted by dreams, Mallarmé explored the nature and being of poetry, his starting point. An age was coming to an end. The invisible which had hitherto hidden discreetly behind words, the invisible which was the intimate friend of cre-

> 'For it is through **science** that I fit
> The hymn of spiritual hearts
> Into the work of my patience,
> Atlases, herbals and rituals.'

Chance. *Colour lithograph by André Masson for the book* Un coup de dés jamais n'abolira le hasard *(A Throw of the Dice Will Never Abolish Chance) by Mallarmé (National Library, Paris)*

ative writers from Virgil to Villiers de L'Isle-Adam, was demanding that writers should form a new relationship with it.

However, can the invisible be the exclusive preserve of either poetry or hermetism? Surely occultism is more than a simple explanation or, to use Mallarmé's words, a 'commentary of pure signs'. Otherwise art can be little more than a mere scrap of something much more fundamental and vast — the invisible revealed through Gnosticism, whose works alone, elusive as quicksilver, provide the ultimate answer to man's spiritual quest.

Meyrink, Gustav

1868–1932

Romantic novels inspired by esoterism

The author of Golem based all his works on ideas taken from esoterism.

Gustav Meyrink was the son of an actress and a minister of state in Württemberg. He discovered esoterism when on the the verge of suicide, after having ruined himself financially on the stock exchange. He then joined various esoteric circles in Prague, Munich and Vienna and took enthusiastically to yoga.

The **Golem** is a clay figure, into whose mouth its creator, a rabbi, would put a slip of paper with the name of God written on it. This brought the statue to life and the rabbi, who was its master, could use it for various tasks. An old Jewish legend from the ghettos tells how the Golem protected Jews during the pogroms.

The Golem is therefore a forerunner of Mary Shelley's *Frankenstein*. Frankenstein the monster was created by a scientist, by scientific means; the Golem by a Cabalist, using mystical methods. Both myths — like that of the homunculus — are very old. They express man's desire to be equal to God but usually end in catastrophe, for presumption must be punished.

The rabbi in Meyrink's version of the story regains mastery of his creature by taking God's name away from him. The Golem is thus obviously a form of Cabalistic speculation: as 'masters of the secret', the Cabalists knew the true name of God, the name that the high priest alone uttered once a year in a secret room in the Temple of Jerusalem.

A literary medium

Meyrink was a talented expressionist writer and has left us a series of novels on the theme of initiation. Gérard Heim, one of his translators, wrote, in his preface to *The White Dominican*:

> Meyrink was certainly the most remarkable medium in European literature. He was passionately interested in occult phenomena and his whole life was a long quest for esoteric knowledge. He is one of the few Europeans who have managed to learn at least one branch of the technique of yoga, and he used this to develop the sensitivity of his body and perfect his powers as a clairvoyant and a medium.

The main character in the above book is, incidentally, John Dee, the English alchemist. Meyrink's best book, which has often been filmed, is however generally reckoned to be *Golem*.

The **Dibbuk** must not be confused with the Golem. It is the spirit of a dead person which takes possession of a living body and can only be driven out by exorcism.

'In every name there is a **hidden force**, and when we repeat that name over and over again, in our heart, without opening our mouth, until it finally fills our being day and night, we draw into our blood that spiritual force which then circulates in our veins and, in time, finally tranforms our whole body.' Gustav Meyrink, *The Green Face*

Milosz

(Oscar Vladislas de Labunovas Lubicz-Milosz)

1877–1939

A poet imprisoned by his visions

Milosz was a great poet, but a lesser master of esoterism.

Milosz was born in Lithuania and died at Fontainebleau near Paris. He was the son of a Baltic baron who was fascinated by Buddhism and, on his mother's side, the grandson of a Cabalistic rabbi. He was a great poet and an interesting playwright whose works are, today, sadly neglected. Milosz also produced esoteric writings, which combine dazzling intuition with a kind of prophetic naïvety. An example of his naïvety, from the *Poème des arcanes*, is his desire to believe in the fusion of the irreconcilable: the teaching of Hiram, the mythical master of freemasonry, with the teaching of the Church. The *Letter to Sorge* (1916) and *The Iberian Origins of the Jewish People* (1933) are works of, at times, great beauty but they are also often bewildering for the reader. Milosz frequently confused symbolism with reality and found it difficult to distinguish between fiction and fact.

The 'Hymn of Knowledge'

In Milosz's writing, the *Hymn of Knowledge* marks the transition from the profane to the sacred:

> To those who, having asked, have received and know already.
> To those whom prayer has led on to meditation on the origins of language.
> The others, who stole pain and joy, science and love, will understand none of these things . . .
> The power of naming objects which can be experienced by the senses, but are impenetrable to the spiritual being,
> Comes from the knowledge of archetypes which, being of the same nature as our spirit, are situated like it in the consciousness of the solar egg . . .
> The language of truth, rediscovered, has nothing new to offer. It only awakens recollection in the memory of the man who prays.
> Do you sense the oldest of your memories awakening? I can tell you here of the sacred origin of your love of gold . . .
> And this is the effective prayer into which the operator must plunge: Keep safe within me the love of this metal coloured by your glance, the knowledge of this gold which mirrors the world of archetypes . . .
> Learn from me that all illness is a confession by the body.
> Real evil is hidden evil; but when the body has confessed, very little more is needed to bring the spirit itself, the preparer of secret poisons, to submit.

Nerval, Gérard de

(alias of Gérard Labrunie)

1808–55

Nerval's poetry is an introduction to hermetism

El Desdichado is a mysterious poem which leads the reader to the hermetic mystery in all of Nerval's work.

Gérard de Nerval was fascinated by occultism. In *Les Illuminés* he speaks of Cagliostro; in *Le Voyage en Orient* he provides a sequel to the legend of Hiram. The critic Jean Richer has established that Nerval copied out long passages from hermetic works and that he knew, almost by heart, *Le Monde primitif* by Court de Gévelin and Dom Pernety's *Dictionnaire mytho-hermétique*.

Nerval's vision of the world is filtered through hermetism, as is shown by the conclusion of *Aurélia*:

> But, in my opinion, earthly events were linked to those of the invisible world. This is one of the strange connections I had not even realized myself, and which are easier to point out than to define ... What had I done? I had disturbed the harmony of the magical universe from which my soul drew the certainty of immortality. I was damned, perhaps because I had desired to penetrate an awful mystery by offending the law of God.

The mystery of the poem

Georges Le Breton points out correspondences between the fragmentary and mysterious *El Desdichado*, and alchemy and the tarot cards.

El Desdichado

Je[1] suis le Ténébreux, — le Veuf —, l'Inconsolé,
Le Prince d'Aquitaine à la Tour abolie:
Ma seule *Étoile* est morte, — et mon luth constellé[2]
Porte le *Soleil noir*[3] de la *Mélancolie*[4].
Dans la nuit du Tombeau[5], Toi qui m'as consolé,
Rends-moi le Pausilippe et la mer d'Italie[6],
La *fleur*[7] qui plaisait tant à mon coeur désolé,
Et la treille où le Pampre à la Rose s'allie[8].
Suis-je Amour ou Phoebus? ... Lusignan ou Biron?
Mon front est rouge[9] encore du baiser de la Reine[10];
J'ai rêvé dans la Grotte où nage la Syrène[11] ...
Et j'ai deux fois[12] vainqueur traversé l'Achéron:
Modulant tout à tour sur la lyre d'Orphée[13]
Les soupirs de la Sainte[14] et les cris de la Fée.

I[1] am the Dark one — the Widower — the Disconsolate,
The Prince of Aquitaine whose Tower was abolished:
My only *Star* is dead, and my lute in its constellation[2]
Carries the *Black Sun*[3] of *Melancholy*[4].
In the night of the Tomb[5], You who consoled me,

Give me back Posilipo and the sea of Italy[6],
The *flower*[7] which so pleased my desolate heart,
And the trellis where the Vine and the Rose are joined[8].
Am I Love or Phoebus? . . . Lusignan or Byron?
My brow is red[9] still from the kiss of the Queen[10];
I dreamt in the Grotto where the Siren[11] swims . . .
And twice[12] as victor I crossed Acheron:
Playing all the while on Orpheus'[13] lyre
The sighs of the Saint[14] and the cries of the Fairy.

1. 'I' here is apparently the Pluto of alchemy. He represents the earth hidden beneath the black colour. This 'blackness' is present at the start of the alchemist's work; it is 'death' and 'melancholy' . . .
2. The first three verses correspond to tarot cards XV (the Devil), XVI (the Tower) and XVII (the Star).
3. The expression 'Black Sun' occurs frequently in alchemy.
4. 'Melancholy' symbolizes the 'rotting of matter'.
5. Alchemists believed that 'a king had to be put in his tomb in order to raise him again from his ashes'.
6. Posilipo (Pansiliphon) is the red (philosopher's) stone; the sea represents mercury.
7. This is a mythological reference to the 'white flower' of Proserpine.
8. The vine-shoot represents the colour of rust and is therefore Mars; the rose is Venus. The philosopher's sun is born of their union.
9. Note that the first quatrain is black, the second white, and the first triplet is red.
10. Sulphur is the philosopher's king; mercurial water, the queen.
11. The siren is Melusine; the grotto is the alchemist's vessel.
12. This line alludes to the second stage of alchemical work.
13. Dom Pernety wrote: 'As a poet, Orpheus is the Artist, who tells allegorically what happens in the alchemist's work.'
14. The Saint is the Virgin of alchemy who will produce the 'matter of the wise men'.
(Extract from the journal *Fontaine*, no. 44–45)

A mystery
It does not seem to be going too far to say that *El Desdichado* is perhaps the most carnally mysterious poem in the French language.

Have these references any real meaning, though? Have they anything other than a purely decorative function? Was Nerval perhaps simply indulging in a little game? Probably not, for the whole poem is steeped in mystery, and Nerval wanted us to sense this mystery and comprehend its grandeur. So is it then a coded message in which Nerval has hidden a secret for us to find? This would be to surround it in a false mystery. The Black Sun is not a rebus, but a poetic image; it is not to be decoded, but simply taken as it is.

A meeting with alchemy

Nerval believed that his literary quest bore strong similarities to those of both the alchemist and the adept of the tarot, and he highlighted these links in expressing his personal experience of the secret.

Hermetism, Gnosticism, and alchemy fascinated many poets, including Shakespeare, Blake, Baudelaire and Rimbaud. However, the secret has never seemed so tantalizingly near (and yet far) as in poems such as *El Desdichado* and *Artémis*. The fact that Nerval dabbled in alchemy to discover himself is an intriguing problem for literary criticism; perhaps hermetism could provide theoretical models for all poets.

Novalis

(alias of Friedrich von Hardenberg)

1772–1802

The Night of Novalis is the one before initiation

In the Hymns to the Night we sense an allusion to a vision impregnated with esoteric thought. This philosophical vision is contained in the Fragments.

Novalis is sometimes likened to Pascal; Maeterlinck was more precise and said he reminded him of a rather dreamy Pascal, for 'Pascal never knew Böhme, Lavater, Eckartshausen, Zwizendorf, Young-Stilling, and the great Böhme never lets go once he has taken hold'. This mysterious German poet was a friend of Schlegel and Schiller, and he often visited the occultist Zacharias Werner, who was apparently the model for the master in *Disciples in Sais*. Novalis's *Hymns to the Night*, his love for the young Sophie (which reminds us of Dante and his Beatrice) and his other works reveal, according to Thomas Carlyle, a 'strange character'. For Novalis, there was always union between man and the universe, whether it was expressed in terms of poetry, magic or love.

The children of God

'We understand the world when we understand ourselves, for we and God are complementary halves of one whole ... We are the children of God, the seeds of divinity. One day, we will be as our father.

We are in touch with all parts of the universe, with the future and the past. Whether or not we develop any one dominant relationship so that it appears particularly important and effective to us, depends on the direction and duration of our attention. A proper method as far as this process is concerned, would be nothing less than the science of divination ...

We are bound more closely to the invisible world than to the visible ... Mathematics only concerns law, or the nature and art of justice; it does not concern the nature and art of magic. Both become magic only through moralization. Love is the principle which makes magic possible. Love acts magically ...

The unknown, or the mysterious, is the result and origin of everything ...

The physical magician can bring nature to life and use it arbitrarily, as if it were his own body ...

Any spell works by partial identification of the enchanter with the bewitched, who can be made to see an object, believe it and feel it as the sorcerer so desires. The magician is a poet. The prophet is to the magician as the man of taste is to the poet ...

Plato

429–347 BC

An initiate of Pythagoreanism?

All we can say with certainty is that Plato was familiar with Pythagoras' esoteric thought and based much of his work on it.

Plato was quite familiar with Pythagorean thought. He is probably of all thinkers the one who has meditated most deeply on notions of 'harmony' and 'proportion', as is particularly obvious in his *Timaeus* with its speculations on number, or rather on the rhythm of the soul of the world. Some experts have gone so far as to claim that they have reconstructed Plato's mathematical and musical scheme, and that it is founded on Pythagoras' tetractys. Plato's main desire, however, appears to have been to generalize his theories and apply them, in social organization (see *The Republic*); in this he was a utopian, with leanings towards totalitarianism.

The mathematical demiurge
The demiurge filled the double and triple intervals by cutting more shares of the original mixture and placing them in the spaces so that in each space there were two middle parts, one of which overlapped the extremes and was overlapped by them by the same fraction of each of them, while the other overlapped one extreme number of which it was overlapped by the other. From the links between the first spaces there arose new spaces of one and a half, one and a third and one and an eighth. Then the god filled the spaces of one and a third with a space of one and an eighth, leaving in each a fraction such that the remaining space was defined by the proportion of two hundred and fifty-six to two hundred and forty-three.
Timaeus

Traces of primitive belief

Some modern writers claim that Plato was nothing more than a writer of genius who popularized the manifestations of the Greek mysteries. Without going this far, it is certainly possible to point to traces of very ancient customs and primitive rites within Platonism which liken it to occultism. This inspiration can be seen in the amatory maieutics of the *Symposium*, in the initiation performed by Diotimos, in the dialectic of one and many, and some and other expounded in the *Parmenides*; the *Cratylus* could even be taken for a real treatise on the theory of magic. The *Timaeus* describes the creation of the world and shows how numbers govern the cosmos, and how relationships are perceived by us through music. Finally, in the *Critias*, Plato invents Atlantis, the fabulous continent symbolizing the origin of all knowledge.

Shakespeare, William

1564–1616

The royal road to hermetism

Alchemy is at the heart of Shakespeare's works.

Shakespeare stands on the threshold of the medieval and modern worlds. It is not surprising that, like Hieronymus Bosch in the artistic sphere, his work should be filled with mythology, magic and esoterism. Shakespeare was also undoubtedly affected by illuminism and Cabalism which were at that time enormously influential in intellectual circles.

Esoteric exegesis

A Midsummer Night's Dream is deeply marked with popular cosmology; *Love's Labour's Lost* carries an Orphic love theme, with the lovers setting one another tests. *The Merchant of Venice* contains Pythagorean ideas:

> There's not the smallest orb that thou behold'st
> But in his motion like an angel sings ...
> But, whilst this muddy vesture of decay
> Doth grossly close it in, we cannot hear it.

In *The Tempest*, we see a magician fighting against the forces of evil and putting young lovers through an initiation. However, alchemy has pride of place, especially in *The Winter's Tale*. The play is saturated with alchemical philosophy and symbolism, as Paul Arnold points out. For example, the striking scene of Hermione's 'resurrection' must surely be based on the alchemical description of the king and queen going down into the tomb and rising again.

Alchemy re-creating itself

However, alchemy has an even more intimate function in Shakespeare's work; it may even be its real heart. This is the process of alchemy re-creating itself. In an allusion to the 'alchemy of the Word', Rimbaud states that poetic creation is an alchemical process. To understand this, one only has to consider the concepts of the 'royal art': transmutation, sublimation, fixation, etc. We should also remember that alchemy is the stage production par excellence, with figures representing and discussing man and the universe at one and the same time. These figures establish an elusive, fleeting equivalence of world and self, arousing the spectator's creative imagination. It could even be argued that any truly creative writer must rely on alchemy.

> 'Wilt thou tell of hidden things denied to common understanding?' *Love's Labour's Lost*

Strindberg, August

1849–1912

The maker of gold

Strindberg really did try to make gold. This may have been simple naïvety, but his 'struggle with the angel' had an esoteric side.

One of the great dramatists of modern times, Strindberg was also a hermetist who practised alchemy in the laboratory. In fact, he almost set fire to a Paris hotel in which he was staying in the course of an experiment. He wrote the following letter on 15 April 1896 to Jollivet-Castelot, who was also held in esteem by the 'makers of gold':

> Dear Sir
> Since you believe it is possible to make gold, I am sending you these samples to ask your opinion on the metallic precipitate . . .
> I dip a strip of paper in iron sulphate. Then I hold it over an open flask of ammonia, for no longer than one minute. After this, I let the paper dry for five to ten minutes in cigar smoke. That is all. The cigar dries it and produces ammonia, and this prevents the hydrated iron oxide from returning to the state of iron . . .
> Here is what happens:
> Ammonical sulphate of iron =
> $Fe\ (AzH_4)\ 2\ (SU_4)\ 6\ aq = 392$
> 196x2
> ↓
> Gold
> Please repeat my experiment and tell me if you think the yellow metal contains gold, even in microscopic quantities (after all, the ore of the Transvaal only contains microscopic quantities).

How could Strindberg be so naïve? It is certainly tempting to attribute his behaviour to some loss of mental balance.

However, perhaps we should remember that genius, far from being close to madness, helps to ward it off. Genius is the 'struggle with the angel', the struggle against the madness that every human being carries inside himself and which the artist alone dares to confront.

The choice of hermetism

For Strindberg, as for Nerval, alchemy is closely bound up with the literary work whose inner secret it reveals. It is certainly most intriguing that so many artists appear to choose hermetism as their ultimate reference.

> Although originally an admirer of **naturalism**, Strindberg then took up symbolism which set him off on a quest foreshadowing, in some ways, that of Kierkegaard, one of the founding fathers of existentialism.

The Surrealists

Love and revolution unite with magic

Alongside Marx and Freud, the surrealists revered Nicolas Flamel and Eliphas Lévi, among others. Love, revolution and magic formed their triple seal.

The interest in dreams, magic and love shared by surrealist writers and artists is well known. As one of the most important movements of this century, the surrealists, including Eluard, Aragon, Artaud, Char and others, inevitably came to discover hermetism. However, they had no interest in esoteric philosophy; their sole aim was to set free all those creative forces which are stifled by social alienation. They were, in effect, following the lead of Marx and Freud.

Are 'super-reality' and 'invisible' merely synonyms?

The critics have perhaps yet to appreciate just how surrealism came to flourish when it was embracing two apparently contradictory trends — hermetism, with its dream-like qualities, and revolution, which represented the dispelling of darkness. However, the very name of the movement — surrealism — shows that the artists involved were seeking a 'super-reality', a 'different' reality, an invisible reality. They wanted to explore this reality, and to succeed where their predecessors had failed; they wanted to 'change life' by writing it into their revolutionary agenda.

A position vis-à-vis the cosmos

It could be said that there is nothing new in this. Kandinsky, the inventor of so-called abstract art, wanted to make visible the invisible, of which form is but the outer shell. Further back in history, classicists such as Watteau, or Poussin (who knew and used the golden mean), and Rembrandt (who was influenced by the Cabala) worked also on the invisible — but discreetly. Such examples only serve to underline the primacy and permanence of the invisible in art. Is there then any justification for making a special case of surrealism? Surely the problem is now to try to understand why the invisible, which impregnates all artistic work, suddenly gave rise in the 1920s to surrealism, as if to signify that it was urgent for man to state his position vis-à-vis the cosmos. All living traditions must have firm roots in the present; by studying surrealism, perhaps we can reach a better understanding of ourselves.

The Surrealists *Surrealism, like hermetism, was an attempt to rediscover the dream dimension. Oil painting by Valentine Hugo, showing André Breton, Paul Eluard, Tristan Tzara, René Crevel and René Char. (National Library, Paris)*

The Symbolists

Creators who declare their occultism

More than any other movement, the symbolists recognized their debt to occult philosophy.

Symbolism inevitably took an interest in the occult — or, to be more precise, the occult was the only possible path symbolism could take. René Terrasson provides the following definition of the movement in his fine book, *Pelléas et Mélisande ou l'Initiation*: 'The time of symbolism may be defined as that superior instant when Art combined with Mysticism to reach the very meaning of existence through privileged metaphysical interrogation.' Symbolism was therefore born of the 'need to return to the sources of Being'. This is not, however, a return to religion, but to the original philosophy, at the stage when it was just separating itself from mythology and still retained all its poetic colour; this was a philosophy which had not yet forgotten how to dream.

An order with eclipses

It is at such moments that tradition re-emerges and esoteric movements flourish, without any plotting or planning; invisible history has no need of these. A sort of spontaneous reaction occurs, which encourages the participants to become alive, once again, to the unconscious, which can only be illuminated through the language of hermetism.

'In the realm of the Arts,' writes René Terrasson, one of the revivers of the Rosicrucian Order, 'Joséphin Péladan, although largely unrecognized, expresses most eloquently the need for this movement which broke all the rules and created a new language from a forgotten word — the Symbol.' This spiritual ferment was begun by Villiers de L'Isle-Adam, Mallarmé and countless others and circles were formed throughout Europe. In Paris, besides the Tuesday group of Mallarmé (who appears also to have been a mason for a while), we might mention the bookshop of Independent Art and the Brasserie des Martyrs as important focuses of the movement.

It should also be noted that the Rosicrucian order was linked with symbolism from the very start. Followers or sympathizers of these sister movements included Keats, Oscar Wilde, Manet and Debussy.

The Rosicrucian Order is a strange association. Jean-Claude Frère called it a 'mysterious brotherhood, in and out of the public eye, which has endured for at least three centuries, whose ramifications are complex and whose outstanding members share the same ideals and a common purpose . . .'

The way through hermetism

Symbolism is acknowledged as the meeting-point of surrealism and hermetism. Perhaps its most important phenomenon was the penetration by occultism of both literary and artistic creation. We are not talking here merely of an influence, or the establishment of a clandestine cell within a literary movement by a secret society; this was something far more fundamental. All creators, of course, engage in some form of hermetism, whether manifest or latent, in the course of their work — secrecy, transmutation and coincidence are suited perfectly to the creation of a work of art. Nevertheless, the symbolists are distinguished by the way in which they made such explicit reference to hermetism in their work.

A drawing by Eliphas Lévi combining various hermetic symbols, including the hermaphrodite, the uroboros and mercury.

Wheatley, Dennis Yates

1897–1977

A master of the macabre

A best-selling novelist who used occult themes in several of his most popular works

Dennis Wheatley wrote more than 60 novels between 1930 and 1970. He was enormously popular; his books were sold all over the world, and were translated into many languages. His life was as full of action and drama as his novels.

Wheatley was educated in England and Germany and saw service with the artillery in World War I before joining his father's wine business, taking over as owner in 1926. His literary career started in 1933 and for the next 40 years he continued to produce books at a rapid rate. During World War II he was on the Joint Planning Staff of the War Cabinet, at one time writing a mock 'invasion plan' which ran to 15 000 words and which he completed in 48 hours, sustained 'by 200 cigarettes and three magnums of champagne'.

Wheatley wrote several series of books. In one, the hero, Roger Brook, was an emissary for the British government in the late 18th and early 19th century, travelling to Europe, Asia and America. This series is notable for the actual historical events – often described in great detail – woven into the plot. In one book Brook saves his own daughter from being sacrificed at a Black Mass on Walpurgis Night.

Gregory Sallust is a more modern hero. Described as 'a satanic looking cynical egoist', he is sent behind German lines during World War II to sabotage invasion plans. In the final volume of the series, *They Used Dark Forces*, Sallust tries to overthrow Hilter by recourse to occult practices. Other Wheatley books featured the Duke de Richleau, including one of his most popular, *The Devil Rides Out*, which was filmed in 1970 with Christopher Lee, an actor noted for his work in macabre films, as its star.

In *To The Devil a Daughter*, the principal character, Copley-Syle, invokes all kinds of occult practices. It was widely believed that Wheatley based this character on the 'Great Beast', Aleister Crowley, a theory denied by the author himself. In the book, Copley-Syle's 'Satanic temple' is described in detail, with black candles, a backcloth of Adam and Eve with the Macrocosm, a large bat, and a broken crucifix. Copley-Syle is engaged on dreadful experiments to produce a homunculus using a young woman as his victim.

Wheatley clearly took a great interest in the occult. He was at one time asked to write a serious study of the subject, but declined, preferring to use the world of dark forces to enliven his novels. He did later write one non-fiction work with an occult theme, *The Devil And All His Works*. He is an interesting example of a popular modern author using many strands of the occult in his work. He has said that Dumas was one of his favourite authors, and as well as the repeated Satanic references, hauntings occur, notably in *The Haunting of Toby Jugg*, one of his best books.

Towards the end of his life, Wheatley acted as editor for a 'Library of the Occult' published in London and running to over 40 volumes.

Reincarnation

Dennis Wheatley was a convinced believer in reincarnation. In his autobiography he wrote: 'The progression of the spirit is based upon the belief that it is a growing thing; that in each life it has some lesson to learn. At times it may slip backward, but in due course it conquers greed, impulses to violence, meanness, injustice and other evil tendencies until it achieves complete serenity and happiness in helping other spirits that are still bound to the flesh to progress'. D. Wheatley, *The Time Has Come*

Esoterism and Reality

Is esoterism, which designates the whole body of the occult sciences, the 'archaic residue' of a way of thinking which has now been elevated to the status of a science? If this is so, it is hard to explain the lasting fascination of this 'residue', and the persistence of a handful of superstitious beliefs. This sort of approach does not get us very far, though. In fact, it simply serves to further obscure the subject.

The relation to reality

Truth in this area is both more subtle and more complex than this. Hermetism (or esoterism, if you prefer) reveals, in a rather confused way, an aspect of reality which, for want of a better word, we can only call 'invisible'. There is absolutely no point in trying to prove whether it exists or not: existence or non-existence is felt rather than proved. The peculiarity of the invisible — its strangeness — is that it cannot be captured in rational thought; it is only glimpsed in analogies. Perhaps it is not esoterism which is fantastic, but the use that is made of it.

Our book does not claim to be exhaustive; it is merely an exploration of the most obvious forms of the invisible, aimed at the average European reader in the late 20th century. Naturally, a journey like this, with initiation and magic at its centre, has spirituality, poetry and parapsychology on its edges. It touches upon these, but cannot be reduced to them alone. We have not ignored what lurks in these nooks and crannies, but have sought, in passing, to define it in the light of our main subject.

How is it possible, though, to talk of light when the invisible, if it exists, only reveals itself in confusion? All becomes clear as soon as we remember that esoterism does not depict reality, but the relationship of the subject to reality. Esoterism does not 'reconstruct' reality or try to seize it in its totality; it concentrates on the failure of various attempts at unification. It gathers up the materials discarded by science, of which art will perhaps be able to make something.

So, if analysis shows that the material of art is the same as that of esoterism, is the latter simply an obscure substitute for the former? In fact, this material appears to lie on the dividing line between art and philosophy. Esoterism reminds us that philosophy springs from the personal poetry of the individual. Utopian and astoundingly libertarian, esoterism invites us all to share the experience that the invisible is 'the most equitable thing in the world'.

Esoterism is, however, much more than merely some form of utopianism. After all, is it really possible to think or live other than in such a utopian way? Surely it is hermetism which holds the key to the myth that supports humanism and science, if only we know how to use it.

Emotion as the 'raw material' of the work

We need, therefore, to take account of our own hidden side. For the occult exists, above all, within us, and our failure to illuminate it is what gives rise to deviant forms of hermetism, whether fanciful, phoney or psychotic. The ploy of passing off such aberrations as true hermitism is all too common.

Let us, first of all, examine the psychotic manifestation, if only to point out that the psychotic is only a degenerate form of normality. It is possible to disentangle and understand the psychotic, although we must be careful not to become contaminated by it. It can be put back on its feet (as Marx said) or rectified, as the alchemists would put it.

To summarize, most alchemical texts are rather abstruse, but contain occasional flashes of insight. These flashes could be said to be pure poetry, and the surrounding obscurity, failed poetry. However, the interest of these texts is not that they compete with poetry but that they try to provide the emotional material which, when it is worked upon, will yield the philosopher's stone.

At the end of every cycle in science — ie when any great hypothesis becomes null and void, as, for example, just before the discovery of relativity — science experiences a crisis. It is then that whatever has been provisionally set aside, ie the 'occult', bursts upon the scene. There is no progress, no new hypothesis, if the occult cannot be transmuted, by rationalism, into some fresh, unexplored form. Science does not proceed by suppressing the 'hidden dimension', but by 'setting it aside', or putting it on 'hold'. This is, however, not a case of burying one's head in the sand, for nothing is discarded without examination.

Fermentation

It must be stressed, however, that hermetism, occultism stripped of its fancies, cannot be tied down to reality. Critics with an enquiring turn of mind have identified certain points of similarity between art and hermetism. We can certainly go so far with their theory, but must part company as soon as it starts to confuse the two. Occultists nostalgic for the Church have, similarly, shown the necessary connection between religious feeling and the quest of initiation; this is justifiable as long as the different approaches to spirituality are not forgotten.

In the same way, many current theories, based on legitimate points of similarity, end up by identifying science with occultism. The underlying idea seems to be that occultism holds the key to the mysteries science has only just discovered. True mystery, however, has nothing to do with science, and simply degenerates into hallucination when anyone tries to use it inappropriately.

Hermetism is all around us — in religion, science and art. It acts, however, only as a fermenting agent: once the process is underway, it disappears, or degenerates. Hermetism does not 'build' reality and ultimately provides no world-view; it only provides the impetus for creativity. Therein lies its mystery.

Words, Divination and Supports

Rimbaud's line, *La vraie vie est ailleurs* ('Real life is elsewhere') points to the first step in hermetism. In the *Mutus Liber*, angels sounded trumpets while the adept slept; the mystic must awaken to a form of reality his crude bodily senses cannot grasp. In this way, he can rediscover the 'true life', from which mankind was cut off by some original catastrophe; he can rediscover the 'lost speech'.

Words are not the clothes of things

Lost speech is the Word, made into a tool by man when he is vested with his part of divinity. It cloaks many coincidences: that of self and other (in which the mystic or initiate discovers his psychological centre, or 'secret'); that of man and the universe (in which the individual is 'a stone of the temple' and discovers his correct relation to things); and that of various moments in one's life. The present is revealed in the light of the coincidence of past and future. Time for one individual is rather like a hologram in which each fragment holds a summary of the whole; each particle is a microcosm playing the part of macrocosm.

So, to find this speech, or to be initiated, is to create that which is named. This is the source of the magic of the name, found among the Egyptians, in the Cabala, esoterism and all ritual, whether initiatory or magical. Every spell or incantation relies on words. The Golem is a spectacular example. This is the clay figure of Jewish legend, brought to life by inserting the name of God in its mouth. The only difficulty lay in finding out God's real name.

How, then, do we define a 'word'? Without entering into the arguments of modern linguistics, we would point out simply that words do not merely clothe things. Words are also the creation of man, springing to life when he discovered his being in the cosmos.

The supports of divination

How can someone living today name something living in the future? How can prediction work? Can everyday words suffice to name the invisible? Or must they be used in new way, according to rules, as the Cabalists or surrealists believed? We use words every day simply to designate objects, but this is not their sole function. In his *Baudelaire*, Jean-Paul Sartre pointed out that the poet did not use words like everybody else; he did not 'make tools' of them. A word is the trace of a more immaterial operation than phonetics. It is breath, and intensity. Intensity, in turn, introduces the notion of number and the rhythm of speech. The universe of the occultist is a universe of rhythms, to which his procedures will bring him closer. Everything in divination or clairvoyance needs a material support: take, for example, the use of tarot cards or fortune-telling by means of tea-leaves. The support must, however, remain just that. Running parallel to this visible operation, there is always an invisible operation. It is just as absurd to reduce occultism to its visible operations as it is to reduce religion to its rituals. This invisible operation proceeds, by definition, 'elsewhere': in an 'elsewhere' which gives rise to the present, roots it in a tradition and draws it on towards the future.

The power of clairvoyance

The occultist believes that he can get in touch with this 'elsewhere' even if, as in modern astrology, he has to pretend to be a technician to do so. Is it really possible to be both here and elsewhere, to escape the present and go elsewhere, even for a moment? Moreover, what is this 'elsewhere'? In order to discover this, we must set off on a journey, without knowing our destination.

Old books of magic and of divination detail countless methods for exploring this 'elsewhere'. The main problem is how to become receptive to them, and this is what is discovered through initiation.

The universe is like a hologram

Hermetism is founded on mythology. Mythology magnifies the powers of perception and reveals that which is significant. Human perception, then, has to be refined, which brings us to Jung's concepts of amplification and individuation.

The process is seen again when the discipline of occultism is reduced to words. But what lies behind these words, or behind this exploration of mythology? The mythological quest is particularly original because it is an 'operative fiction' which allows the operator to enter into the reality it depicts, fully and vigorously. It also enables him to crystallize his relation to the universe, which has finally been achieved. It is of little consequence whether we speak of 'relation' or 'enlightenment': whatever the terminology used, the operator has penetrated the ultimate secret.

In conclusion, for the occultist, the universe is like a hologram: a photograph, produced by a laser beam, which appears to be a meaningless pattern until it is suitably illuminated, and is seen to be a three-dimensional image. Furthermore, if a hologram is produced, then torn into tiny pieces, each of these pieces will still provide an image of the whole hologram. The correspondences between the hermetic axiom — the analogy between microcosm (man) and macrocosm (universe) — and the hologram are quite evident. A final observation may be useful; the operative fiction mentioned above can also be analyzed in psychological terms, culminating as it does in what Jung referred to as synchronism. This idea occurs in occultism, perfected: matter and spirit are two sides of the same coin, but we are unaware of this as long as the bad dream continues. Initiation on the one hand, or divination on the other, enable us to recover this lost unity. Matter is, in effect, the universe seen in terms of a hologram; any support can be a substitute for mythology; success in divination comes from the activation of an 'archaic residue' in the psyche.

Glossary

In this book, esoteric terms are explained as they appear in the text. However, this glossary sums up the meaning of certain terms which might, at first sight, seem self-explanatory, but which have a particular meaning in hermetism.

archetype The pattern, model or type par excellence. From Plato to Jung, idealist thinkers have given it supreme importance, making it a sort of cosmic invariable and then anthropomorphizing it. The same idea is found in books of magic. It is, however, really only an operative fiction.

chaos Chaos is the term for the original state of matter before the Spirit gave it shape. The concept is found in religion and in hermetism and, particularly, in alchemy. Here, far from being a mere notion, it is a reality which can be actualized, or made flesh, at any time, eg at the end of a historical cycle (when matter is reabsorbed) or at any point in individual evolution (in initiation, for example, the mystic descends into himself to discover his chaos).

Corpus Hermeticum The title of the central text of hermetism which comprises 17 treatises. The subjects it covers include: alchemy; astrology; initiation; magic; physics (of a sort where the experimenter is part of the experiment); psychology; sociology; and mathematics (a form based on radically different principles).

dragon The dragon is a symbol of chaos. Its antithesis is the uroboros, which re-establishes cosmic circulation.

handing on or **transmission** In initiation as in any apprenticeship, and in the profane world as well as the sacred, there is a process of handing on. This is not just a question of passing on the technique to a pupil or an apprentice, but also of the manner in which it is given. In hermetism more than anywhere else, great emphasis is placed on the teaching method. The handing on can be from master to pupil or by means of an initiation ceremony. In the second case, it will almost always include the motif of death. This is the symbolic death of the initiate to the profane world and, implicitly, the symbolic death of his teacher too. For, in his new life, the initiate will no longer have any need of a master to lead him.

husks This is a term taken from the Cabala. According to the *Zohar*, reality is like an almond whose kernel continually slips away from us. We can, however, infinitely draw close to it, by removing successive layers of husk or shell (ie by removing our own prejudices).

measure Is it possible to measure mystery or the product of symbolism? Not as long as we rely on mathematics as it is currently conceived. However, things change as soon as we turn to the use of numbers in hermetism. We know, for example, that a non-Euclidean system of geometry exists, referring to a world other than the one our senses immediately perceive. And the world of Einstein's physics does not respond to the sacrosanct principles of Euclid. We might even go so far as to wonder whether there is a geometry of the invisible.

mystery The mystery of hermetism is quite different from the mystery of revealed religion. It is not an act of faith, but a mystery the philosopher reflects upon, and which anyone of any sensitivity can feel. It is not a question of bowing down before this mystery, but of attempting to approach it (the Cabalists were considered heretics by orthodox Jews because they wanted to be 'masters of the secret'). The best definition of mystery comes from the Christian existentialist philosopher, Gabriel Marcel. He explains that we are bathed in mystery, so that it cannot be an object for us, and this is why scientific methods are inappropriate as a way of grasping it. Besides, it is not so much a question of grasping the mystery as of enlightening oneself in its 'dark light' (as Corneille said in *Le Cid*). Hermetic texts offer various approaches to mystery. Strictly speaking, there were in antiquity not only great mysteries, but also small mysteries, corresponding to two different levels of initiation with different ceremonies, often several years apart. This would appear to correspond to the degrees of apprentice and master in freemasonry, or white and red in alchemy.

mystic A person about to be initiated or undergoing initiation.

operative fiction Proudhon, who was a freemason, called God 'a necessary hypothesis'. The phrase is paradoxical, but very useful. Proudhon remained an atheist, but found that he was obliged to confront the idea of God as a unifying principle, in order to understand things. The world of science is based on monism, so Proudhon 'made a tool' of God, using God as he might use mathematics. So, for Proudhon, God was an operative fiction (as he is for hermetism in general). He is used, like imaginary numbers, to solve concrete problems. It may even be that the whole of hermetism is one vast operative fiction.

psychocosmic Man is, according to hermetism, both psychic (and therefore measurable) and cosmic (a mystery coming from elsewhere). Inner freedom consists in balancing these two qualities. Equilibrium is not acquired once and for all, though; it is the fruit of a ceaselessly renewed conquest.

reality Reality is complex; there is no need of philosophers to tell us that. But do we fully accept this complexity? We must, for example, accept dreams for what they are, a particular dimension of reality, and not as some strange negation of it. Similarly, the invisible and the symbolic are other dimensions of reality. This being so, it must be stressed that nothing is more damaging than the confusion of the various orders of reality. To take dream for reality is fanciful. However, the confusion of real and symbolic leads to serious error — for example, identifying freemasonry as the driving force behind the French Revolution, or Plato's error (in the *Republic*) in excluding poets from the city. All extreme political views arise from such errors.

religious feeling In its original state, without any ritualization or dogma, religious feeling is the 'raw material' of the work of alchemy, and of initiation in particular. At its heart are the questions the human race asks itself and which Gnostic philosophy expresses. The hermetist sets out to 'work' upon this religious feeling, refining and transmuting it, to make explicit the being-in-the-world, the purpose of the experiment. (Hermetism works neither on the being nor on the world, but on the being-in-the-world, which is the only accessible reality for it.) Opinions diverge when we ask what to make of this religious feeling. Some would say it is the way to rediscover the esoterism of religion; others, that it must be rejected entirely. Still others would hold that it must be transmuted, either into philosophy or poetry.

sacred intoxication This term describes the sense of elation that comes of the word of God — that of Pythia at Delphi, or of a shaman or a Cabalist. Nostradamus said that he had composed his *Centuries* because he was prey to an intoxication which gave him the second sight. It is evident in the paintings of Van Gogh and the writing of Rimbaud. The problem with intoxication, sacred or otherwise, is how to intensify it, while remaining master of the creative process it releases; how to stay afloat and not be swept away with the tide. This intoxication necessarily starts and ends every esoteric operation, but can also occur at any intermediate point in it. Divination can give rise to the conditions of a real experience of controlled intoxication, artificially and on a limited scale. The science of numbers also claims to know its rhythms. This intoxication comes from the dizziness felt on being swept away in the whirlwinds of the cosmos, and from the knowledge that we may be little more than dizziness ourselves.

sacrifice In reality, sacrifice in the hermetic sense is always symbolic. Think, for example, of Abraham's sacrifice of Isaac, a turning-point in history, marking the shift from actual to symbolic sacrifice.

simulation Hermetism is founded on simulation, since it depends on symbols to create itself. This simulation reveals another, invisible reality. In this, hermetism is like art. We might even see hermetism as the path to creativity.

soul As an intermediary between body and spirit, the soul joins together two dimensions: the masculine *animus* and the feminine *anima*. The perfect balance of the two, an ideal, is symbolized by the hermaphrodite. In reality, however, sexual differentiation is the rule; every being has animus and anima in varying proportions, according to whether he is man or woman. The individual (microcosmic) soul corresponds to the (macrocosmic) soul of the world, without which the Great Architect of the Universe, the demiurge, would have lacked sensitivity and been incapable of creation.

superstition René Guénon points out that superstition is, in some ways, the debased remains of traditional knowledge. It is part of the 'wisdom of nations', or collective unconscious, and describes a truth which failed to find expression and aborted. Thus, 'Third time lucky' is, and remains, a superstition, but the fact that we say it reveals a deeper, unconscious, need for symbolic reflection on numbers. But, for example, if we want to wear a certain item of clothing 'because it is lucky', this is merely childish or neurotic behaviour. Nonetheless, superstition seems to correspond to a real need, which different cultures and societies satisfy, each in their own way.

union of opposites This is, in a way, a more concrete version of Hegel's style of dialectic. Hegelian logic, influenced by the philosophy of Jakob Böhme, is unlike Aristotle's formal logic in that it believes it arrives at the heart, or essence, of things when it 'seizes their constituent contradiction' (Lenin). Philosophically, this goes right back to the pre-Socratic problem of self and other, explored by Empedocles or Heraclitus, among others. (Pythagoras tried to express the problem in numbers.) However, Hegel provided the best definition, which was the one later adopted by Lenin. The union of opposites is a similar philosophy, but is distinguished by the fact that it takes account of the analyst. On the other hand, Leninist dialectic, claiming to be objective, had no need of an analyst. However, in hermetism, the analyst, or human being, is the only point where the union of opposites — like the coincidence of sun and moon, sulphur and mercury, animus and anima — can be achieved.

universal In older esoterism, the word 'universal' was applied exclusively to the universe. Ever since the Enlightenment and the rise of freemasonry, however, the word has also been used to refer to the whole of humanity. There are, therefore, two problems:

1. How is it possible to be completely human and, at the same time, belong to the universe? Is the human not governed by nature? Alchemy supplies the answer, by stating that the human is a transmuted, refined fragment of the cosmos. The work of alchemy is part of nature, but transcends it at the same time — an interesting dialectic, a union of opposites between nature and culture.
2. How is it possible to be universal and singular at the same time, as initiation ceremonies promise? This is another union of opposites. Montaigne provides a solution here when he suggests that he will find his own singularity by discovering the whole of the human condition within himself. This brings us back to the concept of 'singular-universal' implicity found everywhere.

For hermetism, the universe can be unveiled only in the singular-universal. Objectivity is revealed only in, and through, subjective encounters, eg dialogues. This explains the need for initiatory societies such as the freemasons and the earlier operative masons, and is, moreover, the basis of the sociohistorical axioms of the invisible.

word The Word can be thought of as language, in the sense that the first language was able to create the things it named. This is not magic, which is limited to reproducing what once existed or making spirits with certain powers manifest themselves. The Word truly creates by naming, as God did in the beginning. There are only two cases nowadays where the Word comes into play: poetry, for a great poet creates what he names, and his poem reveals a new world; and initiation ceremonies, where the mystic is called upon to manifest himself and is thus created.

Index

Entries in **bold type** refer to item headings on the pages referred to in the book